THE ESSENTIAL SOCIAL WORKER

To my father,
Tom Brett Davies

The Essential Social Worker
An introduction to professional practice in the 1990s

Third Edition

Martin Davies

Ashgate

Aldershot • Brookfield USA • Singapore • Sydney

361.3
DAV

First published 1981 by Heinemann Educational Books Ltd
Reprinted 1983
Second edition published 1985 by Wildwood House Ltd
Reprinted 1988, 1989, 1991, 1993

Published by
Ashgate Publishing Limited
Gower House
Croft Road
Aldershot
Hants GU11 3HR
England

Ashgate Publishing Company
Old Post Road
Brookfield
Vermont 05036
USA

Reprinted 1995, 1998

British Library Cataloguing in Publication Data

Davies, Martin
  Essential Social Worker: Introduction to
  Professional Practice in the 1990s-
  3 Rev. ed
  I. Title
  361.30941

ISBN 1 85742 100 0 (Hardback)
      1 85742 101 9 (Paperback)

Printed in Great Britain by M.P.G. Limited Bodmin

Contents

Part IV In conclusion

Preface to the third edition

The Essential Social Worker in its third edition continues to serve the same purpose as its predecessors. It is intended to be both an introduction to the subject of social work, and a reflection of one man's attempt to make sense of its role in society.

When, in 1985, I wrote the preface to the second edition, I noted that much had changed in the four years since the book had first appeared. The same, of course, is true again. Partly because of its heavy dependence on constantly reformed legislation, but also partly, and more worryingly, because of changing fashions and fancies among social work personnel, any piece of social work writing is going to have a limited shelf life. The problem has been compounded in recent years by the way professional terminology has been pinpointed as a potential source of political incorrectness; hence, words which ten years ago were in common parlance are now taboo. Doubtless, the process will continue. I wish I could be confident that those people in social work (and elsewhere) who are vehemently insistent on the importance of not using discriminatory language were equally 'correct' and reliable in practice – it doesn't always follow.

The major change to the structure of the book is the addition of a new Part I; there, I have sought to explain the historical and the policy context of social work practice in England and Wales. By so doing, I have been able to present parallel accounts of how child care, community care and criminal justice policy have evolved over two decades. It is certain that the trend towards specialisation in each of these three client-group areas will gather pace. Nonetheless, this book suggests that there remains a central core of social work culture which justifies a common approach in training and in the development of a professional identity.

The whole book has been extensively revised. I have excluded a lot of redundant and outmoded material, and have added new passages to take account of developments relevant to the 1990s. But the central thesis of the book – that maintenance theory best explains the role of social work in society – remains intact. If anything, events in the years since I first struggled to formulate the argument have strengthened my conclusion that it fits the available empirical evidence better than either of the previously dominant psychotherapeutic or Marxist models.

I have shared my professional life with two social work generations. In that time, I have seen groundswells of evangelistic and sometimes intolerant enthusiasm for post-Freudian ideas, for radical or Marxist theory, for feminist interpretations of society, and most recently for the CCETSW-inspired (and therefore dangerously powerful) commitment to so-called anti-discriminatory practice as the required orthodoxy. The ideologies have all had two things in common. Firstly, they have all had *something* relevant to say to social work theory and practice, and for that reason they have each left their mark upon it.

But secondly, in each instance, there have been fanatics who seemed to see in their respective body of ideas – Freudian, Marxist, feminist or anti-discriminatory – a system of belief that could and should overrule all other perspectives and that therefore must be thrust on those around them. Often the fanatics were in significant positions of responsibility in social work training, and the combination of the seeming validity of some of their arguments with the need often felt by students for reassurance and certainty has meant that in each decade of my working life I have had to live with a different orthodoxy.

Such confident disciples of certainty produce homogeneity in their textbooks and, most recently, through the medium of CCETSW, they are even trying to brief their agents to police the political correctness of course assessment – not usually in regard to anything as mundane as practice competence but with an emphasis on the use (and even the repetition) of acceptable words and phrases. Such advocates of a 'total' system have no truck with those who, in search of rational evidence and in pursuit of the ever-unattainable 'truth', choose to adopt a more cautious and often more sceptical approach. A sceptical emphasis has been, of course, the starting point – and even the endgame – for *The Essential Social Worker* since it was first conceived and developed in first-year classes for graduate social work students at the University of East Anglia.

For me, the great pleasure and privilege of being in social work lies in the quality and commitment of its front-line practitioners, the best of whom deliver a creative and professional service to people who for the most part command few services. Personal style and methodological variety, self-belief and nonconformity remain, I am convinced, at the heart of the best social work practice. God forbid that politicians, managers or social policy analysts should ever be allowed to squeeze such qualities out of a system now approaching the end of its first century.

The Essential Social Worker, in its third edition, emphasises continuities in practice. Fashions will come and go, but research has shown that the skills, the knowledge and the qualities of the mainstream social worker are remarkably constant. The civilised world may not always realise or acknowledge it, but it has good reason to be grateful to the essential social worker – in the 1990s and, undoubtedly, into the 21st century.

Martin Davies
Norwich, July 1993

Permissions

The author and the publishers would like to thank the following for kind permission to reproduce their material in this book: Richard J. Bealka; *British Journal of Social Work*; *Community Care*; Her Majesty's Stationery Office; John Jamieson; Nottinghamshire County Council; *Social Work Today*; C. E. Wakefield.

Acknowledgements

The Essential Social Worker is very much a personal statement about my relationship with a particular subject, and it is right that I should acknowledge the influence on me of three men and one woman over the two decades that preceded its original composition. Tom Simey at Liverpool University imbued me with a critical sensitivity to the dangers of social work dogma that has never deserted me; Peter Westland and Arthur Rogers, then probation officers, taught me how to combine academic awareness with a commitment to and a feeling for the clients' lives in practice; and Jean Heywood, at Manchester University, at a critical time reinforced for me the conviction that good social work must combine intelligence and warmth. Both qualities are crucial: without intelligence or critical sensitivity social work loses its way; without warmth, commitment or feeling, it loses its identity.

More recently, my thinking has been stimulated by discussions with my students and colleagues in Norwich, and especially by conversations with my friend, David Howe. For the first edition, I consulted with and remain grateful to Juliet Cheetham, Tony Hall, Nancy Hazel, Rudolf Klein, Bill McWilliams, Rolf Olsen and Colin Pritchard.

Colleagues at the University of East Anglia have been generous with their time and their advice during the final stages of work for the third edition: Caroline Ball, Jo Connolly, Diana Hinings, Raymond Jack, Ann Lewis, Ann McDonald, Steve Rashid, Gill Schofield, Clive Sellick, Nigel Stone and Tracy Wild. I wish to express my gratitude to them all.

Part I

A framework for the 1990s

1 The historical context

By the year 2000, the practice of social work will be four or five generations old. Its beginnings lay in the work of the 19th-century poor law officials who moved destitute people into and out of the workhouse – or, when they misbehaved, into the police court and the local bridewell (or lock-up).

At the beginning of the 20th century, in London and other big British cities home visitors from the Charity Organisation Society dispensed alms, encouragement and advice to needy families; police court missionaries were called on by magistrates to help offenders in trouble; school-board men tracked down truants and returned them to their classes; and a host of voluntary organisations, often linked with the churches, made it their business to help orphans, pregnant girls and destitute women. Help for people who were old or psychiatrically ill, or who had physical or learning disabilities, always lagged behind, but existed in some degree. (The terminology of the time was, of course, different: 'lunatics, imbeciles and cripples' were unashamedly viewed as a class apart.)

In the 1930s, the beginnings of social work professionalism could be detected, and by the 1950s, probation officers, child care officers, hospital almoners and psychiatric social workers all enjoyed an independent existence, with the first university-based qualifying courses firmly established. During the 1960s, the common elements in social work training programmes were widely acknowledged, and generic preparation for practice became the norm.

Scotland led the way towards a new unified superstructure with the establishment of social work departments in 1968. In England and Wales, the Seebohm Report (1968) similarly recommended that most social workers should be brought together in the same public sector organisation, and the policy was enacted in 1970 with the creation of social services departments under the control of local government. In England, Wales and Northern Ireland the probation service alone remained independent, but in Scotland it too was absorbed into the local authorities.

There are many social workers now practising who were not even born when the Seebohm Report was published, but the structure that was created in its wake has held firm – and this despite many changes of emphasis, of style and of substance. In the United Kingdom, social workers are overwhelmingly employed either by local authorities or, in the case of probation officers outside Scotland, by committees made up largely of magistrates. United Kingdom social workers are almost all public servants and find themselves working for much of the time within a tightly defined legislative framework, or rather three legislative frameworks. The probation service operates within the system of criminal justice; work with children and families is governed by child care legislation and especially by the Children Act 1989; and almost all other categories of client fall within the purview of mental health legislation, the National Assistance Act 1948 and the National Health Service and Community Care Act 1990.

The power of the legal statutes and the different kinds of demands that they make on social work in the 1990s mean that the short-lived generic tradition is under threat. Although the boundaries between the three legislative categories are not absolute, it seems increasingly likely that social work at the millennium will have committed itself again to the value of specialist skills suitable for use in different settings.

Growth within any organisation tends to lead to greater specialisation of focus and function, and social work has certainly grown steadily since the creation of the new local authority departments in 1971 (Table 1.1).

Table 1.1
Central government expenditure in the public sector: growth/decline in real terms 1971–1991

	1971–76 %	1976–81 %	1981–86 %	1986–91 %
Defence	− 12	+ 18	+ 10	− 27
Education	+ 26	− 5	− 10	− 2*
Health service	+ 38	+ 29	− 5	+ 13
Social security	+ 22	+ 50	+ 30	− 24
Housing	+ 125	− 46	− 86	− 60
Personal social services	+ 150	+ 32	+ 1	+ 10

* Only the 1989–1990 figure is available for education at the time of writing, and the statistic is adjusted accordingly.
Source: Monthly Digest of Statistics, HMSO.

The personal social services had an enormous boost in expenditure immediately following the implementation of the reforms prompted by the Seebohm Committee's Report; its growth was second only to social security in the quinquennium 1976–1981. In the first half of the 1980s, like most other areas of public expenditure, its expansion was tightly squeezed (though not so much as education); and in the period from 1986 to 1991, only health and social services were allowed any real-term growth. Of course, compared with the other spheres of public expenditure, the personal social services started from a low baseline, but by 1990–91, the total level of expenditure on them had risen to £5.6

billion, compared with £28.6 billion on the health service and £53.8 billion on social security. But, taking the 20-year period as a whole, British social work has grown in budgetary significance and the trend shows no signs of losing steam.

The real nature of the expansion is illustrated in Table 1.2, which shows that the total

Table 1.2
Workforce in statutory social work offices 1975–1991

	1975	1985	1991
Social services departments in England: total numbers employed (or whole-time equivalents)	179 070	217 013	236 043
Social services fieldwork staff employed in England	20 400	24 773	30 675
Number of probation officers in post (wte) in England and Wales	4 998	6 220	7 153

Source: Statistics issued by the Department of Health and the Home Office.

number of staff employed in local authority social services departments grew by 32 per cent from 1975 to 1991, that the number of social workers there rose by 50 per cent in the same period and that the number of probation officers increased by 43 per cent. Bearing in mind that the period has seen high levels of unemployment in all corners of society, one fact becomes clear: social work has offered one career opening that provided continuing opportunities for new recruits.

It is simply not possible to say in any absolute sense what an *appropriate* level for social work expenditure is in any particular economic climate. Rising standards of living mean that expectations of welfare also rise; and an escalating total population combined with longer life-expectation, higher divorce rates, increased levels of crime and a growing number of people who survive life-threatening illnesses means that the client-groups traditionally targeted by social work are burgeoning. In most local authorities, the social services department is now second only to education in the scale of operations.

Understandably, the Treasury tends to get nervous about such expansion and to insist on the need not only for quality control but for clearer targeting of resources. The 1990s are a time for continuing debate about the respective merits of a needs-led or a resource-led programme of welfare provision. In truth, of course, needs are ultimately unassuage-able, and social workers, both individually and corporately, are liable to identify expectations of service far beyond a level that will be politically or economically feasible. Hence the primacy, in a democratic society, of parliamentary authority; the only 'absolute' level of provision possible in the public sector is the one from time to time determined by government – and that, of course, is not absolute at all, but related to social, political and economic considerations operating at the time.

The emergence of a mixed economy of welfare in which the allocation of public resources sits side by side with market-led provision by commercial or non-profit-making voluntary operators is likely to lead to further changes in the shape and direction of social work during the 1990s. Notwithstanding criticism from the New Right, however, the role of social work in modern society is rarely challenged at the highest levels of politics; on the contrary, concern on all sides about child abuse, teenage crime, loneliness and vulnerability in old age, and homeless people sleeping on the streets of the nation's cities tends to lead to arguments for more and better social work intervention rather than less.

The collapse of the Iron Curtain between East and West Europe has exposed a particularly intriguing historical episode, one whose implications have not been lost in social work circles. Romania in the 1950s had a perfectly satisfactory social work system with a focus on child and family care not dissimilar to that found elsewhere. However, the country's autocratic dictator, President Ceausescu, decreed that, because under his rule there were no social problems, there could accordingly be no need for social workers either. As a result, for 25 years until the revolution in 1989, no child welfare was practised and many of the children in greatest need were banished to crudely administered orphanages shut away behind closed doors. No social workers were trained and none were employed; no community work was practised. When, in 1990, UNICEF agents arrived on the scene following world-wide television exposure of horrific images from the ill-resourced orphanages, it quickly became apparent that the outlawing of social work had created a situation which could only be rectified by a major programme of training and the employment of a new generation of professionals.

The irony of the fact that it was the failure of a regime based on socialist ideology which has provided the ammunition to counter New Right scepticism about the legitimacy of social work in society will never be lost. On the contrary, it splendidly illustrates a fundamental assertion: social work is incompatible with dogmatic ideological perspectives, whether they emerge from Left or Right.

Social work reflects a centrist policy commitment, concerned to hold the balance between vulnerable individuals and a compassionate state. It is not a comfortable or complete relationship and it is one which is always open to exploitation. But my own involvement in the Romanian renaissance has reinforced my view that social work will never be redundant in an urban world. I accept, however, that it is both politically and economically important to ensure that social work always maintains an appropriate and properly budgeted approach to the specific tasks allocated to it.

Above all, social work can never be a law unto itself.

2 The policy context

Child protection

written with Elsbeth Neil

The great majority of child care social workers are employed by local authorities and are expected to carry out statutory duties. Although there are some voluntary and private sector agencies, particularly in the provision of residential care, they are heavily dependent on state finance, and generally provide facilities under contract to local authorities or central government. Child care social work in Britain is therefore a manifestation of public policy and of family-related legislation.

But of course what social workers actually *do*, albeit constrained by a legislative framework, is influenced by ideas and values which reflect the climate of opinion in society (especially as reported in the media) and by the professional and personal standards they themselves bring into the job or absorb during and after training. These ideas, values and standards are in turn influenced by research findings, changing ideologies and, to some extent, fads and fashions.

Child care policy in the 1980s

Child care policy in the 1980s was based largely on laws passed in 1969 and 1975, and reflected the struggles of social workers throughout the decade to achieve a satisfactory balance between the interests of the vulnerable child and the problems faced by families in trouble.

Under the Children and Young Persons Act 1969, social workers were authorised to use place of safety orders to protect children in emergencies (Dyde 1987). Such orders meant that a child could be detained in a safe place for up to 28 days if a court could be persuaded there were reasonable grounds for concern about the child's well-being. The

7

magistrates could grant such an order without hearing from the parents in the case; indeed, the parents did not even have to be informed that an application was going to be made. It was assumed that the short-term interests and the safety of the child were paramount, and that the informed judgment of the social worker was sufficient basis upon which to make an order.

The Children Act 1975 restricted the rights of natural parents, and permitted under certain conditions the freeing of children for adoption against parental wishes. As a result, the Act strengthened the position of foster and adoptive parents compared to birth parents.

The Child Care Act 1980 imposed a duty on the local authority to diminish the need for children to come into care by offering 'voluntary supervision'. It also enabled local authorities to receive children into care on a voluntary basis, but the parents of such children did not have the automatic right to remove their children from care on demand. Local authorities had the right to make a full care order if certain conditions were met and, if not rescinded, it would last until the child's 18th birthday. Once such an order was made, parents lost all their rights and duties in respect of that child.

During the 1980s, because of public concern about a succession of child abuse scandals, a great deal of government energy was devoted to the establishment of appropriate child protection procedures: area review committees were set up with an inter-professional membership, case conferences were regularly called and child protection registers were created in all local authorities

Child care practice in the 1980s

Basing its conclusions on work done between 1979 and 1982, a Health Department research programme into social work practice in child care said that the patterns of practice identified were 'disturbing and depressing' (DHSS 1985). Social workers were very pessimistic about admitting children into care and tried to avoid it at all costs, with the result that their practice was characterised more by tactical evasion than by positive planning. Their attitudes did not, in fact, lead to a reduction in the numbers being taken into care, but often only in admissions being unplanned. Not nearly enough preventative work was being done – the provision of respite or day care in order to reduce the risk of family breakdown, for example.

One finding of considerable importance was that social workers seemed to have very different perspectives from those of the parents with whom they had to deal. Parents said they felt misunderstood and not sufficiently involved in the care of their children or in decisions that affected their children's welfare.

Social workers frequently undervalued the contributions that parents could make to their own children's welfare. Once a child was admitted to care, parents were often neither consulted nor kept informed. Inevitably, from that point on, many children lost contact with their birth families.

Practice was heavily influenced by an important ideological debate about 'permanence'

– an emphasis on the child's need for long-term stability and security (Morris 1984). Initially, it was believed that confusion was likely to occur if there were more than one 'family' in a child's life. Hence permanence, it was argued, could best be achieved by removing a child from parents who could not cope and placing him with foster or adoptive parents on an exclusive basis – cutting off parental contact in order to avoid psychological confusion. Such an approach was usually attractive to the substitute parents.

The contrary argument in the permanence debate has been described as 'the kinship defender position' (Fox 1982). It stresses the importance of the blood tie and asserts that it is social and economic factors which make it difficult for birth parents to cope with their children. If, the argument goes on, social workers were able to deal with the problems of poverty, housing and other structural matters, then a policy of 'permanence' in the child's own family of origin could be pursued more frequently.

Social workers themselves often complained that, although they might be in direct contact with children for whom they bore a heavy responsibility, they were often unable to pursue an effective strategy because of their lack of influence over resources. As a result, all too often, birth parents were left to struggle and a 'wait and see' tactic was adopted, often leading to a situation in which children in care continued to drift from one unplanned placement to the next.

Child care policy in the 1990s

The Children Act 1989 was designed to improve upon the conflicts and ambiguities that had characterised child care social work in the 1980s. The Act has been described as 'a watershed in the history of British child care', reflecting major changes in attitudes and practice (Department of Health 1990). The Act created a family court structure designed to deal with matters of both custody and care; it redefined legal powers in regard to child protection; and it outlined the principles that should characterise the care of children in the public domain.

The foundation of the Children Act 1989 lay in the presumption that children are best brought up by their own families. It replaced the negative preventative emphasis of the 1980 Act with a positive requirement that families should be provided with support in order to enable them to stay together.

The Act introduced the idea of 'a child in need'. It provided a definition which focused on three things: the likelihood of the child either achieving or maintaining 'a reasonable standard of health or development', the probability of any impairment in the child's health or development, and whether the child had any disability. If the circumstances deemed that the child was in need, then the Act required the social worker to provide a service.

The Children Act replaced the notion of parental rights with that of parental responsibilities; these responsibilities are not lost if the child is in care and can only be legally removed by adoption. The Act says that statutory agencies should work in partnership with parents, and demands that the provision of care and services should always be done by the least restrictive means – meaning that it should be done on a voluntary basis whenever possible. Parents now have the right to be party to any proceedings concerning their child.

Voluntary care is replaced by the idea of 'accommodation', which must be made available for any child apparently in need of it. The change in terminology was introduced especially to deal with the stigma and the sense of parental shame that had become associated with the idea of a child 'being taken into care'. Parents may remove children from accommodation without notice.

The grounds for using compulsory measures under the 1989 Act are restricted to situations where the risk of 'significant harm' to the child can be proved, and where it can be convincingly argued that the making of an order will be more beneficial than making no order. Thus, crucially, children are now protected not only from harmful parents (whose existence is undeniable) but also from potentially harmful, desultory or disjointed interventions of statutory social workers – a risk that, not long ago, would have been discounted by most professionals but that has been demonstrated incontrovertibly by research.

The 1989 Act introduced emergency protection orders which can be of only eight days' duration: a period of time which demands a concentration of effort and a tightness of focus in social work assessment previously missing. Under an emergency protection order, there is a normal presumption that the child will be allowed 'reasonable contact' with his parents, thus ensuring continuity in the relationship wherever possible.

In child care social work in the 1990s, both the interests of parents and the wishes of the children have to be taken into account. The 1989 Act retained the principle that the welfare of the child is paramount. To this end, it requires that children's wishes must be ascertained by the social worker, and that their age, gender, health, personality, race, culture and life experience must all be given due weight. Children have enhanced rights to participate in proceedings that concern them.

The 1989 Act represents an attempt by policy-makers to deal with the renowned problem of children who drift while being 'looked after' by the social work system. It emphasises the need for a social worker to operate quickly and decisively: 'Time is a crucial element in child care and should be reckoned in days and months rather than years' (Department of Health 1990).

For the first time the Children Act placed an obligation on social workers to 'advise, assist and befriend' young people leaving care at the age of 16 or 17, and to continue to do so until they reach the age of 21. The assistance may be in kind or, 'in exceptional circumstances', in cash, but 'it is not intended that local authorities should assume an income maintenance role' (Ball 1991: 29).

The 1989 Children Act provided a completely new legislative framework for child care social work. It replaced a system that was widely regarded as 'confusing, unnecessarily complex and in places unjust' (DHSS 1987), and it was designed to redress the balance between professional power and family rights, while at the same time strengthening and modernising the crucial task of protecting children from abuse whatever the context of their domestic lives.

Child care practice in the 1990s

Child protection has become the highest priority in child care practice, but, as in other fields of social work, the personal style of the worker remains as important as it has always been. However, the policy changes encapsulated in the 1989 Act – heightened awareness of the rights of children and their parents, and sensitivity towards (even apprehension of) public and media concern about the abuse of children – have all become influential factors in any attempt to determine what constitutes good professional practice.

Factors which have further complicated an always demanding job include the emergence of sexual abuse in childhood as an apparently much more common event than was once thought (Osborn 1990), the problems associated with the increased scale of unemployment and homelessness, and debate about the extent to which the growing number of single parents affects the welfare of children.

The Act reiterated the pursuit of permanence as a principal objective in child care social work: 'continuity of relationships is important and attachments should be respected, sustained and developed' (Department of Health 1990). But the case for permanence has been modified since it was first pressed upon the profession in the early 1980s. Thoburn (1985) argued that, in its earlier form, the idea was too rigid. Instead, she shows that there are as many as 16 different ways of achieving permanence in a child care setting – with or without contact with the birth family. Thoburn's analysis did much to defuse what had become a somewhat sterile debate about the respective rights and responsibilities of birth parents or substitute families, and led to a widespread acceptance that a child's need for stability and security demands that the social worker should consider all the options available. Social workers have come to believe that contact between the child and the birth family is appropriate and desirable, and can bring positive benefits in the development of a sense of identity.

The 1989 Act explicitly recognises the needs and interests of black families. Race, culture, religion and language must be taken into account when placements are determined, and reference must be made to the wishes of the children and of those people who are important to them.

Conclusion

In child care, as elsewhere in social work, policy and practice are different. While policy-makers deal in generalities and to some extent even in abstractions, the practitioner is faced with everyday reality – with the uniqueness of a specific situation, with the constant realisation that personality (her own and the clients') and social reality often make a mockery of her best laid plans. Social work is about negotiation, judgment, compromise and discretion; ultimately, it is more of an art-form than a science. And although attempts have been made to restrict decision-making in some areas (for example, with regard to trans-racial placements), the professionally sensitive view remains that good-quality social work requires its practitioners to retain the highest level of discretionary power wherever possible.

The enormity of the dilemmas facing social workers was regularly rehearsed in public during the 1980s in a sequence of reports emerging from panels of enquiry into child deaths and other events (for example, Lambeth 1987, Blom-Cooper 1985, 1987). Social workers were criticised for obeying 'the rule of optimism' – wanting to believe the best of abusive parents and as a consequence not looking adequately for contrary evidence. They were criticised for failing to fulfil statutory responsibilities in a proper manner and for neither knowing nor understanding the laws relevant to child protection. And they were criticised for failing to investigate reports of abuse sufficiently quickly and efficiently. There was clearly much that was wrong with the standards of disciplined practice in some departments.

However, in 1988 social workers found themselves under attack in the Cleveland Enquiry for erring in the opposite direction and for being *too* assiduous in their removal of children from homes where, it had been alleged, there were grounds for suspecting incidents of sexual abuse (Butler-Sloss 1988). The Cleveland case (followed in 1991 by another in Orkney) demonstrated that the pressure on social workers to be 'efficient' in their efforts to cut the incidence of child abuse in society to negligible proportions is not easily compatible with public expressions of concern about the inappropriateness of removing children from their homes on the basis of allegations which may be unfounded or even malicious and which are often exceedingly difficult to prove.

Child care practice in the 1990s is carried out by staff with specialist responsibilities for children, and often with advanced qualifications. It puts particular emphasis on the important art (or skill) of communicating with children. It focuses its attention on the assessment of risk, and is alert to the possibility of sexual abuse in a way that could never have been anticipated in an earlier generation. It operates in a relatively structured fashion, according to well-defined procedures, and with a keen awareness of statutory requirements. It is flexible in the options it considers for a care plan and looks at a wide range of 'permanence' alternatives. It seeks to ensure that the child will maintain contact with his birth parents whenever possible. It usually uses written agreements with all parties involved (birth parents, foster and adoptive parents, children), and it tries to pay special attention to the wishes of the birth parents. It aims to involve parents in any conferences or discussions that take place about the child, and it emphasises openness in the decision-making process.

Child care social workers cannot escape from the fact that the tasks they are called on to perform are often of a severely stressful nature. Like it or not, they operate in an environment that can be both unstable and hostile, and the child protection duty and the child-caring role must take precedence over all other considerations. One major step forward in the last decade has been the recognition of *time* as an overriding factor; what may seem good and sensible in the short term (the removal of a child from home) is now known to contain the seeds of worse effects in the long term. It is the social worker's job, above all, to weigh the probabilities in the balance, and to take a decision in the light of all the available evidence and on the basis of her accumulated professional experience. When you consider that a decision may affect the child's whole life, now and in the future, it is an awesome responsibility, and it is right that the variables should remain of public, political and professional concern.

So much of what happens to children in their families occurs in complete privacy with no impartial witnesses. Social workers in practice have had to 'learn by doing' the job of policing the domestic environment, and it would be misleading to claim that they have yet got it right. What can be said is that they are a lot wiser than they were, that the skills of assessment, decision-making, reporting, advocacy and negotiation are qualities of a high order, and that the need for care planning in every case is taken seriously. What is less certain is whether a full and proper *modus operandi* yet exists for cooperation and collaboration with parents who may often be in conflict with the worker, or whether the need for fully independent representation of parental interests will, within the decade, become recognised.

Children with disabilities

written with Maya Rawal

Children may be deemed to have disabilities of various kinds, be they learning disabilities, physical disabilities or emotional and behavioural problems. Some children may suffer multiple disabilities. The guiding principles that have influenced recent policy developments, and therefore legislation, include the following: the value of normalisation, the desirability of community integration, the primacy of the child's rights and the importance of parental participation and partnership.

As recently as the early 1980s, the statutory framework determining provision for children with disabilities was disjointed and piecemeal. The children's interests were covered by different Acts dealing with health, education, disability and income maintenance. Disabled children were defined according to ten categories of handicap, including 'educationally subnormal' and 'maladjusted'. They were often housed in large residential institutions redolent of the poor law, without the protection of regular reviews and often a long way from their parental homes.

In 1979 the Jay Committee reflected the growing feeling that it would be better if children with learning disabilities who were unable to live with their birth families became the responsibility of local authorities so that they could be protected by child care legislation in exactly the same way as if they were not disabled. Research had suggested that smaller residential units could achieve better results than the traditional hospital settings (Russell 1989: 178), and Jay argued that foster care could also provide a fruitful way forward.

In 1978 the Warnock Report, of the committee of enquiry into the education of handicapped children and young people, prepared the ground for the Education Act 1981, finally implemented in 1983. The Act embodied the principle of integration, and it replaced the previous rigid distinction between 'handicapped' and 'non-handicapped' people with a *continuum of needs*. The ten categories of handicap which had long been employed in systems of assessment were outlawed, and the term 'learning difficulties' was introduced in their place. A learning difficulty was defined as a significantly greater difficulty in learning than would be the case with the majority of children the same age, or a disability which prevents the child making use of educational facilities of the kind usually provided for children the same age. The Act emphasised that 'the main focus should be on the child himself rather than his disability'.

Section 7 of the 1981 Act introduced the 'Statement of special needs' procedure, or as it has become known, 'statementing', involving a multidisciplinary assessment team and the participation of parents. Following an assessment, the local education authority has an obligation to make appropriate provision, preferably in mainstream schools, though local special schools can be used if they represent the most positive option.

The statementing process was a well-intentioned innovation, but it has been criticised in practice, particularly on the grounds that the provision of special facilities has tended to be resource-led rather than needs-led. Stone (1991), writing as the mother of a nine-year-old son with cerebral palsy attending an ordinary school, says that 'when children with disabilities are currently integrated within ordinary schools they have to fit into an education structure which is not designed for them and which frequently provides inadequate support'.

Referring to the way in which her son's annual review was carried out, she says that 'it appeared that if additional support was unobtainable the need for it should not be registered'.

Special problems have been identified among ethnic minority families caring for disabled children. The families have been quoted as being dissatisfied with an absence of translation and interpreter facilities in schools, and with a lack of adequate opportunities for representation and advocacy among minority groups (Russell 1989).

The introduction of statementing (though not itself a specifically social work innovation) was an attempt to put in place a policy requiring interdisciplinary collaboration, but in some ways it can be viewed as a classic example of how much easier it is to get well-intentioned reforms onto the statute book than to implement them in full in practice, especially when they have significant resource implications or when they assume the ability or willingness of all parties involved to cooperate in achieving difficult objectives.

The Disabled Persons (Services, Consultation and Representation) Act 1986 was a second major piece of legislation affecting disabled children and their families. It put in place a system designed to ensure that social workers would liaise with schools as children with disabilities approached the end of their schooling. At that time, a social services department, having earlier determined that the child is a disabled person, is required to carry out a multidisciplinary assessment in order to focus attention on the child's need for further education, training and for possible employment arrangements.

Gradually during the 1980s, the importance of carers came to be acknowledged by the government, and legislation in 1986 (the DPA) and 1990 (the NHS and Community Care Act) for the first time explicitly recognised the importance of assessing the needs of the carer as well as those of the disabled person. The Griffiths Report (1988) had stressed the value of informal networks of care and accepted that families, friends, neighbours and other local people would 'continue to be the primary means by which people are enabled to live normal lives in community settings'. Of course, in reality, it is almost always the parents of disabled children who carry the heaviest responsibility. 'Most mothers take on the additional burdens willingly, accept it as right that they should do so, and are prepared to adapt their lives and expectations' (Abbott and Sapsford 1988).

The Children Act 1989 represents the culmination of the policy that children with disabilities are children first and foremost. It is the first statute to combine local authority obligations in child care with their duties to disabled people, and as a result children with disabilities now benefit from the powers and responsibilities which local authorities have towards all 'children in need'. Services must be provided in such a way as to 'minimise the effect on disabled children in the area of their disabilities, and to give such children the chance to live lives which are as normal as possible'.

The Children Act says that local authorities must seek out, assess and make provision for children in need, maintain a register of disabled children, and make available information about the services they provide.

Local authorities have a duty to provide appropriate systems of day care for children in need, and they may offer counselling, home help, assistance with travel or holidays and access to family centres.

Following on the heels of earlier legislation, the Children Act recognises the need for a close working relationship between different departments: health, education and social services. But social workers also have to collaborate and consult with parents and children at all stages of assessment, at decision-making meetings and at case reviews. The ideas of partnership and of client participation are given headline treatment in the policy context, although it is recognised that the practice implications will take some time to work out.

The requirement that social workers should involve children in the process of planning their own futures is crucial to future developments; but if the child is especially young, has complex needs or experiences difficulties in communication, then the principle will be of little value unless the practitioners are in place who can develop specialist skills of a high order.

This is a good example of how policy developments impinge upon the world of practice, and need to be taken into account by those responsible for training, practice and management.

People with learning disabilities

written with Ashok Chand

Language and terminology have assumed major importance in a number of social work fields in recent years, but nowhere has this been more apparent than in respect of people with learning disabilities – or, as they would once have been called, the moderately or severely subnormal or the mentally handicapped.

In 1982 the World Health Organisation put out definitions of the following terms:

- *Impairment:* a permanent or transitory psychological, physiological or anatomical loss or abnormality of structure or function.
- *Disability:* any restriction or prevention of the performance of an activity, resulting from an impairment, in the manner or within the range considered normal for a human being.
- *Handicap:* a disability that constitutes a disadvantage for a given individual in that it limits or prevents the fulfilment of a role that is normal depending on age, sex, social and cultural factors, for the individual.

Ashton and Ward (1992) have said that the most common term used for people with psychological problems was 'mentally handicapped person', now by prescribed conventional usage replaced by 'people with learning disabilities'. Ashton and Ward argue that labels like these are not insignificant because 'experience has shown that terminology is important in determining peoples' attitudes and expectations and in avoiding misconceptions'.

Normalisation

Policy regarding people with learning disabilities is unusual in the 1990s because it has not been significantly influenced by legislation specific to the client-group. But practice has certainly been radically influenced by a series of policy documents produced down the years, and most recently by the passage of the NHS and Community Care Act 1990.

'Normalisation' is a key concept in work with learning disabilities. The purpose behind the idea is to secure for the client a way of life that is as near to normal as possible. Wolfensberg (1983) suggested that normalisation meant 'as much as possible, the use of culturally valued means to enable, establish and maintain valued social roles for people'. Such an approach is crucially related to the policy of moving swiftly in the direction of community care and away from the kind of extreme institutionalisation that mentally handicapped people have long suffered.

Nirje (1970) outlined ten areas for normalisation:

1. People with learning disabilities should experience the same cycles and rhythms of the day, week and year as others.
2. Children should experience a normal family atmosphere.
3. Schools should cater for all children so that they may learn together.
4. Problems of self-image suffered by adults with learning disabilities and of their acceptance as adults by others should be tackled.
5. People with handicaps should experience change.
6. In old age connections with earlier periods of life should not be severed.
7. Time should be taken to find out the viewpoints of people with learning disabilities and their views should be respected. ·
8. The sexes should not be separated.
9. People with learning disabilities should receive and handle basic financial privileges.
10. The standards of living enjoyed by their families should not be significantly different from those of the general population.

A key document in United Kingdom policy – and one which is still influential in practice – was published in 1971: the White Paper, 'Better services for the mentally handicapped'. The paper recognised the need for clients to move from traditional large long-stay hospitals to a comprehensive care programme based largely in the community. It was argued that people with learning disabilities needed domiciliary and personal services rather than medical treatment, and it set out a 20-year deadline for the achievement of its outlined policy. Since the paper was published much has changed, but much remains to be done.

In 1982 the Barclay Report outlined two primary tasks for social work: to plan, establish and maintain the provision of social care; and to provide face-to-face communication with clients in order to help them to tolerate or change some aspects of themselves or of their circumstances. The first of these tasks is clearly central to the job of helping people with disabilities survive in the community; and the second is similarly important but requires special skills to enable communication to occur with people 'who are often robbed of their speech because other people do not believe that they have ideas or that any ideas they might have would have any value' (Anderson 1982).

Barclay suggested that community social work should be directed towards the support and strengthening of informal networks in order to prevent problems arising. He acknowledged that this must involve the provision of resources for carers, and his report suggested that the way ahead for social work lay with a policy of promoting partnerships between informal carers and statutory and voluntary services. This is the way 'most likely to meet the needs of citizens with social problems'.

In 1983 an All-Wales Working Party report provided guidelines for good practice in work with learning disabilities. It laid down the right of handicapped people to normal patterns of life within the community and to be treated as individuals; and it emphasised that, if people with learning disabilities are to develop their full potential, they will always require help from the communities in which they live and from professional services.

As policy has since evolved, five elements have come to be recognised as crucial:

partnership, advocacy, individual care plans, multidisciplinary working and, of course, community care. But all of these can be said, so far as people with learning disabilities are concerned, to be directed towards one overriding goal: that of empowerment. Adams (1990) described it as 'a process by which individuals, groups and/or communities become able to take control of their circumstances and achieve their own goals, thereby being able to work towards maximising the quality of their lives'.

In 1988, the Griffiths Committee reviewed community care policy and made recommendations for its improvement. The Minister of State at that time, Virginia Bottomley, defined community care as being 'about providing the services and support which will enable people affected by . . . disability to live as independently as possible. The aim is to support people in their own homes or in "homely" surroundings wherever this can be done.'

In 1989, a White Paper committed the government to provide services for people with disabilities and to develop them by means of a multidisciplinary assessment of needs. An assessment should include the opinions of the clients and the carers, thus embodying, at least to some degree, the idea of partnership.

According to the White Paper, the care manager (who may or may not be a social worker) would be expected to carry out an appropriate assessment of an individual's need for social care, in collaboration with medical, nursing and other caring agencies, before deciding what services should be provided. She would then design a 'package' of service tailored to meet the assessed needs of the individual and that person's carers; and agencies would be expected to establish procedures for receiving comments and complaints from service users and for monitoring the quality and cost-effectiveness of services.

Partnership and the social worker's role

It is the job of the social worker to prepare the ground for an individual's return to his own home by providing advice and support for those involved. She has to help clients adjust to new settings following any move, paying special attention to the importance of overcoming difficulties of communication and/or mobility. She has to have knowledge about facilities for occupational, social, cultural or recreational activities. And she has to help find permanent accommodation outside the family home if the client desires it.

Social workers performing these functions need to have several skills: they need a good knowledge of carers' needs, of benefit systems and of local voluntary services; they need skills in advocacy, negotiation and counselling; they need sensitivity in the way they handle the partnership role; and they also need to be able to help carers improve their own skills and to become adept in the assertion of their rights.

The idea of partnership is critical to the successful pursuit of policy in the sphere of learning disability. The intention is that, in place of the social worker or the nurse determining everything, full account will be taken of the client's and the carers' opinions before decisions are made.

A Law Commission consultation paper (1991) highlighted the issue of advocacy when working with people with learning disabilities. The client might well be capable of making a decision, but incapable of communicating it. The social worker, acting as an advocate, could plead the cause of her client and take such action on his behalf in order to secure valuable services and enable him to enjoy his rights to the full.

The Disability Manifesto Group argues that it is often not the disability itself that handicaps people but rather the way in which they are treated because of it (Ashton and Ward 1992). The difficulties faced by people with learning disabilities, therefore, may be due to the reinforcement of their limitations by those who stigmatise and discriminate against them.

The NHS and Community Care Act 1990 brought a decade of planning and debate to fruition, and emphasised the need for individual programme plans which would 'favour environmental rather than service provision; and reflect the informed choices and wishes of the consumer and the carer'.

Carers say that what they want from social workers is continuous support and care in helping to alleviate the loneliness that many feel, together with practical assistance and advice. They want social workers to have specialist skills (rather than a generic background) and detailed knowledge about working with learning disabilities. They like their social worker to be in close touch with other relevant agencies, such as education and health. And, most of all, they want to be able to share their feelings with an understanding person (Glendinning 1983).

A particular need for respite care to ease the burden on home carers was recognised by the Disabled Persons (Services, Consultation and Representation) Act 1986. One parent's view of respite care included 'the freedom to be spontaneous and just going where you want. Jane's got used to me being around and she can get a bit selfish about me going out. As much as I love her, it's lovely to go out without her occasionally.'

Revolutionary changes have been brought about in the world of learning disabilities in a relatively short period of time; they have been designed to make life better for an always vulnerable and potentially high-profile group of people on the fringes of society. They have not been implemented without dissension and controversy, and there remain many problems. Four in particular look likely to run and run: first, the institutional problems of securing effective collaboration between different agencies (especially health and social services); second, the extent to which the idea of normalisation introduces a wholly artificial or spurious idea of what is 'normal'; third, public awareness that the caring role is traditionally assumed to be women's work which therefore makes it a feminist issue; and, fourth, the question of whether sufficient funds will follow needy clients into the community and wherever they may move on to – especially if they have no domestic family to settle down in.

These dilemmas also reflect the fact that the boundaries around both social work and nursing in the area of learning disabilities are especially fluid, with the real possibility that by the end of the 1990s the differences in the work of the two occupations could have blurred to the point where professional separation (and therefore training distinctions) are no longer defensible.

Elder-care

written with Rachael Davis and David Parry

Social policy debates concerning the care of older people in our society are dominated by an irresistible demographic fact: the number of British citizens over the age of 85, having risen steadily throughout the 20th century (and very quickly during the 1980s), will continue to grow into the 21st, though with a temporary respite after 2011:

Table 2.1
Number of elderly people in Great Britain: 1901–2041

	Age 75–84		Age 85 and over	
	Number (000s)	% change	Number (000s)	% change
1901	450		57	
1971	2 074	(+361%)	462	(+711%)
1981	2 501	+21%	552	+19%
1991	3 050	+22%	875	+59%
2001	3 165	+4%	1 144	+31%
2011	3 081	−3%	1 291	+13%
2021	3 412	+11%	1 287	0%
2031	3 997	+17%	1 454	+13%
2041	4 604	+15%	1 656	+14%

(2001–2041: projections)

Source: Adapted from the Family Policy Studies Centre: Fact Sheet 2 – 'An Ageing Population', 1991.

Faced with the complex demands implicit in this underlying trend, two clear strands can be identified in recent elder-care policy-making and implementation. First, there has been a growing emphasis on the role of community care as the preferred public sector approach. And second, we have seen a significant increase in the proportion of people living in privately owned residential homes rather than in those provided by local authorities.

Community care

Community care means different things to different people, has different applications to different client-groups, begs the question of who provides the care and glosses over the need to define the words 'care' and 'community'. For older people, Bamford (1990: 7) has defined it as 'domiciliary support to remain at home rather than face a future of residential care or hospitalisation'.

The NHS and Community Care Act 1990 provides the first embodiment of a structural concept of community care in legislation, although, both as a theoretical idea and as public policy, community care was first enunciated in the build-up to the Mental Health Act 1959. Its growing importance since then can be tracked steadily through a sequence of official documents.

The Seebohm Report (1968) 'referred to a wider conception of social service, not directed only to the care of social casualties but to the well-being of the whole community' (Bulmer 1987: 4); and it created an expectation that the profile of social work with older people would be raised and the professionalism it required be acknowledged.

During the 1970s, 'the dominant paradigm of social welfare for elderly people was the "continuum of care", by which increasing disability was matched to a progression through different services, from domiciliary care to residential and then geriatric [nursing] care' (Bebbington and Charnley 1990: 410).

The Barclay Report of 1982 has been described 'as an important statement about the character of community care in the late twentieth century' (Bulmer 1987: 9). At the same time, the long period of Conservative rule had begun with the New Right's emphasis on the tactical value of introducing market forces in public sector management, an emphasis on a traditional model of family responsibility, and the idea that the state's role in welfare was that of providing a safety net rather than a total package of care designed to meet all 'needs'. Because of the long-recognised high cost of residential provision, the idea of community care was welcomed by politicians in power because of the way it seemed to promise reductions in public expenditure.

Bebbington and Charnley have suggested that there was effectively no model of social care for the elderly operating through the 1980s, and it can certainly be argued that the decade was characterised by transitional stages of development in policy and practice. But, in reality, the mixed economy of public, private and voluntary residential provision, the significant scale of home care facilities provided by social services and health departments, and the experimental idea of turning social workers into care managers represent, if not a model, then certainly a framework for practice which absorbed large sums of public money and laid the foundations for a still humane and efficient system of providing for the rising numbers of older people.

Residential care

Despite the arguments put forward in favour of community care, 'residential care has remained a dominant form of provision for elderly people' (Phillips 1992a: 46). Greatest growth has come in the private sector. The November amendment to the Social Security Act 1980 famously (and, it is widely believed, unintentionally) made the social security system financially responsible for old people entering private residential care if they could show that they did not have the means to pay for themselves. This led to an enormous boom in private residential homes. Bird, in his study of one English county (1984), found that the number of private homes in Norfolk grew from 35 in 1979 to 92 in 1983. By the end of the 1980s, it was over 300.

Nationally, in 1981 there were 39,000 private places and in 1986 93,000 (Sinclair *et al.* 1990: 14). The cost to the Exchequer was enormous: annual spending on supplementary benefit payments for people's fees in private residential homes rose from £6m in 1978, to £190m in 1984 and to £460m in 1986 (Phillips 1992a: 34).

While private residential provision expanded during the 1980s, the numbers accommodated in local authority homes were at a standstill.

A policy for the 1990s

In 1986 the Audit Commission, faced with the explosion in supplementary benefit costs caused by the ease of access to the private sector, drew attention to the conceptual conflict between the government's community care policy and the apparently automatic availability of private residential provision at public expense.

Following the Audit Commission's report, a committee was established which led to the publication of the Griffiths Report in 1988, which laid firm foundations for major legislation. Griffiths proposed that local authorities should move away from their role as significant providers of care and instead take on the job of arranging and purchasing care services from 'providing agencies' (Phillipson 1988: 30).

The 1989 White Paper, 'Caring for people', reiterated the view that 'enabling people to live as independently as possible in the community is at the heart of community care. Community care means providing the right level of intervention and support to enable people to achieve maximum independence and control over their own lives.' As well as emphasising the value of independence to older people, the White Paper wanted to see them being given more choice in their use of service facilities and more encouragement to live at home.

The White Paper insisted that there would have to be prioritisation of needs, and the new regime would demand not only close collaboration and liaison between health and social services, but also the active cooperation of their agents with relatives and informal, voluntary carers.

'Caring for people' aimed at a marriage between the language of welfare and the language of the market place, and it necessarily stressed the need for efficient systems of business management, given the big sums of public money involved. The terminology bequeathed to the 1990s was virtually unknown a decade earlier: purchasers and providers, consumer options, care management, coordination, and packages of care.

The culmination of the period of preparation, experimentation and planning came with the passing of the NHS and Community Care Act 1990. Its six key objectives echo those spelt out in the White Paper: people are encouraged to live at home; carers can expect to be supported; needs must be assessed; the independent sector (private and voluntary) is crucial; local authorities' responsibilities are to be clarified; and there must be value for money.

Implemented in 1993, the Act requires that social work with older people focus on care planning, case assessment and care management, and that there should be extensive use of the independent sector. The Act lays down that residential and nursing homes, together with long-stay hospitalisation, should all be regarded as part of the overall 'community care' strategy, thus pushing towards a fully integrated approach in practice.

A central issue that emerged in the wake of the 1990 Act concerns the conflict between needs-led assessments (the desirability of which is implied in the Act) and resource-led assessments which are thought to be inevitable in the pragmatic world of service provision. The unlimited satisfaction of needs remains a mirage of ideological purity – well-intentioned, but ultimately not a realistic foundation for social work practice.

Some people have expressed doubt over whether the care manager's role can be appropriately categorised as social work. But there are of course no narrow limits to what constitutes social work: 'social work is what social workers do', and the NHS and Community Care Act has made a radical contribution to the evolutionary process in social work practice characteristic of the late 20th century. In work with older people, as elsewhere, social work is best defined in whatever way serves the needs of a policy-based system of service provision, set alongside clinical operators like nurses, physiotherapists and doctors. The social worker can perfectly happily be made responsible for case assessment, for the purchase or the provision of care, for care management, for one-to-one counselling, for case advocacy or for gatekeeping.

Assessment

Assessment is neither a new nor an unusual role for social workers, although the specificity of focus required by the 1990 Act means that the process is very different from earlier forms of casework. It is still concerned with psychosocial diagnosis, but in addition it must draw on inter-professional guidance and take material and environmental factors into account in order to relate the client's 'needs' to the 'resources' available. Moreover, to complicate matters further, the policy-makers' insistence on the need for choice has introduced a shift in the balance of power between worker and client; and it is a shift which, when it involves purchasing 'packages of care' from the private sector, not all social workers are comfortable with.

Phillips and McCoy (1990) have identified wide variations of attitude among social workers towards the private sector. At one extreme – often among hospital-based practitioners – there is total acceptance, while at the other there is implacable hostility. They note five types of practice:

1. The social worker makes a pragmatic response, in which circumstances (including a lack of public sector resources) mean that she is forced to refer people to the private sector.

2. The social worker judges a particular private home to be well-matched with the client's needs, and makes a positive referral.
3. She acts as an advocate for isolated elderly people, including some already in private homes.
4. The social worker makes herself fully knowledgeable about the private sector as a whole, and acts as an advisory service.
5. She has strong political views, either for or against the private sector, and she allows her ideological perspective to influence her work.

Under the Act, social workers have had to improve their knowledge of the availability and suitability of all local homes for different people (and indeed of all packages of care in the community, an increasing proportion of which are likely to be privately managed).

Social workers, employed by the state, remain in key positions of responsibility: assessing, referring, registering homes, purchasing services and inspecting practice. There has never before been such a vivid example of how the social worker's role is *necessarily* subordinate to political developments which, though subject to professional debate, are ultimately the product of democratic decision.

The traditional skills and qualities of social work can surely coexist with the strategic developments built into the 1990 Act. Marshall writes of the need to achieve a balance between the dynamism and the enthusiasm that characterise new developments and the experience and skill already existing in conventional social work methods (1992: 109).

Provided that social workers continue to pursue a commitment to the best interests of the client, there is no reason why the emergence of a mixed economy of care should not be successfully absorbed into the professional tradition. Certainly the principle of enabling people to remain in their own home for as long as possible (which, almost all research agrees, is the preferred option for most people), and the principle of matching needs to resources according to professional assessment, are easily assimilable into historical patterns of social work practice.

Mental health

written with Deirdre Shores and Louise Wensley

By the late 1970s, most of the large Victorian asylums in Britain had been closed down or reduced in size and many psychiatric patients transferred to general hospitals. At the same time, a new generation of general practitioners had emerged who were, according to Butler and Pritchard (1983), better trained and more interested in mental health than their predecessors. Tranquillisers had been developed which were capable of controlling symptoms without 'reducing the patient to a state of stupor' (Butler and Pritchard: 96), thus allowing some long-term patients to return to the community, and in some instances to return to work and enjoy normal family life and social networks.

The Mental Health Act 1959 emphasised the value of informal rather than compulsory admissions, and laid the foundations for the community care policy that remains at the heart of treatment and maintenance systems today. The Act's intention was to ensure that psychiatric patients were treated in the same way as other patients, setting them free as a consequence from 'the straight-jacket of the past' (Hoggett 1990).

What of social work in the social services departments after 1971? Goldberg and Warburton (quoted in Hudson 1982) found that local authority social workers had minimal involvement with the mentally ill: 'On the whole the impression was gained that social workers were holding a watching brief unless a crisis forced them to arrange the care of children or the admission to hospital of adult clients.' Goldberg and Huxley (1980) were harsher: 'the social work role in relation to the mentally ill client has . . . become stagnant'. Others were agreed that social workers, after Seebohm, were confused about their role in mental health and lacking in professional confidence. By 1982, with the emergence of community psychiatric nurses as a professional group, it was being suggested that social workers might be reduced to a welfare rights role and to a policy of crisis intervention.

The two main developments of the 1980s came with the Mental Health Act 1983 and renewed advocacy of community care policy.

The mental health pressure group, MIND, had taken a campaigning lead during the 1970s with the aim of reforming the law relating to mental illness. It argued that every mentally disordered person should be able to expect to have their rights safeguarded: compulsory admission, when necessary, should be carried out according to clear regulations; compulsory care should be given in the least restrictive conditions possible; the professionals concerned should be adequately trained and their competence assessed; and the quality of care and treatment should not fall below an accepted minimum.

The Mental Health Act 1983 was designed to meet these demands as far as possible, and is generally regarded as having been an effective piece of psychiatric legislation. The 1983 Act deals with the detention of patients who are a threat to themselves or to others; with the position of patients who need treatment but who refuse it because of their mental disorder; with aspects of the admission of patients who are mentally disordered and who need hospitalisation; and with the need to ensure legal protection for patients detained in hospital.

Mental illness is not defined in the 1983 Act, its identification being left as a matter for clinical judgment. Definitions are provided for mental impairment and psychopathic disorder ('a persistent disorder or disability of mind which results in abnormally aggressive or irresponsible conduct'), but Hoggett (1990) criticises the Act for not adequately distinguishing between those forms of mental disorder that warrant long-term civil commitment and those which permit a therapeutic rather than a penal disposal of criminal offenders.

Part II of the Act deals with compulsory admissions to hospital for assessment (Section 2) and for treatment (Section 3), emergency admission (Section 4) and guardianship (Section 7).

Compulsory admissions can only be made if 'the patient is suffering from mental disorder to a degree which warrants detention in hospital' and 'detention is necessary for his own health and safety, and the safety of others'. Applications for assessment can be made either by the patient's nearest relative or by an approved social worker (that is to say, a social worker who has undergone special training in mental health skills). There must be recommendations in writing from two medical practitioners, only one of whom need have special experience in the diagnosis and treatment of mental disorder. A Section 2 admission may last up to 28 days, but Hoggett (1990) argues that, 'once in hospital, the treatment which can be given to the patient is the same as that which may be given to long-term compulsory patients', and she suggests that this constitutes a serious intervention in the patient's life.

Admission for treatment under Section 3 is made only if the patient's disorder is judged to be treatable; it can last for six months. Section 4 is used for urgent and emergency admissions as normal procedures would cause delay; only one medical opinion is required initially, but a second opinion must be provided within 72 hours, and the applicant and the doctor must have seen the patient within the last 24 hours. There is criticism of the fact that under Section 4 the medical recommendation for admission may be given by a doctor who does not know the patient and who has no experience in the diagnosis or treatment of mental disorder (Hoggett 1990).

Section 7 concerns applications for guardianship which can be made on similar grounds to those for compulsory hospital admission by the nearest relative or social worker. The local social services authority may be named as guardian, or any other person approved by them. The patient's guardian can require the patient to live in a certain place and attend for medical treatment, employment and therapy.

The Mental Health Act 1983 transferred to approved social workers (ASWs) the functions previously entrusted to mental welfare officers. ASWs are officers appointed for the purpose by a local social services authority. They came into being in October 1984. The intention was to create a body of professional expertise competent to operate in a sensitive area of human welfare.

The legislation gives approved social workers specific roles: to gain access to mentally disordered people living in the community who may need help; to recapture compulsory patients who may escape; to arrange compulsory admission. The legislation requires the social worker to play an independent third-party role in order to defend the patient's rights, but there is a widespread view that many ASWs find it hard to withstand the pressure put upon them by doctors (who have medical and psychiatric expertise behind them) and by relatives (who are left with the burden of coping with a potentially difficult person if admission to hospital is not effected). Hoggett (1990) notes the discrepancy between the idea of social work independence and the difficulty of achieving it in practice. There remains doubt as to whether the 1983 Act has rectified the problem which Bean (1980) had earlier described: 'The doctors are likely to see him [the social worker] at best as a junior member of a professional team which is devoted to securing the best possible care and treatment for the patient. At worst, they will see him as little more than a messenger to supply the forms, arrange transport to hospital and smooth over any difficulties with the patient and his family.'

The general duties of a social worker working with mentally ill people under the terms of the 1983 Act may be summarised: to investigate the patient's social situation and to look at how social and environmental pressures may have contributed to the patient's behaviour; to use her skills as a professional to help reduce any social, relationship or environmental difficulties which might have contributed to the crisis and to make use of appropriate community resources; to form her own opinion, after interviewing the patient and those closest to him, as to whether compulsory admission is necessary, and to consider alternative solutions. Fisher *et al.* (1984) note that 'social work was not concerned with the alleviation of the mental health problem; rather effort was directed at ameliorating the environmental stresses associated with it'.

Olsen (1984) argues that it is the role of the local authority to provide services for the mentally ill: social work support by specially trained social workers; day care facilities to help with the re-integration of anyone who has suffered mental illness; residential facilities for those who have no home to return to after their illness. There is great variation among local authorities in the effectiveness with which they fulfil these roles.

Community care

The idea of community care for mentally ill people was first enunciated in the context of the Mental Health Act 1959, and has been pursued more or less assiduously ever since. It is designed, above all, to avoid the worst effects of institutionalisation – the circumstance in which the residents of a long-stay hospital become disabled, not by their psychiatric illness, but by their long experience of life in a protected environment.

The 1986 Audit Commission report, 'Making a reality of community care', said that it was being implemented too slowly and too unevenly. In 1988 the Griffiths Report proposed an ambitious programme of collaboration between central and local govern-ment, health and social services, statutory, private and voluntary sectors in a 'mixed economy of care'. It recommended that the local authority social services department should be required to assess community care needs in its area, and then to 'enable' the provision of the necessary services using a mixture of informal care and professional support systems. Griffiths emphasised the need to plan for the ultimate closure of all large mental hospitals, while at the same time insisting that 'no person should be discharged without a clear package of care devised'.

The eventual White Paper (1989) and the NHS and Community Care Act 1990 stressed normalisation and choice. They paid special attention to people with mental illnesses, acknowledging the importance of providing adequate short-term services in hospital, and sufficient places in hostels and sheltered lodgings, for those needing residential rather than medical care but who were unable to survive in the community without structured support. The three tenets of the White Paper were: the provision, where necessary, of continuing health care; the availability of capital for building new facilities; and the efficient provision of social care to ameliorate the pains of mental illness.

Advances in chemotherapy (as with the use of lithium to control manic behaviours) have made possible the release into the community of patients who previously would not have been tolerated by other people. But the arrival during the 1980s of homeless people on the streets of London and other cities — many of them with psychiatric conditions — has shown that not everything is working as it was intended, and the task of achieving effective liaison between different elements in the public sector has proved particularly problematic. MIND argues that there is a continuing need for additional resources to ensure the success of an advanced community care policy, but there is also a need to ensure the optimum use of those resources already available — and that, as always, is trickier to guarantee than many advocates initially imagine.

One of the most significant events in recent years — the strengthening of the power and the influence of self-help groups — owes nothing to legislation or to public policy, but could well emerge as the development most likely to change for the better the lot of those suffering from different forms of mental illness.

Probation

written with Jenny Carter

The responsibilities held by the probation service (traditionally known as the social work service of the courts) have gradually increased in range and variety over the years. While still fulfilling their long-standing roles of supervising offenders placed on probation and providing reports for sentencers, probation officers in the 1960s took on major responsibilities for prisoners and parolees. Under the Criminal Justice Act 1972 they also took on board the Community Service for Offenders scheme, widely regarded as one of the few penological success stories of the last half-century. The main aim of the probation service, outlined by the Home Office in 1984 in a Statement of National Objectives and Priorities (SNOP), that officers 'should ensure that, wherever possible, offenders can be dealt with by non-custodial measures', remains valid, even though, paradoxically, the size of the prison population in the United Kingdom has continued to rise inexorably.

The Criminal Justice Act 1982 built on the experimental foundations that had been laid ten years earlier, and made possible the steady development of probation day centres for offenders – places which could combine such subjects as counselling with craft work, literacy teaching with a disciplined introduction to the Highway Code, and therapeutic groupwork with offence-related correctional programmes. The centres were designed as real alternatives to custody, and their aim was to convince sentencers that they offered no soft option. As a result, they were generally run in a more restrictive fashion than previous ordinary probation orders.

In 1984, because of the Home Office's determination to reduce what was judged to be an unacceptable degree of personal autonomy among probation officers, SNOP was published. The statement indicated the order of priorities which it expected the probation service to follow:

1. To ensure that, wherever possible, offenders can be dealt with by non-custodial measures.
2. To prepare reports for the criminal courts.
3. To fulfil its statutory obligations to prisoners and ex-prisoners.
4. To make 'an appropriate and effective contribution to wider work in the community'.
5. To undertake civil work.

SNOP was the first step in a persistent, and still continuing effort by government to introduce performance indicators and measures of efficiency, economy and effectiveness into a service which had traditionally concerned itself with just 'doing the job' that it was given. The government's approach, together with an emphasis on the importance of quality control and accountability, meant that people started asking incisive questions about the objectives of probation – questions that had been in the air for a long time, but which could sometimes be difficult to answer in a way that was both empirically defensible and politically persuasive.

One of the issues that lay at the heart of the debates and developments throughout the 1980s concerned the question of the place of 'social work' in the probation service's sphere of activities and interests. A corporate document produced in 1987 by the three main elements in the service – probation committees, chief officers, and the main-grade union, NAPO – reaffirmed their commitment to some of those areas to which the Home Office had allocated a low priority in SNOP. Research published in 1989 (Davies and Wright) provided analytical evidence to demonstrate that, although the Home Office ministers and the Conservative government might *want* to see a correctional approach to community supervision, those employed as probation officers (together with their managers) were unambiguously identified with the social work tradition. Social work is not itself either restricted in definition or immutable in structure or function, but it has firm professional foundations and a long history. Through their training and by a process of cultural osmosis, probation officers, like other social workers, have a firm idea of the value base which governs their working style and a sense of what is acceptable and what is unacceptable in function or objective.

The government's criminal justice perspective was indicated in a 1990 White Paper (*Crime, Justice and Protecting the Public*): 'punishment in proportion to the seriousness of the crime . . . should be the principal focus of sentencing decisions' (para 2.2). It was made clear that the Home Office therefore expected punishment to be incorporated into community disposals and to be administered by the probation service; the government, it was said, could see no problem in principle in view of the fact that the probation service had been administering the community service system since 1972.

The White Paper wanted to see offenders getting their 'just deserts', and proposed that probation orders should become sentences of the court, not, as had been the case since 1908, deferment of sentence. This would, it was felt, provide a more appropriate framework for the regular inclusion of tough additional requirements in probation orders in order to make society's displeasure with the offender more apparent.

O'Keefe (1988) spelt out the probation officer's dilemma in an article that pre-dated the White Paper. The probation officer's role, he suggested, would no longer be 'to advise, assist and befriend' as had been the case since the origins of the service in 1908, 'but to monitor, enforce and punish'. The 1990 White Paper offered a compromise approach, reflecting the two different approaches of corrections and social work. It said that probation officers are first and foremost officers of the court, and have the responsibility of protecting the public and preventing re-offending, but that they also have the job of successfully re-integrating offenders in the community.

Despite shifts in probation policy in recent years, and the obvious conflicts of perspective between the representatives of the service and the government, Parsloe (1991) has argued that probation officers themselves have not in practice been asked to inflict punishment on their clients. She also argues that all the probation-related developments emerging from policy documents in the 1980s (and later incorporated in the Criminal Justice Act 1991) could be defended as being compatible with social work values.

The Criminal Justice Act 1991 provided firm foundations for probation practice in the 1990s. It made probation a sentence of the court for the first time in Britain. It provided for the possible implementation of curfew orders and electronic tagging as a means of controlling the movements of convicted criminals, whether or not probation officers are responsible for administering them. And under the Act, probation officers are required to prepare pre-sentence reports (PSRs) in which they are expected to offer not recommendations but a range of community sentence options.

The Act was followed in 1992 by the publication of *National Standards for the Supervision of Offenders in the Community*, intended to 'give a clear statement of expected practice, setting out the objectives of supervision'.

Among the practices described, the statement indicates that the first meeting between the officer and the offender should take place no later than five days after the making of the order; that the officer should explain clearly the meaning of the order to the offender; that a supervision plan should be drawn up with the offender and be regularly revised; that the offender should see the supervising officer 12 times in the first three months of the order, and less frequently thereafter; that breach action should be initiated after three failures to comply with the terms of the order; and that all orders should be terminated for good progress if the circumstances warrant it.

The objective of the 'national standards' was to achieve accountability, consistency, equal opportunities, good practice and good management.

In 1992, the probation officers' national association published what they called a damage-limitation document in which they acknowledged that the Criminal Justice Act 1991 had not itself altered the essence of probation practice. 'That will only happen', said NAPO, 'if workers in the probation service allow the punitive philosophy behind the Act and the mechanistic enforcement procedure of National Standards to control their work.'

The changed face of probation

Davies and Wright (1989) found in their analysis of probation practice at the end of the 1980s that, although the social work tradition was still powerful, this did not in itself appear to be incompatible with the objectives of the criminal justice system. Most probation officers seemed to have little difficulty working within a correctional framework, 'although their commitment to the interest of the client always makes them anxious to emphasise client rights and to react against any implicit prejudice in the system'. The researchers also found that the probation service provides a wide range of different working opportunities for its main-grade staff, and that officers uneasy with an excessively structured or disciplined approach to supervision could often avoid extensive involvement in those parts of the service where it was required.

Indeed, the most unexpected finding of the study was that almost a half of all main-grade officers are engaged in largely specialist duties – although fieldwork practice with a mixed caseload is still the single most common role.

There are seven principal areas of specialist practice: prison-based work; civil work (dealing with marriage breakdown and child welfare); court-based work; day centre work; through-care for prisoners and their families; community service supervision; and running probation and bail hostels.

Some of these specialist areas require managerial skills, such as the ability to engage in public relations work or the recruitment and supervision of staff, especially those concerned with day centres and community service. Those who work in prisons have to be able to adapt to the institutional culture without losing their professional identity as probation officers. Those in civil work need to have knowledge of relevant child care and family legislation and to develop high levels of skill in communicating with children. Those who work in day centres have to have a range of qualities and abilities more akin to those of a youth worker than a caseworker. And POs in prisons, community service and hostels have to be prepared to adopt a firm and disciplined approach to their work with clients, and to be particularly alert to the risks of trouble if the boundaries between acceptable and unacceptable behaviour are blurred. In most of the specialisms, the idea of the probation officer working primarily as an office-based one-to-one caseworker is largely redundant.

The contemporary role of the probation officer has been described as one which requires them to hold the balance between the offender and the community (Boswell 1989). Always the probation service (like the police and the prison service) has to work within legislative guidelines laid down by parliament. But, given that constraint, it is remarkable how probation officers have, over the years, earned the respect of the public for the way in which they manage to achieve a happy marriage between their commitment to treat the offender as a responsible individual (in the social work tradition) and their acceptance of the need to supervise him in a disciplined manner (as required by their place in the penal system).

The great problem during the 1980s and still with us in the 1990s – and it is a problem which cannot be glossed over – lies in the fact that the social and psychological sciences have been almost wholly unsuccessful in providing neat formulae which can be used to bring about the reform of individual offenders. We know that environmental manipulation – such as strengthening the design of public phone boxes, introducing driver-visible mirrors in double-decker buses, or creating defensible space in housing estates – can reduce the incidence of some kinds of crime. We know that some offenders, once convicted, never again return to court; but we also know that whenever offenders do return, that very fact increases the probability of them doing so again – and again. What, however, has virtually defeated 20th-century analysts of criminal behaviour is a therapeutic method which could be employed by the penal system in order to reduce the likelihood of convicted criminals re-offending. It is a matter of considerable frustration to politicians, to administrators and to magistrates and judges; most probation officers have learnt to be fairly philosophical about it.

For a long time, it was hoped that the probation service could take on an effective role of corrective intervention. Some researchers today continue to offer to politicians and policy-makers the alluring idea that criminal behaviour can be 'treated' successfully – if only in a small number of cases. But in practice, those who proffer such a model have so far failed to produce systems of diagnosis and assessment that can be used to determine the most likely method of achieving crime reduction in specific instances.

If penal system managers, including those at the helm in the probation service, commit themselves too rashly to a crime reduction strategy as their primary objective, the outlook for social work in the penal system could be distinctly gloomy – not least because of Treasury pressure on the Home Office to justify its constantly rising penal system budget.

The important thing for probation – as for all branches of social work – is to be entirely open and honest about its aims and purposes. The supervision of offenders, the provision of a wide range of community-based sentencing options, and the unflinching pursuit of a humane and humanitarian penal system lie at the heart of British probation history and are as important now as ever.

Those are sufficiently ambitious and challenging goals, and they avoid the trap of giving false assurances about the probation officer's ability to reform all deviants. Social work can promise no such thing.

Centrifugal tendencies and social work's primary objective

This wide-ranging review of social work's policy context in the 1990s demonstrates how far apart the various specialisms have now moved, and shows that all of them require their social workers to engage in close relationships with other professional groups: doctors, teachers, nurses and health visitors, the police, magistrates and the judiciary.

Despite these centrifugal tendencies, however, there remain many generic elements in social work practice, and some common factors in the skills, knowledge and qualities required in a good practitioner. In particular, there is one overriding common objective in social work no matter what the client-group or agency setting, and it is the aim of this book to explain the basis of that assertion.

Part II

The theory and practice of maintenance

3 The social worker's role

Sometimes it seems as though everybody has a separate or different opinion about what social workers do or should do. Even within social work, there are widely differing views on the matter – much more so, I think, than is the case in parallel professions, such as teaching or nursing or the police force.

Traditionally two myths have been held about social work, and there have always been those within the profession or on its fringes who believe that one or the other – or both – are necessary to its existence. This book argues that it is not so.

The first myth claims that social work is primarily a left-wing political activity, and that all social workers must therefore accept a campaigning role, the mantle of the activist. The second myth holds that social work is always directed at client therapy – in a quasi-psychological sense. Both myths are born of the idea that the social worker is, or should be, first and foremost an agent of change. There is evidence that these myths flourish partly because of the personal needs or the evangelical fervour of many who enter the profession. But they also exist because social workers feel pressurised to fulfil the sometimes exaggerated expectations of policy-makers on both the Left and the Right of the political spectrum. Some politicians and government administrators look to social work to be a channel for social reform; others seek from social workers the successful delivery of measurable behavioural changes in deviant clients. It is not surprising, therefore, if social workers are seduced into believing that the achievement of either or both of these objectives provides the *raison d'être* for their existence.

There are, of course, slivers of truth in all these myths – and this can make it all the more difficult to refute them, especially when they are morally worthy or politically attractive to the onlooker. It has also been strangely difficult for social work to arrive at a helpful definition of its own role, and this book through all its editions has struggled to contribute to that objective.

There are some other false emphases in social work, and it is as well to dispose of them before moving forward.

1. *Social work is an impossible job, and it leads to personal burnout.* It isn't, and, properly practised, it shouldn't.
2. *Social workers need to be in tune with their inner selves in order to cope with the complex problems found in other peoples' lives.* Certainly a balanced personality and a degree of self-awareness are important professional qualities in any job but a narcissistic concern with self-knowledge is not a prerequisite for effective social work practice.
3. *Social workers are better than other human service professionals at understanding the problems of their clients.* Not so. They simply see their clients' problems from a different perspective.
4. *All social workers are socialists, or should be.* The first assertion is simply incorrect, and the second depends on the validity of the political myth. The functions of the social worker do not depend on political conformity for their satisfactory performance, though empathy with, and sensitivity to, the feelings of the underprivileged citizen *are* prerequisites for effective practice, and there is as a result a natural tendency for the majority of social workers to be politically left of centre.

In so far as there are common elements in social work they are best described by the general notion of *maintenance:* society maintaining itself in a relatively stable state by making provision for and managing people in positions of severe weakness, stress or vulnerability; and society maintaining its own members, without exception, by a commitment to humanist endeavour. The pragmatically humane approach to social policy has had an impact on 20th-century Western society that should not be underestimated. Most social workers would recognise and support Julian Huxley's assertion (1961) that 'existence can be improved, that vast untapped possibilities can be increasingly realised, that greater fulfilment can replace frustration'. They might disagree on the kinds of effort required of the social worker to activate the client's and society's potential, but a fundamental belief in the capacity of man to improve his own circumstances without necessarily doing so at the expense of others is central to the social worker's philosophy of practice.

Social work, like tourism, computer programming and the leisure industry, has emerged in a particular historical context. Its existence reflects the economic buoyancy of 20th-century industrial societies, coupled with the growing recognition by the state of its obligation to provide for the deviant and the disadvantaged, the depressed and the disabled, the child at risk and the elderly, and to do so in terms and according to standards which avoid the degradation and dismissiveness of the past and of less humane societies. This recognition remains common to all political parties, though there is disagreement about the extent to which governments should encourage and subsidise private commercial initiative in the welfare sector, and about the scale of public expenditure on the personal social services.

Social work can usually be characterised as operating in response to human needs. But that is not to say that social work is always and everywhere available as a free service to those who demand it. For the *needs* might as often be those of society as of the individual in distress. Social work's obligations to the state are as legitimate as its obligations to the client, and the end product of social work is necessarily a negotiated settlement between the state and the various individuals with whom the social worker is deputed to deal. The conflicts and tensions that exist in any open society will impinge on the social worker's field of action, but it is unlikely that any one influence will emerge as carrying undue force.

Social work can only be understood by observing what it does and then by reflecting upon the contribution that those activities make to the way society ticks. As good a way to begin as any is to demonstrate how today's social workers operate from the cradle to the grave; indeed they are involved before the cradle is bought and after the body is buried.

Thirteen varieties of social work – from cradle to grave

1. *The social worker counsels pregnant women who apply to have an abortion. She may prepare a report which could influence the decision of the consultant gynaecologist.*
    Practice may vary according to policy variations in gynaecology departments. In one Lancashire town where requests for abortion are almost never refused, the social worker merely fulfils a counselling and advisory function. In another, where a more restrictive policy applies, social workers have to assess carefully the social and psychological circumstances of the applicant and make a recommendation in the light of this. If, in the social worker's opinion, there is no reason why the woman should not give birth to the baby and raise it satisfactorily, the recommendation is likely to be negative.
2. *The social worker has almost absolute power to facilitate or prevent the process of adoption. She selects adoptive parents, advises the birth mother, and allocates the child.*
    Adoptions may involve the transfer of a child to a complete stranger, with the social worker counselling the birth mother, allocating the child to a previously selected adoptive family and then superintending the exchange. Other adoptions may involve the assumption of full parental rights by relatives of the mother's – her parents, for example.
    In some cases (for example, where the birth mother is withholding consent to the adoption), an independent social worker, the guardian *ad litem*, may be asked to investigate the circumstances surrounding the adoption process and to report back to the court before a decision is taken. A social worker can also be appointed as reporting officer with the duty of reassuring the court that birth mothers who have given consent fully understand the implications of doing so.
3. *The social worker is expected by the community to play a key role in preventing child abuse. She has the power to recommend the removal of a child whom she believes to be at risk of being harmed.*

Prevention has become a fashionable concept in social work but its theoretical foundations are somewhat shaky. Nevertheless both the NSPCC (with *prevention* encased in its title) and other social work agencies are expected to take such steps as they consider appropriate in order to avoid child abuse. Detailed manuals are provided which set out the steps required by local authority departments, and case conferences abound. A small but growing number of children are now removed from their parents at birth. But it seems reasonable to fear that social workers will find it difficult to improve on their recent record in prevention: even with regular visiting and close knowledge of a delicate situation, deaths and child abuse will continue to occur. And, however much the sequence of events can be thought to have been predictable with the benefit of hindsight, it is foresight that matters. No social worker will ever be able to claim 100 per cent certainty in that.

4. *The social worker works in day centres designed to provide non-custodial facilities for juvenile or adult offenders.*
   The centres offer education, social skills training, crafts or sporting activities, and groupwork or counselling often designed to focus on the participants' law-breaking behaviour. Intermediate treatment (IT) for juveniles provides a virtual *carte blanche* for social workers to develop their own creative ideas in youth work, although social services departments vary in the scale of their budgetary commitment. Day centres for adult offenders are becoming more numerous, but there is controversy over the extent to which they should incorporate a strictly disciplined regime. On the one hand, such an approach may be alien to social work principles; on the other, it may be essential if the courts are to be persuaded to use them as an alternative to prison or youth custody.

5. *In respect of children with learning disabilities, the social worker expects to play a significant part in helping the child make the transition from childhood to adulthood.*
   There may be an attempt to help the child find a job if the handicap is not too severe, or arrangements may be made for attendance at a day centre or sheltered workshop. There is evidence from a number of research studies to suggest that there is considerable room for improvement in practice – both so far as the frequency of social work help is concerned, its relevance and sensitivity, and in the degree of commitment shown by the social worker, not only to the disabled teenager but to the family bearing the heavy burden of caring for him day in, day out.

6. *The social worker organises the community service programme for offenders, whereby men and women of all ages do useful work under supervision instead of going to prison or being otherwise punished for crimes committed.*
   The Community Service for Offenders (CSO) scheme is the most radical departure made by the British penal system since the introduction of probation and borstal at the turn of the century. It gets away both from institutional containment and from a unidimensional approach to supervision in the community. It is not *social work* as traditionally understood but its successful absorption by the probation service, working hand-in-hand with the community, has demonstrated the inherent flexibi-

lity of a social work service, and accurately reflects the influence of social work values.

7. *The social worker is responsible for organising and running day care provisions for those who have been or who otherwise might now be in a psychiatric hospital.*

Joint funding between the health and social services and the stimulus of central government grants through urban aid have led to the establishment of many day centres such as the one in Warrington described by Cosgrove (1983). It is available on a drop-in basis, and is characterised by informality; it relies heavily on voluntary help, and the open-door policy and the friendly atmosphere have made it acceptable to people who are psychiatrically damaged. They play games, prepare meals, participate in group meetings and have a full educational and activity programme. The social worker reports great improvement in many of those who attend despite the lack of any formal treatment plans.

8. *The social worker, usually employed by a voluntary agency, provides a long-term support service to families in severe straits. Sometimes the commitment extends over several years.*

The Family Service Unit is the agency traditionally associated with this kind of long-term work; it is common for a unit to work with a family for four or five years, and there will often be examples of cases which have remained open through two or three generations. The social worker may see the family at least weekly, varying the emphasis from time to time. The mother might come into the unit with her children, get material help, be taught – and often taught again and again – how to budget on a limited income. Relationships are close – often on first name terms – and the social worker might act as a godparent, bridesmaid and mourner at one time or another. But, though close, the worker will always have a long-term strategy, and will plan, one day, to withdraw.

9. *The social worker, in partnership with the client, pursues a policy of empowerment.*

Clients are often oppressed people, and the social worker may choose to strengthen the long-term position of her client by using an empowerment model of practice. This requires a radical shift of attitudes on the part of the traditional social worker, one which enables her to take the client into partnership in order to improve his position. She can act as an advocate on his behalf, both within her own department and outside; but she must accept the client as a knowledgeable co-worker and allow him freely to influence her practice on his behalf. This approach is of particular value in work with carers (Holdsworth 1991).

10. *The social worker coordinates the range of services made available by the local authority to make life easier for a severely disabled person.*

The most pressing needs of disabled people are not normally for company – though a survey of disabled housewives has shown how desperately depressed many of them are – but for improved living conditions, adequate financial support and better mobility. One problem is the scale of the demand: even the most modest estimate puts the number of disabled who 'suffer disadvantage and restriction of activity' at well over a million, and although disability and old age go together, there are said to be around 400,000 disabled people under the age of 65 in England alone. The last two decades have seen a surge of social services concern for this client-group, but the pattern of social work activity that is both appropriate and adequate has never been properly spelt out. It needs to be.

11. *The social worker as care manager assesses the needs of an elderly person and allocates resources accordingly.*

    The care manager has a statutory responsibility to carry out an assessment in any case where residential care might be needed for an old person. Wherever possible the social worker will make arrangements for domiciliary care to be provided so that the client can remain at home for as long as possible. If residential care is deemed to be essential, then the social worker will either arrange for admission to one of her department's own homes, or she will 'purchase' a place from the independent sector (Phillips 1992b).

12. *The social worker is responsible for arranging and superintending a pauper's burial.*

    'Who will bury the dead?' Nothing is quite so sad as the total isolation of a corpse without friends or relatives to see to the final rites. Rees (1978) has a nice story of the former welfare officer in a Scottish social work department who volunteers to fulfil the department's statutory responsibility for public burial of the destitute. 'I do most of the funerals in this area. That's another thing that nobody seems keen to do. Simply because I have done them before I still get them. My colleagues are always saying, "I'll come with you the next funeral you do", but I'm still waiting.'

13. *The hospital social worker provides stillbirth counselling for young parents.*

    The bereaved mother is visited in the ward as soon as possible and again at home shortly after her discharge. 'It has been found that the first six weeks after stillbirth can be a period of great isolation and sadness, when feelings of inadequacy and failure are not always appreciated even by family and friends' (Atkins 1981). The social worker's role is therefore to allow the clients to bring their feelings out into the open. A third and final contact is made after six months.

Social work practice – and its critics

Whatever the reason, a large number of people – especially in neighbouring occupational groups, such as the police, medicine and teaching – often fail to appreciate either the breadth or the subtlety of social work practice. Criticisms can still be heard of the allegedly undue influence of Freudian thinking, and of the social worker's consequent obsession with 'potty-training in infancy'; magistrates will attack the probation officer for adopting what they perceive as an unduly sympathetic stance towards a violent criminal or a confirmed recidivist; and the media and the general public alternately fault the social worker for either doing too much (taking children into care unnecessarily, for instance) or too little (failing to prevent hypothermia in the old or child abuse in families).

In fact, as the panning-shot just used demonstrates, the elements in contemporary social work are not overwhelmingly concerned with *treatment* in a quasi-medical or psychotherapeutic sense. There is a strong emphasis on counselling and verbal support, but also a clear recognition of the responsibilities that society invests in the social worker to operate on its behalf in a preventative or restrictive fashion. A major task is to enable the citizen to retain his independence in the community for as long as possible, and to superintend his movement into or out of institutional care in a way that serves both the client's and the community's long-term interests. It is a central tenet of social work that no-one should feel demeaned or abused as a consequence of statutory intervention, and that psychological independence should be encouraged.

The practice of social work takes place almost wholly as a result of *either* statutory legislation *or* policy decisions taken by politicians in central or local government. The functions of the social worker and the focus of her work are not self-selected, but are politically sanctioned and authorised by the agency which employs her. To point that out may beg as many questions as it answers, but it does at least indicate the source of social work's legitimacy, and emphasises that social workers are not, and can never be, a law unto themselves.

The idea of social work as *maintenance* has drawn the wrath of critics on the political Left. Leonard (1976) pinpoints the origins of this criticism: 'Marx saw the governmental machinery of the state and the organisations related to it as performing one crucial function above all others, namely maintaining the rule of the dominant class over the subordinate classes.' 'Maintenance', then, is a dirty word. What is the virtue of maintenance if it merely perpetuates poverty, degradation and discrimination? And from that rhetorical question it is but a short step to the assertion that social work, so defined, must be a sham, a defender of privilege, and social workers the lackeys of capitalism.

It is true that a working contact with many of the social services' clients strongly reinforces the feeling that Disraeli's two nations survive; that, despite undoubted material improvements in most sectors of society, there are still the rich and the poor, the powerful and powerless, the establishment and the nobodies. But must such a realisation lead to the conclusion that social work, as currently practised, is in error?

Some socialist critics of social work, outside the profession, seek its destruction. Others, inside, or more usually on the fringes, argue for a radical model of practice, one which will align the worker with the client *against* the state and the forces of oppression. The problem with this position, attractive though it undoubtedly is to those with a romantic tendency to believe in the coming of the millenium, is straightforward: can a social worker employed by the state continually denounce the objectives of her own department, and can she freely engage in political confrontation with a view to undermining the foundations of social and economic power?

Such an approach might be employed once or twice, provided it is done discreetly, but beyond that it seems improbable that the strategy can be pursued successfully other than on a short-term basis in a society ripe for revolution. There is nothing logically impossible about social workers, along with other groups, pursuing radical ends with a view to overthrowing the present balance of power. They might even choose to do so *as a result of* what they have seen and experienced in the course of their social work duties. But for them to claim that what they are then doing *is* social work seems of doubtful validity. Social work, as it has emerged in the 20th century, undoubtedly depends for its existence on its acceptability to the political regime within which it is practised (and significantly social work exists as an occupational activity in nations of many varied political hues). It demands of the majority of its practitioners that they are prepared to tolerate, with a greater or lesser degree of enthusiasm, the political complexion of the state which employs them.

Inevitably this tips the balance of attitudes towards a consensus model of practice, though it certainly does not preclude the conviction that societies evolve and improve as a result of conflicts within them and that the social worker's perspective can and must contribute to desirable changes in policy and practice. It does, however, tend to reflect the view that all societies have imperfections, that the business of social work is necessarily concerned with ameliorating the pains of these imperfections, and, furthermore, that without underestimating the importance of structural reforms and corporate planning, the individualist approach of traditional social work is both necessary and sufficient to justify the existence of the profession. If social workers were not around to perform the functions outlined in these pages, any urban industrial society would find itself having to rectify the omission whether its political complexion were capitalist or socialist.

Criticisms of social work are not, of course, confined to the political Left. But those normally expressed by right-wingers are more difficult to pin down. Conservative critics do not usually postulate a preferred alternative; they simply argue that social workers are undesirable and unnecessary appendages to a society which has gone soft at the edges. The right wing starts from the complacent assumption that society would be better if the principles of self-help, free competition and law-and-order were linked to the primacy of the work ethic and the self-sufficiency of normal family life to produce a smooth-running society in which the natural instincts of men and women would ensure justice for all and altruistic support for the helpless. The social worker is disliked because her very existence questions the legitimacy of this idealised view of life in a civilised society. Ironically it is the social worker's emphasis on individualism which is despised by the radical Left and which leads her to undermine the corporate model of family and community life beloved by the Right. The social worker sees the anguish of the poor, shares the pain of a mother coping with a Down's syndrome child, experiences at close range the degradation of the dole queue, realises that the offender is never all bad and so recognises the naivety of ideological attempts to manage human affairs wholly at arm's length and only according to economic theories.

Most critics of *The Essential Social Worker* in its first edition branded it as being either right-wing or, at best, centrist in its orientation. Certainly it is not a socialist text. Nor would I be so naive as to lay claim to ideological neutrality. *The Essential Social Worker* pays particular attention to accounts of practice and to the political context within which they take place. Social work in a capitalist society or a mixed economy is both theoretically problematic and yet an empirically self-evident phenomenon. The reasons for its existence, its relationship to state finance and legislation, and where it fits into contemporary patterns of power and privilege are all fascinating questions of political philosophy that deserve more study than they have so far received. This text is faced with the unenviable task (as are all social work teachers) of setting down guidelines for good practice in the full knowledge that, on the face of it, there is no clear consensus of opinion about aims or objectives in social work. Hence, in the course of presenting arguments about the nature of professional competence and how to prepare for it, I am compelled to indicate the framework within which I believe contemporary social workers are expected to operate.

Socialist theories in our field have been significantly better at providing structural critiques than offering empirically testable alternative guidelines for practice. In this book, we start by accepting *a priori* the statutory base and the administrative structure of social work (given that each is the product of democratic decision-making), and attempt to relate both to the traditions of social work literature, the personal motivations of staff and the known interests of client-groups. The end product is noticeably less exhilarating than any Marxist critique would be; in compensation, it hopefully offers some clues to the embryonic social worker about the whys and wherefores of the paid job to which she has made a commitment. It is my belief that social work practice under different political regimes is very much less variable than is often assumed by those who criticise its manifestation under any one – though the precise form in which it exists in the United Kingdom clearly reflects the strongly social democratic influences of the 20th century, tinged as they are with the continuing power of capitalism and an ideological commitment to the idea of personal freedom however defined.

Social workers – and therefore social work students too – are unlikely to be comfortable in their work if they aspire to revolutionary socialism, to a *laisser-faire* society in which all forms of state welfare intervention are proscribed, or to a counselling role in which the client-worker relationship exists independently of the agency by whom the worker is employed. Failure in the past to clarify the nature of these exclusions has led to difficulty in practice, in training and in management. In particular, it has become important to recognise that objective clarification, efficient administration, controlled discretionary budgeting and quality control are all elements as important in a public service operation as they are in commerce or industry, and that an emphasis on their achievement is not in any sense indicative of malign reactionary intent.

4 Clients point the way: Eight lessons to learn

It is only in the last 25 years that the client's voice has come to be heard with any persistence in the social work literature. The publication of Mayer and Timms's *The Client Speaks* in 1970 was a major landmark in this respect and it has been followed by a steady stream of papers, books and articles presenting the point of view of those on the receiving end of welfare interventions of various kinds. The client may not always be right in the judgments he makes about social work but what he has to say is relevant and his conclusions – where they seem to make sense in the context of social policy – should be taken into account when planning future practice.

Research into client opinion is one of the few fields in which sufficient empirical work has been done for firm conclusions to have become possible. Despite methodological problems and the fact that clients constitute a highly heterogeneous group of people who may be expected to want different things from social workers, it is easier now than it was a few years ago to spell out the lessons that we can learn from what the clients tell us.

Lesson 1

Improve the pathways to social work service

There are four ways in which the pathways to service might be improved. First, there is a clear need to increase the public's awareness of the existence of social service agencies. Time and again research studies recall how much difficulty clients experience in discovering where they should go to meet a particular need – how to set about applying to adopt a child, for example, and how many different options might be open to the would-be applicant. Social work offices should be prominently located (perhaps decentralised into residential areas), their facilities should be advertised and deliberate efforts should be made to educate the public about how social workers can help them. Some studies point out that those clients who were personally acquainted with a social worker had an unfair advantage over other clients. If a service exists, *all* members of the public have an equal right to know about it and to have easy access to its facilities.

49

A second point is linked to the first. We know that virtually every visitor to a social services or probation office feels some stigma in being there. (Even I, as a member of the profession, when visiting a student on placement in a social work office, experience a slight feeling of being put-down when the face behind the grille tells me, not always politely, to take a seat. What have *I* done that I should be frequenting such a waiting-room? And I look round uneasily at my companions, knowing that they are looking round uneasily at me.) We also know that it is exceedingly difficult to counteract stigma. But attempts should nevertheless be made to do so – partly, perhaps, by a process of public education, and partly by emphasising the universal availability of social services facilities and the public's right to them. Most social work offices receive regular referrals from a limited number of sources: doctors, councillors, the court, solicitors. The evidence from client-perspectives research shows that such referrers often display considerable ignorance of the social worker's role and convey either no idea or wrong ideas to the client of what is likely to befall them when they arrive. Particular efforts should be made to educate the sources of most referrals and so avoid the serious misunderstandings which can damage a social work relationship before it has begun.

Finally, a problem emerges with casual referrals who appear to be less likely to receive a full service than those sent to the social worker by significant others – councillors, magistrates, psychiatrists, and so on. All referrals should be treated equally. Those who have been referred inappropriately should be told so, irrespective of the status of the person who sent them, while those who have come in under their own steam should be assured of just as full a response as any sent by doctors or social work colleagues.

Underlying these four points lie two imperatives. First, it is essential for social work to establish and defend professional standards in the pursuit of publicly recognised objectives; and second, it is important for the client in particular to grasp the nature of social work, because research has shown that an absence of understanding can reduce the quality of help offered to him, can lead to reduced client satisfaction, and thence to higher drop-out rates.

Lesson 2

Handle the intake process with imagination, sensitivity and tact – put clients at their ease

As in all public service agencies, a pervasive problem is that each new arrival represents a familiar, even a routine, process for the worker, while for the client the occasion is probably unique. Many new clients have described how much grim determination they needed before they could bring themselves to cross the agency threshold. If, having done so, they are greeted with a casual, cavalier or downright hostile attitude, they are likely to turn tail and run. Not only are the clients in a strange, even alien, setting; most of them have intensely emotional reasons for being there – hence the need for even more sensitivity and tact than is required of a dentist's receptionist or a building society counter clerk.

The importance of the intake process to the client is shown by the fact that, long after the social worker has forgotten it, the client can recount every detail of what happened. And the conclusions to be drawn from the literature are, first, that the receptionist should treat every newcomer equally seriously; second, that as a matter of principle the agency should attempt to provide *some* positive response to every initial request; and third, that if a referral to another agency is unavoidable, it should be made helpfully and, whenever possible, a personal introduction arranged.

Rees and Wallace (1982), in their review of client-perception research studies, confirm the sense of stigma felt by many who come for social work help and, as well as emphasising the importance of an unhurried approach, a friendly reception and a non-judgmental response to all applicants for help, they say that it is especially important for intake staff to learn the art of enabling the client to ask for help. 'The ability and willingness of the worker to anticipate and articulate what help is required has been described favourably by clients.' If the social worker does accurately anticipate the request, it relieves the client of discomfort and embarrassment, and serves to convince him that the social worker and the agency are truly caring.

A particular fear expressed by some clients concerns the agency's reputation for authority and power, and, although (as lesson 6 acknowledges) this is not wholly unrealistic, it can sometimes induce unnecessary apprehension. Lishman (1978) has an excellent example of this when she confesses how surprised she was to learn, long after the event, of the intensity of one mother's feelings during the intake interview at a child guidance clinic. 'I was frightened,' said the client, 'I thought they would say I was a bad mother and take him away from me. When they took him away from me [to see a psychiatrist while she stayed with the social worker] I wondered where he was going. I did not ask.' Lishman was the social worker and she admits to having been quite insensitive to this woman's feelings, and there is evidence in other studies that such discrepancies are not uncommon. Certainly many clients do view social workers as potential takers-away of their child, and such unspoken fears will inevitably have an effect on conversation and the relationship.

At intake the public sector social worker must always be sensitive to the fears and anxieties that the client might have of her perceived role.

Lesson 3

Be concerned with the client as a person. Handle the personal in a professional manner. That is the heart of social work .
Client-perspective studies have greatly helped in the task of defining professionalism in social work. It is clear that the *true professional* is not someone who is cool, detached, career-minded and disinterested, but is the worker who can display friendliness (not necessarily friendship in the conventional sense), understanding and a warmth of manner which convinces the client of her active interest in and concern for the client's plight. And clients are remarkably sophisticated in being able to recognise that such professionalism is part and parcel of the social worker's formal occupation. 'With lawyers it's mainly a professional job for them, they don't take a personal interest in it. They wouldn't show

any feelings and not really any interest. The social worker didn't behave as though it was a job, even though it was' (Rees 1978).

The establishment of such a professional relationship gives the social worker the power to exercise considerable influence over the client – to set limits, to give firm advice. There is clearly an element of acting in this, but the performance emerges as crucial to good social work in the eyes of the client. Professionalism is the projection of a concerned interest in the client's welfare.

Rees and Wallace (1982) identify some positive and negative factors which can be defined as good or bad professional practice:

> It often pleases a client when social workers take an interest in them outside the perceived scope of contact. For example, asking clients about their families, taking an interest in their hobbies and activities. visiting outside official working hours – such actions do much to convince people that the social worker's interest is genuine. He or she is not just 'doing a job'. This reinforces the clients' perception of the social worker as a 'friend' rather than a 'professional'.
>
> It is important to the client that the social worker does not appear bored, and that he or she listens attentively to what the client has to say. Things like the social worker staring out of the window while the client is talking, keeping the client waiting, failing to apologise if the interview is interrupted by a phone call, breaking appointments at the last minute – all these have caused some distress to people expecting a more personal approach. When such things occur, social workers confirm the expectations of some clients that social workers are, in fact, no different from other officials.

Lesson 4

Identify the client's expectations and relate these to the agency's obligations and resources. Be active. Be alert. Be helpful. And don't string the client along
Client-focused research has demonstrated frequent instances of misunderstanding between client and worker – what Mayer and Timms dub the 'clash in perspective' – and these must be avoided or overcome if an effective working partnership is to be established. Mayer and Timms (1970) quote the case of the market-stall holder who, because of illness and unemployment, could not afford to buy stock for his stall. He and his wife were advised to go for help to the Family Welfare Association (FWA) and several interviews took place. The clients' only idea was to receive financial aid at a time of desperate need, and the stallholder's wife was particularly resentful that the social worker's focus seemed to imply that their marriage was in difficulties. She said that she asked questions about 'what our marriage was like, were we happy together, were the children contented and things like that. It had nothing to do with what we wanted. It was financial help not any other help.' Eventually the FWA did give the couple a grant, but the client's wife said that 'she would let her children starve before seeking professional help again'.

So numerous are such examples in the literature that one might be forgiven for thinking that what have been called 'pervasive disagreements' are an inherent part of the social work process. They arise partly because of the client's frequent misunderstanding of the social work role, or his misconception of agency resources, but also because of the failure of many social workers to recognise that the responsibility for providing clarification is undoubtedly theirs. Having carefully and sympathetically allowed the client to state his business (providing sufficient time for difficulties of communication), the social worker must accurately assess and honestly explain whether or not the agency can respond. She must tell the client how, to what extent, and for how long help can be given – and on what conditions, if any. If the agency is not in a position to respond, this should be quickly made clear, at the same time providing advice on possible access to other sources, if there are any. If there are not, the social worker may nevertheless feel justified in asking whether there is any other way in which the agency might help. But the client should never be led to expect more than is available. The research literature is full of examples of clients who felt they were 'strung along' by well-meaning social workers and then let down when the reality was eventually made known to them.

When the client's needs or expectations have been identified, there is clear evidence that an active response by the social worker is greatly valued. 'By "doing things" or attempting to do things for clients, social workers confirm their concern and willingness to help. Clients frequently regard worker activity as being denotive of genuine concern' (Rees and Wallace 1982). Clients often stress their material problems and are glad of tangible assistance; many tend to measure both their troubles and potential solutions in concrete rather than abstract terms. Of course, social work has to aim at achieving a balance, not to the total exclusion of counselling or general support roles; nevertheless the recipients of social work service remember appreciatively when they received practical help that was both immediate and relevant to their needs.

Lesson 5

Be a good counsellor
One of the reasons why client studies have tended to emphasise the value of tangible help, is because counselling skills – like good acting or writing – tend not to be noticed when they are present; it is only in their absence that you realise something is wrong. Warmth, informality, genuineness and non-judgmental empathy are traditionally associated with effective practice, and there are adverse comments in the research literature on social workers who failed to reach acceptable standards in these respects.

Lesson 6

Remember that the social work role puts you in a position of power and privilege. You cannot escape or deny it. And you must be honest and open about your agency's responsibilities
Many social workers, especially those with a strong commitment to an egalitarian society, find it difficult to reconcile themselves to the power and authority which are implicit in almost all their working roles. But the message from clients is that any attempt to deny the reality of their position is confusing and results in inefficient practice.

In child care, mental health and probation, the client may well be apprehensive and fearful of whether the social worker is going to respond in a way that will be perceived as punitive; in other spheres – adoption, fostering, requests for material aid – the client knows that the social worker can give or withhold favours or facilities. It is the social worker who holds the initiative, and only when this is acknowledged can it be used sensitively and to good effect.

Sometimes the client's fears are based on fantasies about social worker power, and the worker must do everything possible to counteract unnecessary apprehension by honestly spelling out the aims, responsibilities and functions of the agency. She should give reassurance where possible, but never mislead the client into a false sense of security if she knows that critical and possibly unwelcome or painful decisions may have to be taken.

The fact of the social worker's authority carries with it two obligations: first, it is her job to give structure to the working relationship, to direct and make positive use of verbal exchanges, to focus on appropriately restricted issues, always to explain procedures, and to be absolutely certain that if further appointments are thought to be needed, the client is aware of the fact and knows that the social worker remains available. The second obligation is the traditional one accorded to the privileged person in a service relationship: always to use her influence on behalf of the client where it is pertinent and feasible to do so.

One way in which the worker's power can be used to good effect is in the field of anti-discriminatory practice – an approach to social work that has in the 1990s assumed almost doctrinal qualities. The worker is expected to take the lead in counteracting the heavy burden of discrimination weighing down on the client – whether it be because she is a woman, a member of an ethnic minority group or a person with disabilities. 'Empowerment' is another way of pursuing similar ends, enabling clients to take responsibility for their own lives and their own destiny. In either case, the 'power equation' is turned on its head, with the worker using *her* power to strengthen the client's position in relation to the social environment.

Lesson 7

Use your knowledge and experience for the benefit of the client. Keep it up to date. Use the working group to supplement it
Rees and Wallace (1982) identify three elements looked for by clients:

1. They like social workers to have sufficient experience of life and the world to be effectively unshockable. Violence, deviant behaviour, degradation and psychological fantasies are often a part of many clients' lives, and it is no help to them if the social worker gazes open-mouthed at their personal revelations, adopts a condemnatory attitude towards apparently outrageous behaviour or is salaciously inquisitive without an obviously helpful intent.
2. They like social workers who have self-evidently had the opportunity to learn about the clients' problems through their own life experiences. Clients criticise excessive youthfulness, naivety or a sheltered background in the worker; they are sceptical of

how much help they can expect from someone who is childless or unmarried if their problems concern complex family dynamics; and, in some situations, clients definitely prefer a worker of their own sex.

3. They like workers who have specialised knowledge about a client-group — the disabled, the mentally handicapped, and so on. A worker who is a jack of all trades and a master of none is not viewed with equanimity.

The worker has a responsibility to have at her fingertips detailed, accurate and up-to-date knowledge about the law, welfare rights and local community facilities, and to be willing to turn for help to others in the agency if questions arise with which she feels inadequately qualified to cope.

Lesson 8

Always be trustworthy. Always be reliable

Clients frequently express appreciation of the moral goodness of social workers. They are not, in this, passing judgment on the worker's private life, but are referring to their experience of the worker's performance. Openness and honesty are seen as assets in social work. And any worker who lets a client down after building him up to expect something better is rarely forgiven. 'Children, like adults, appreciate honesty in all their transactions and can forgive almost anything more easily than being told lies or being misled' (Timms 1992).

The need for honesty is even greater in situations where the exercise of unwanted or unpleasant authority is called for. The parents of children in care are often hostile towards social workers, but there is evidence that, at least in retrospect, they are willing to give credit to those workers who confronted them with the reality of their child's — and their own — situation.

Conclusion

Social work has not emerged entirely unscathed from grass-roots criticism, but neither are the comments wholly negative. There are many expressions of appreciation and of pleasure in almost all the client-perspective studies. Even those concerned with wholly authoritarian settings, or those concentrating on unsuccessful cases, record interviews with clients who remembered individual workers with affection and respect.

There are quite clearly two component parts to the practice of good social work, as postulated by the client-perspective research studies. First, the quality of the relationship established is a prerequisite of success: conversation must be easy; there must be friendly concern, commitment and trustworthiness; and the client must be able to feel confidence in the professional knowledge and ability of the worker. Second, the relationship must produce results. The worker must demonstrate an ability to provide help of a kind appropriate to the felt needs of the client within the restrictions imposed by society. The help should normally have a strongly practical (not necessarily material) component for at least part of the time, and must be offered in a way that does not undermine the carefully constructed 'professional friendship'.

It can be concluded that one of these qualities without the other is either not useful or is not social work, so far as the client is concerned.

5 Towards a theory of maintenance

There are a great many elements that contribute towards maintaining and developing a society and its people. Agriculture, industry, trade and commerce provide the wherewithal for material survival; defence policies and policing protect it; education lays the foundations for future growth; the health services ensure physical well-being; and so on. To an increasing extent, in all countries, the state plays a major part in pursuing policies which harness human and natural energies to meet social, political and personal needs.

An assumption in all societies is that, beyond statutory provision and within the framework of the wider social and economic community, individuals and families will maintain themselves, exist in relative self-sufficiency and derive personal satisfaction from the way they make use of opportunities that are presumed to exist. The fact that these opportunities may be unequally accessible is a source of continuing political controversy in all nations, but the underlying assumption about the ultimate primacy of the human unit living his or her own life to the best of his or her ability is common to all communities.

Of course, it has always been recognised that some citizens will need to be looked after by others – hence the central role of the family throughout history. Social work has emerged in the 20th century, and has developed as a major complementary force to compensate for deficiencies in the level of support that families can provide, to encourage them to do better, to protect vulnerable individuals against exploitation and, ultimately, to provide total support for social isolates whose 'natural' support systems have collapsed or disappeared.

Although social workers have many roles, it is the central theme of this book that they are all subsumed under a general theory of *maintenance*. Social workers are the maintenance mechanics oiling the interpersonal wheels of the community. They do so at the end of the spectrum where dysfunctioning has either reached chronic or epidemic proportions or where its effects are spilling over into the lives of vulnerable people. They may use a variety of strategies, directive and non-directive, but their underlying aims are to maintain the independence of adults, to protect the short- and long-term interests of children, and to contribute towards the creation of a community climate in which all citizens can maximise their potential for personal development.

If social workers sometimes act as social control agents, they do so because, for some purposes, it is necessary to maintain stability in the social setting, the better to enable the client to thrive. If social workers operate therapeutically, they do so not to bring about magical change as though their clients were putty in the worker's hands, but to enable the client ultimately to assume a normal role of self-development, once freed of the encumbrances, restrictions or handicaps which prevent normal functioning.

The maintenance strategy is two-pronged – or rather it is concerned with the interface between the individual and society. On the one hand, social workers are employed by the state to curb some of the excesses of deviant behaviour; hence the part they play in protecting children, in supervising convicted criminals, in arranging for the compulsory admission of mentally disturbed patients to hospital and in recommending the reception of delinquent children into care. All of these acts are intended to contribute to a smoother-running society, to *maintain* it.

But social workers are also concerned with ameliorating the living conditions of those who are finding it difficult to cope without help. Their agencies' objectives lead them to make attempts to improve the quality of life of married couples in conflict, out-of-work teenagers, handicapped housewives, terminally sick hospital patients. Social workers in such instances are striving, first, to hold the line, to prevent deterioration in performance, to combat the client's feeling that life can only get worse, and, indeed, to do such work in the environment that will reverse any strong-running momentum that might make decline inevitable. Next, by their continuing contributions, they hope to reach the point where the client's own capacity for self-help begins to re-emerge, and where growth and improvement – and therefore *change* – become feasible. These are all acts of *maintenance*. Motor mechanics hope to produce improvements in the running performance of vehicles after a routine service; they aim to get the car back on the road after a breakdown. For most people, most of the time, the human way of life ensures self-maintenance; but for a minority, either because of defects at birth, deprivation during childhood, the onset of sickness or old age, the experience of an accident, the shock of bereavement or job-loss, or the ill-effects of political, economic or social planning or discrimination, self-sufficiency runs out, and the need for a maintenance mechanic becomes apparent. This need pinpoints the heart of the social worker's role.

The social worker is contributing towards the maintenance of society by exercising some control over deviant members and allocating scarce resources according to policies laid down by the state but implemented on an individualised basis. She is maintaining members *in* society by exercising control, by allocating resources, and by the provision of a wide range of supportive strategies designed to maximise self-respect and develop the abilities of individuals to survive and thrive under their own steam. These two approaches not only overlap, but also, although they can be distinguished conceptually, are often difficult to disentangle in practice. For example, work with a problem family can involve pressure to get a man to work and careful surveillance to guard against child abuse while simultaneously there are warm friendly relationships between the worker and her clients. Part of the uniqueness of the social worker's role lies in her ability to handle simultaneously aspects of behaviour and relationship which, in the eyes of the naive, appear to be both incompatible and in conflict.

An essential step towards the improvement of the social worker's maintenance role is for her to exert an influence on decision-making processes within her own authority and to negotiate improved conditions and additional resources to the extent that they impinge upon the welfare of her clients. Such maintenance functions might occasionally be carried out by the social worker as an individual, but they are more likely to be effective if they are carried out through the corporate strength of the department as a whole. It thus becomes essential for the social services or probation departments to ensure free lines of communication between grass-roots practitioners and influentially-placed administrators. The role of client pressure groups and professional organisations is also significant in this area, although the temptation for the professional associations to campaign primarily for their own members' interests rather than those of the clients appears to be difficult to curb or resist.

The role of the social worker in society can be represented quite simply in diagrammatic form, as in Figure 5.1. The social worker is concerned with maintaining

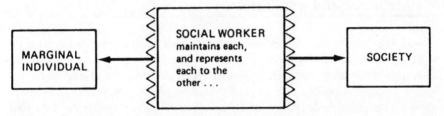

Figure 5.1   The role of the social worker in society

each individual and society as a whole, and with negotiating the interdependent relationship *between* each individual and society: it is a policy of reconciliation. The social worker frequently finds herself defending or at least explaining the laws of the land to a client who has offended against them or feels himself to have suffered from them; and the fact that the social worker's position in society is relative is illustrated every time the law changes or by observation of the different patterns of social work in different countries and within different legal systems. But the social worker also finds herself defending or explaining the behaviour or the plight of a client in the face of social pressure and public criticism. She has to reconcile marginal individuals to their social position, while helping them to improve it; and she has to reconcile society to the existence of marginal groups while simultaneously working to secure improved conditions for them. It is this two-way process that makes social work a unique occupation, and goes a long way to explaining why, at different times, it comes under fire from both directions, but why it survives and generally retains the respect of employers and clients.

The existence and survival of social work is dependent, then, on two conditions: first, its practitioners, implicitly or explicitly accepting a consensus view of the state, must retain broad respect for the political and economic viability of their society and for its underlying political philosophy; and, second, the state itself, as represented in particular in the governing class (whatever its philosophical foundations) must retain a broad commitment to a fair, just and humanitarian society, in which the rights of each individual, and especially of each most vulnerable citizen, are given due consideration. Whenever one or other, or both, of these prerequisites is missing, the consequences for social work will be far-reaching. On the one hand, social workers themselves will be divided, with some setting up in rebellion against a repressive state, and others aligning themselves with the oppressors of the individual, and so denying their basic social work identity. On the other hand, the state will begin to attack its social work services because of the way in which the social worker draws society's attention to the rights and the needs of oppressed minorities. An attack on social work is of necessity an attack on the vulnerable, and to that extent social work, like law, is a sensitive barometer of the social climate in a free society and of its concern for the deprived. The social worker, as an apostle of latter-day gradualism, emerges as a key figure in contemporary social evolution.

Maintenance and general care

In 1967, Peter Nokes, drawing on Max Weber, showed how the *general care* role in the welfare professions (as elsewhere in medical care, penal administration and school teaching) is undervalued and under-rewarded. He pointed out that people's dreams of being a doctor, a scientist, a concert pianist or an air pilot are an accurate reflection of where free ambition leads because of the attraction of such *virtuoso* roles. They have glamour; they enable the practitioner to demonstrate skills and to reveal distinctive know-how; they carry effective autonomy; they produce observable and measurable outcomes; they are characterised by being concerned with limited objectives, clearly specified; and they usually involve a degree of social distance which is institutionalised by occupational structures. It follows that any occupation which tends to be the reverse of these things carries low status.

Nokes's analysis enables us to understand instantly why social work has been so anxious to emphasise its *change* perspective. Such an identity would not only take it in a quasi-medical direction (with the expectation of high status by association), it would give the social worker relative status *vis-à-vis other* general care staff – ancillaries, prison officers, nurses, home helps and their organisers, social security counter clerks. It is an essential part of my argument that the social worker's emphasis on a change perspective is not only unjustified and misleading (because of the relatively marginal nature of change as a virtuoso-type activity in social work), it is and has been counterproductive for the client. An insistence that *maintenance* is the true role for social work has the immediate effect of placing the profession back in the mainstream of welfare practice, of justifying quality of function between the various participants, and, above all, of establishing a springboard from which the general care role in society might come to be recognised as the crucial activity that it undoubtedly is. Social work may well have succeeded too well in espousing a decision-making, therapeutic role and turning its back on general care. Its achievement has meant that the possibility of upgrading care in the wake of social work's strengthened base has been lost because of the profession's determination to separate itself from those beneath it and to encapsulate its differentials in salary scales which merely reflect traditional patterns of social and economic discrimination.

Nokes concludes, gloomily, that 'general care roles are not generally admired, nor understood, nor do they attract theoretical interest'. But such a conclusion should not be regarded as inevitable, and it is more likely to be reversed if the social work caring task is recognised for what it is: a large-scale maintenance business, involving a variety of different occupational groups all with equally important contributions to make.

Underlying the problem are two aspects that, in themselves, need to be tackled. The first is the crude distinction that is drawn between maintenance and change – a distinction that I argue is wholly false, for good maintenance work, in which, for example, the domestic staff in residential care can and do play an important part, will itself induce change. The second is the traditional gender distinction in which the virtuoso performer is thought of as the male, and the general carer as the female. Even if it were thought that there are personality characteristics in the sexes which produce such differences (a point obviously contentious in itself), there is no reason why the roles should have such different statuses. Indeed, again, it is more important to achieve recognition of the equal value of the two roles than merely to open up the virtuoso role to women, for that would not, in itself, do anything to upgrade the general care role, which is fundamental to the idea of maintenance.

Society's failure to recognise the legitimacy and the centrality of the general caring role has led not only to false trails in search of stages upon which virtuoso performances might be given, but directly to the reduced status of work with elderly or disabled people – groups for whom maintenance is obviously crucial.

All social work research has demonstrated the central position of caring in practice. Critical gatekeeping decisions and the occasional therapeutic group may attract public attention, but for almost all the clients of probation and the social services, and especially in residential care, it is the day in, day out routine that truly identifies the nature of social work.

If client change occurs, it will come only slowly, and often as the result of a long programme of selected inputs: social work is about removing obstacles, providing facilities, giving extensive verbal support, freeing the client's mind from restraining fears, opening up new perspectives, fighting for improved conditions, encouraging self-development, resisting decline in body and mind for as long as possible and counteracting negative pressures whencesoever they may come. Such processes are an integral part of a caring approach, and have been employed time and again by ordinary social workers who have thereby earned the gratitude of the client. The yearning for an instantly observable breakthrough, a miracle cure, a revolution in attitude or behaviour is understandable but almost always illusory; perhaps it is important for social workers to believe that one day they will achieve it, just as every journalist yearns for a Watergate scandal and every athlete for an Olympic medal. It may be necessary for personal motivation, but it is not necessary for good social work.

The objective of social work is maintenance, and the acknowledgement of that argument has led to a whole new programme of teaching, research and experimental development in practice. Let us consider now four areas which illustrate the point.

1.   The provision of active support for families

Family casework is the most traditional of all forms of social work, and it still plays a dominant part in both training and practice. It is obviously of critical importance in child care, but support for the family also often enters into the programme of work in probation and is a major contribution towards the provision of welfare facilities for the elderly and handicapped. There is some controversy over the right of the social worker to adopt a family focus in all cases. In probation, for example, there is occasional resistance from families to any active intervention by the officer on the grounds that the court order only gives her the right of access to the offender himself, and although limited visits are sanctioned, undue intrusiveness is not. Sometimes, during the entire period of a probation order, the personalities of parents or spouse will remain quite shadowy.

One field in which work with the family has been identified as being particularly crucial is in respect of learning disabilities. The presence of a child with severely limited intelligence is likely to affect family life quite seriously: it can lead to social isolation, reduce the chances of holidays or recreational activities, affect career opportunities and precipitate housing and financial problems. Above all, it imposes a day-to-day strain that frequently reaches crisis proportions. Many studies have suggested that the kind of help currently given by social workers is insufficient to meet the needs of these families, and it has been suggested that part of the problem may be that social workers have often been trained only to operate according to a clinical model, in which they concentrate on treatment and the reversal of problems. But the families of the handicapped (like those of the elderly) need a preventative and developmental focus.

> Many of the families who care for the handicapped are not faced with acute crises, rather they are normal families who are under pressure from long-term, chronic management problems. They require support and need to feel that someone is interested in them. They want someone to take the time to listen and to provide them with useful information. Finally they need relief and practical help. (Moroney 1976)

What, then, should be the standards aspired to by social workers in the provision of support services for families caring for a child with learning disabilities?

1.   Routine surveillance of a detached and occasional kind is not sufficient. Where there is real stress (and this also applies to other client-groups, such as physically handicapped housewives and families in severely deprived circumstances), there exists a need for regular, reliable and warmly committed support of the kind pioneered by the family service units. If the local authority departments can no

longer provide this, then they certainly have a responsibility to devise strategies whereby it might be developed – either by voluntary societies, community volunteers or an organised system of network support. Without some such facility, community care for families in need is falling far short of the ideal.

2. Social workers must be knowledgeable about available facilities and services. If *they* do not have expert knowledge, it is difficult to know who should have it. They must develop their skills as the providers of useful information.

3. Youthfulness need be no disadvantage and it is certainly not a sin, but both training courses and departments have a responsibility to ensure that social workers have enough sensitivity and skill to be able to do a useful job with clients whose experience of the world often far outstrips that of a typical new graduate recruit to the social services.

4. Ways must be found to overcome the situation that prevails in some departments where work in the field of learning disabilities is placed low on the list of priorities. Even where this is a justifiable administrative procedure in the face of political and economic pressures from other client-group areas, any spillover into staff attitudes must be avoided.

5. Interdisciplinary contacts with medicine and education should be developed, and social workers should become skilled at encouraging and enabling parents to learn the arts of structured teaching for their children.

6. Parents must be drawn into partnership with the professionals.

7. Emergency residential care should be available when needed.

8. Social work involvement is essential shortly after the birth of a disabled child and before and after school-leaving. Close liaison should also be provided with the schools.

There is no client-group which so clearly illustrates the contemporary dilemma of differentially allocating responsibility between society and the individual or the family. We expect those with problems – disabled children, delinquent children, alcoholic members, the sick elderly – to carry the burden for as long as possible, and although the involvement of social workers and others in the provision of help for such families is partly a humanitarian commitment, it is partly (perhaps mainly) an economically sensitive strategy to *maintain* the family in the business of community care in the full knowledge that, should it break down, the costs to the state of residential provision will be significantly greater. Even so, as we have argued, the evidence suggests that the quality and extent of active support for burdened families is in need of radical improvement if practice is to conform to the normal expectations of a social work model.

Presland and Roberts (1983) have suggested ways in which a community and group-work approach can be used with families in which there is a child with learning disabilities. Operating over a four-year period, not according to a predetermined plan but in response to opportunities as they arose, they created a climate in which the parents began to work together for their mutual benefit. They surveyed parents' opinions, increased the regularity of supportive visits to families, created an efficient maintenance network of parents, volunteers and professionals and set up a dialogue between the client-group and the department which ensured a more responsive strategy.

On the face of it, parents' groups, summer playschemes, coffee mornings and encouragement to self-help are modest enough gains, but in a situation where they did not exist their introduction is a major step forward, and Presland and Roberts demonstrate the challenge to social work's flexibility in emphasising the critical importance of taking the lead in such initiatives and in maintaining them once begun. 'Even if problems cannot be removed perhaps we can help parents to feel that there are ways of adapting to situations – that might bring some comfort.'

2.   The provision of foster care

'We have reached the conclusion that almost every child, however handicapped, would be better equipped to face the adult world if growing up in a family rather than an institution.' This assertion by a council fostering organiser accurately reflects the majority view in the social services today, although there is a minority view that a secure and stable base in a children's home is preferable to a fostering placement in which the child is unhappy, discriminated against, or unable to settle.

Fostering is our society's prime strategy for the provision of maintenance for children placed in the care of the council and there are significant signs that parallel steps are being taken to develop similar programmes for the elderly, the handicapped and those discharged from psychiatric hospitals. The system, at its most modest, provides shelter, accommodation and food. Additionally it should give a warm and sensitive social environment in which the child can live as normal a life as possible. At its best, foster care gives a stimulus to development and growth, a framework within which disturbed and disruptive attitudes and behaviour can be, first, contained, and then countered, in a fully therapeutic process.

The organisation of foster care is a large-scale business, and many departments have moved towards the appointment of specialist personnel. The backbone of a first-class fostering service is partly organisational and partly dependent on professional practice skills. The two qualities cannot be divorced from each other: good organisation is quite simply impossible without a practice component – it would then not be *good* organisation – and there would be nothing to practise on unless foster parents were identified and maintained.

Key components in the process can be described:

1.   Publicity and recruitment are essential in order to find potential foster parents. Increasingly adventurous techniques are employed in a field where it is now accepted that marketing strategies are relevant. Radio, television and newspaper advertising and the exploitation of editorial opportunities are now commonly used.
2.   Potential foster parents must be trained and prepared. From a situation where training and preparation were almost non-existent, most departments now recognise that they have a responsibility in this respect. The goals of one training course are

listed as: providing basic knowledge; sensitising participants to situations which may occur; developing participants' self-awareness; helping them understand the role of the agency and principles of good child care practice; developing a group identity with other foster parents and stimulating further learning (Crowley 1982: 29).

3. The aim should be to provide support for all foster parents, before, during and at the end of each placement. Foster families need to be maintained, just as they are contributing to the maintenance of children at risk.

4. Increasingly, foster parents themselves are being involved in the fostering process much more actively – through groups, newsletters, and so on.

There is an expectation that most birth parents will maintain contact with any child for whom the local authority assumes responsibility, and foster parents will need to be briefed on the nature of the controlled access which the birth parents will have.

The most exciting developments in recent years have been in the recruitment of professional foster parents who receive sums of money significantly greater than the modest allowances normally payable, and who in return accept children who would generally be considered unsuitable for fostering. The scheme was pioneered by the Kent Social Services Department, following the realisation that some European countries had developed much more radical fostering policies than Britain's. In Sweden, for example, more than 80 per cent of children in care are fostered, compared with 57 per cent in England in 1991. Sweden has long used specialists rather than generic practitioners and the foster parent was given considerable autonomy and responsibility.

The Kent experiment was widely regarded to have been a success. Recruitment was no problem; salaries for foster parents were generous, but the scheme still cost less than half the money needed to provide equivalent placements in community homes. There were four principles underlying the project – again all drawn from Swedish experience:

(a) *normalisation*: ensuring that any child separated from his parents leads a normal life in a family and community rather than in an institution;

(b) *localisation*: any child has the right to remain in his region of origin;

(c) *voluntariness*: the child and his family should always agree with the decisions except in situations which are either urgent or dangerous;

(d) *the right to participation*: the child and his family should participate in an active fashion in all the decisions which concern them.

Foster parents in the Kent project met fortnightly and gained greatly from mutual support. Any applicant for fostering joined a group for two or three months and was assessed by the group – including themselves. 'We lay down no guidelines for foster families. Nobody really knows how to assess them. Groups seem to be the best way of selection, and people discover for themselves whether they are suitable.' Children were referred by Kent's social workers; families and children were then seen by one of the project workers who emphasised that the foster care system was primarily working to reunite the original family, not to provide a substitute family. When a matching had been made, contracts were drawn up between the various parties involved – the child, his natural family, his foster family and the project workers – and the goals of the placement were established. The tasks to be undertaken were written down together with a forecast of the time needed. The project was providing more than storage in foster care – it was a form of treatment prompting optimism about its effectiveness.

Case example: Successful fostering

Mary, aged 16, was in an adolescent psychiatric unit. She'd been in a variety of institutions since her early childhood and was said to be violent and uncontrollable. Her psychiatrist said she was schizophrenic and her behaviour had been 'stabilised' in the unit with drugs. Referred to the project, she was placed happily in a foster home and managed to hold down a part-time job. Mary complained that the drugs, which the psychiatrist had said would have to be continued, had unpleasant side-effects and made her feel worse. A second psychiatric opinion agreed that an effort could be made to wean Mary off drugs. This was successfully done over four weeks, bringing her back to normal, a happy, though not very bright, adolescent girl, far more alert and far more human. She can be very rude, especially to her natural parents who opposed the ending of drug treatment, but she is never violent. After a year's fostering, Mary had changed so much that 'you wouldn't believe such a transformation possible' (Knight 1976).

The success of the project demonstrates the critical difference between storage (or warehousing) and maintenance. The maintenance approach, though modest in its objectives, and always prompting pleasant surprise at such achievements as Mary's, is positive, planned and consciously strategic. It never implies resignation to failure, but always expresses a belief in the capacity of human beings to grow, given the right conditions and adequate and appropriate facilities.

3.   Maintaining elderly people

Elderly people are the largest single client-group confronting social workers. Their numbers are rising all the time, both in proportion to other client-groups and in absolute terms. Given their numerical importance, our knowledge about the services they need is exceedingly patchy, although recent years have seen a growing number of significant developments in practice.

The two prime areas for social work activity with elderly people are in the community and in residential care. The focus of community care is heavily geared to the provision of services which will preclude the necessity for residential admission. For example, for many elderly people, the 'solution is to remain in their own home in an area familiar to them' for as long as possible, and social workers can facilitate this 'by ensuring that adequate day care services, home helps, meals on wheels, financial advice, counselling, support and adaptations are available' (Fellows and Marshall 1979).

Although there are significant variations between authorities, the range of services available to old people is now considerable and adds up to a major programme of community maintenance. Day centres and luncheon clubs have made extensive use of voluntary help and community support: the local press is often extremely helpful in an area which is probably less stigmatised than most spheres of social work. Boarding out or fostering schemes have been tried, and Kent Social Services Department carried out an especially important initiative in its community care project (Challis and Davies 1980, Challis, Davies and Holman 1980).

Recognising the need to strengthen the contribution of social work to the welfare of elderly people, a strategy was drawn up intended to give field social workers more discretionary powers in their attempt to maintain old people in their homes for longer than was previously possible. The policy hinged on money – both spending it and saving it. The aim was to improve the range of services available and so to postpone or even avoid admission to residential care where previously it would have been thought necessary. Each worker was given a budget per client with which they were able to buy-in services; this enabled maximum individualisation of response to meet personal needs. The client was herself involved in decisions about the services required and the various helpers were recruited either by advertising, word of mouth or personal contact. Most of them were remunerated for each task performed, although the payments were at a level likely to be of symbolic rather than economic value. The programme laid heavy responsibility on the social worker who made the assessment and then coordinated and developed the programme. Challis, Davies and Holman commented that

> the work draws on a number of aspects of social work: on elements of a casework model in achieving a successful assessment and on groupwork and community work principles in recruiting and sustaining local helpers in their caring role. It particularly draws upon specific knowledge of the needs of the client group in question and the available resources, formal and informal, for caring within the local community.

So successful was the Kent project that it was rapidly introduced in other areas, and eventually served as the model upon which the NHS and Community Care Act 1990 was based. The 1990s is a decade in which support by social workers in the community will be more wide-ranging and more entrepreneurial than ever before.

4. The contribution of social workers to health care in hospitals

A detailed analysis carried out in Scottish hospitals (Connor and Tibbitt 1988) has provided a copy-book demonstration of the maintenance role of social workers: where they are present, the organisation of the health-care system runs more efficiently (in particular with regard to the unblocking of beds, thus leading to a speedier service for patients) and the quality of provision available to patients both in the hospital and afterwards in the community is much improved.

Connor and Tibbitt summarise their conclusions like this: 'The greater inter-disciplinary liaison over social care issues in the higher [social work] staffed units tended to ensure higher proportions of patients with social care needs had these attended to, and with less delay. In particular, those areas of social care which were markedly better performed the greater the hospital social work availability in the hospital were:

– on admission: assessment of the patient's home circumstances and arranging any necessary steps to secure property or the care of others left at home;
– formulation of treatment and social care plans: the provision of background information about the overall living circumstances of a patient to enable a realistic plan or rehabilitation targets to be set;
– in-patient support: responding to the worries and anxieties of individual patients, and offering support to them, their relatives and carers in coping with the consequences of illness or being in hospital;
– preparation of the patient and carer for discharge: exploration of alternatives and their implications to allow the patients and their carers to reach a decision and to accept the consequences;
– access to and coordination of services for the support of the patient after discharge, including the provision of information on matters such as welfare rights.'

Connor and Tibbitt cleverly explored what happens when social workers are *not* available in hospitals, and they noted, in two different units, groups of patients who 'consistently suffered unnecessarily when no social work help was readily to hand'. In the geriatric units, the people who suffered from an absence of social work support were:

'– patients who were the sole source of information about their own home circumstances, as in their anxiety to get home there was a risk that they would underestimate their own problems or over-sell the willingness or ability of relatives and neighbours to provide extra support;
– people who drifted into long-term hospital care in the absence of any positive decision about their future;
– people who had left dependent relatives at home: spouses, siblings, friends/neighbours, and ill or disabled "children" of any age.'

In the paediatric units, the people who were the most vulnerable were:

'– children admitted for social reasons, where the cause of the problem was never addressed;
– families of children suffering from a long-term and/or potentially fatal condition;
– parents who were not visiting their child;
– families who were known to be under strain from another cause such as employment difficulties, other family illness, bereavement or matrimonial problems.'

Connor and Tibbitt found that the health care professionals greatly valued the role of the social workers, and were agreed that nobody else could provide the package of maintenance, support and facilitation that was available from the social work team.

Conclusion

Critics of the theory of maintenance consistently misconstrue both its conceptual foundations and its political intent.

Unlike many theoretical models with which social workers have toyed over the years – Freudian, Marxist, behavioural, even feminist ideas – maintenance theory is descriptive and analytical, not prescriptive or assertive. Maintenance theory has emerged out of research studies into the nature and function of social work, and it tries both to describe what social workers do, and then to *make sense* out of their actions in the context of their agency. Most other so-called theories of social work are in fact more ideological than empirical: they reflect what their advocates think social workers *should* be doing. The emergent obsession in the 1990s with the primacy of anti-discriminatory practice is an excellent example of this: it is more akin to a religious doctrine than to a scientifically developed theory.

The maintenance model is neither static, nor pessimistic, nor limited in its potential for good. It can – indeed must – incorporate a commitment to raise the minimum standards of provision and performance.

There is a problem of attitude that is nicely illustrated by three quotations from Birmingham social workers (Black *et al.* 1983: 163):

I would say a social worker is a person who tries to help someone else with a problem they can't deal with themselves. And because as workers you're given resources you can pass them on. You're a relieving service, not always a solving service.

I'm trying to get people to cope as best they can with the situation they're in and get the most out of that situation.

I see social work in very simplistic terms as supporting people and trying to change their environment ... I accept that sometimes all I can do is to help them cope within the environment they've got even if it's a lousy environment.

These three accounts of work in hand certainly reflect a commitment to maintenance, but they also, in varying degrees, convey a mood of disillusionment or dissatisfaction with the role, or at least a sense of the social worker needing to defend its shortcomings. It may be that such an approach is not sufficient, and Black discusses the hazards of agencies trying to embark on more innovative and developmental work. But it *is* the core of the discipline, and all else follows from it.

Perhaps the word *maintenance* is at fault, with its connotations of work done on motorcars or washing machines or other inanimate objects. For no machine is like any human being. The whole point of providing maintenance in the human arena is that, once given, its recipient can always respond actively as a unique pro-active personality and can grow, change, develop and interact. Human nature is such that it confounds any limited perspective.

The theory of maintenance is preferable to a central theory of change, because it better and more accurately reflects the true nature of the normal relationship between the client, the worker and the agency. If change occurs, it will generally do so only because of the will of the client – not because of the magical effect of social work. To speak of social work as therapy is both to exaggerate the powers of the worker, to overestimate the plasticity of the client's personality and to risk denigrating the wide range of maintenance functions which, taken as a whole, properly characterise the nature of the profession.

The impact of an erstwhile if erroneous medical model in social work dies hard. Social work is not about curing, and failure to recognise that can lead to absurdities, such as the situation in which a department decides that it can no longer provide a support service for the families of elderly people in which all hope of a cure or improvement is said to be medically unachievable. Those are *precisely* the kind of families in which social work support is critically needed.

This chapter has provided four examples of mainstream practice which undeniably demonstrate the maintenance emphasis in social work: support for families, foster care, work in hospitals and the care of the elderly. Corby (1982) has pinpointed the high degree to which social workers practise a form of maintenance with long-term clients, but he found that neither their training nor their theoretical assumptions had fully prepared them for the role. He says that practitioners need to be able to discriminate more clearly between maintaining or monitoring situations and intervening more actively, and he concludes that the social workers he studied both undervalued the maintenance role and lacked the techniques for intervention.

It is the argument of this book that such shortcomings reflect a chronic loss of confidence in the field of practice. It is not so much that one needs to *discriminate* between maintenance and intervention, as to recognise that maintenance is the goal, and an interventive strategy may often be the way of achieving it. In other words, social workers must be careful not to confuse maintenance with benign or passive neglect; the whole point of their occupation is that they should adopt an active stance when confronted with the needs, the fears, the vulnerability of their clients. There is a middle course between 'solving the problems of the world – or at least of the client and his family' – and 'doing nothing': it lies in a commitment to maintenance.

The theory of maintenance is neither simple nor yet as well developed as it deserves to be. In the next three chapters, I shall argue that it contains within it but supersumes elements of statutory and agency responsibility, a commitment to pursue change strategies and the use of skills in pro-actively involving the worker in the community. Self-evidently and additionally it presumes a degree of personal and agency support for the client at risk. Because of the organic basis of human nature and society, the successful pursuit of a strategy which has as its goal the maintenance of society and its members will *necessarily* produce growth and a dynamic response. But this can only be so to the fullest degree in a climate which values consensus, not conflict – and to that extent social work and the maintenance model are not ideologically revolutionary.

Of course, there are many outstanding issues. How, for example, do you encourage independence in the client without being callous? How do you avoid inducing degrees of over-dependence which might waste scarce social work resources? And, especially in residential work, how do you prevent a premature decline into client passivity? How do you provide care while still allowing the stimulus of risk-taking behaviour in residents?

Such questions are to do with the psychology, the sociology and even the economics of maintenance, and they deserve more active research investigation within a unified theoretical framework. The model may appear to be modest in its objectives, but its acceptance legitimises much of contemporary social work and represents a major step towards a more ambitious goal: the conscious and planned provision of general care facilities as a high priority for a compassionate society. We have moved more or less steadily in that direction for more than a century in Western democracies and social work's acknowledgement now of its maintenance role can lead, not only to the political recognition of the importance of caring, but also to new and more positive approaches to applied social research and to far-reaching developments in the design of social work training and the structure of the profession.

6 The achievement of change.

Nothing better characterises the disjunction between textbook idealism in social work and the real world of everyday practice than the concept of *change*. From the days of the police court missionaries at the turn of the century, through years of therapeutic commitment by the Freudians and post-Freudians, to the yearnings for conscientisation and social revolution in the 1970s, there have always been teachers anxious to imbue would-be social workers with an evangelical fervour to reform the client. The poor have to be educated, the children to be saved; egos have to be strengthened, insight achieved; criminal tendencies must be excised, marital conflict resolved; communities must be developed, residents led into battle; the deprived must be empowered, the depressed given renewed vigour to face the world.

And students have responded with a will. They want to see people change just as a gardener revels in the cycle of growth from the planting of the sweet pea seed in the spring to the cutting of the sweetly scented blooms in the summer, just as a parent glows with pride as the child's developing skills become manifest – in football, mathematics or music – and just as the sculptor experiences the satisfaction of seeing an artistic shape emerge from a slab of stone or a trunk of wood. Social workers are human, and they live in a society which praises achievement more than it values service; little wonder, then, that the temptation to regard the client as a seed to be cultivated, as a child to be encouraged and shepherded, as material to be shaped is too strong for many to resist. And it might, therefore, be thought unfortunate that much of the social work literature has consistently encouraged the social worker's potential delusions of influence by tending to concentrate on aspects of practice which confirm their currency. Casework texts have sought case examples which illustrate therapeutic effectiveness; advocates of radical practice choose clients who conform to their political interpretation of family conflict; and behaviourists concentrate on those more specific aberrations of human behaviour that lend themselves to a learning theory analysis. But empirical studies of social work practice have shown that such interpretations are at best half- or quarter-truths in any local authority or probation setting: in addition to the important client-perspective accounts, detailed investigations of probation practice (Boswell 1989) and of local authority social work (Black *et al.* 1983) have served to place the concept of change in perspective, and to show that too many writers on social work have made the unforgiveable error of confusing 'is' with 'ought': they have been so concerned to develop a model of instrumental intervention as they think it *ought* to be that they have paid insufficient attention to the real-life context of professional social work – how it *is*.

This is not to say that changes never occur – either in clients or in communities. 'Change is inevitable, change is constant', said Benjamin Disraeli; and the clients of the social services are no different from the rest of us: they experience stress, they grow older and more experienced, they have good and bad luck, they learn to avoid trouble or they plunge ever deeper into it; they have rows, they kiss and make up; they have fantasies and they see reality with brutal accuracy; they make love, or feel frustration; they become absorbed into a new social group, they lose their job or their husband or their children or their budgerigar. All of these daily events, involving as they do complex patterns of human and psychosocial interaction, produce change – for better or worse, and sometimes in the opposite direction to that which common sense might envisage.

Nor is it to say that social workers never do anything to bring about change. For example, the social worker becomes, to a greater or lesser extent, an integral part of the client's own social system – that conglomeration of people and groups whose interactions with him constitute his whole social life: his employer, his foreman and workmates, his friends, the police, the doctors and nurses in a hospital, his family, his landlord, the lodger, his pet dog, and so on – and as a participant in the environment, the social worker may well play an influential role in the client's decline or growth. Indeed, there is one sense in which the social worker can and does have an enormous impact on the client: by effecting, or at least being a party to, his removal from home to an institution – an assessment centre, a mental hospital, a prison, an old peoples' home. That, perhaps, is not what the textbooks normally have in mind when they write about the social worker's achievement of 'change', but we know from the literature that those *are* the changes often most strongly associated with social work in the client's mind.

Many of those who come within the orbit of the social services inhabit such a 'turbulent field' of disruption and confusion that the addition of a social worker to it is no more than a further irritant in an already chronic existence. The social worker couldn't make it worse, because it couldn't *be* worse. But the research evidence suggests that there is little chance of the social worker making it better either; even the physical removal of the chronic client to a sheltered setting – which may well be the only feasible strategy – might fail because of the tortured state of the client's mind and the self-defeating, masochistic nature of his personal relationships.

Finally, of course, and, it might be said, contrariwise, there is evidence – limited evidence, but nonetheless evidence – that most (perhaps all) social workers do play a positive part in the lives of some clients by effecting beneficial change: some of the poor have been educated, some children have been saved; some egos have been strengthened, some insight given; some marriages have improved with counselling, while other partners have been helped to face up to the inevitability of separation or divorce; some communities have responded to the leadership of a community worker; some of the oppressed have found new hope in spirited radical leadership; and some in the throes of depression have been helped to relish the dawning of a new day once again. But what is important is to recognise three facts. First, such *effects* are not the sole *raison d'être* of social work; they are an integral part of the maintenance objective, but only a part, and their significance should not be overestimated. Second, the changes achieved are not necessarily either permanent or complete, nor are they sometimes as effective as the client or his family would choose. Third, although the social worker may facilitate change, the will and the determination to bring it about are the client's.

Changes do not normally come about as the direct result of a magical specific called 'social work'. They occur in response to a wide range of possible variables reflecting either the agency or the worker, or more commonly both together. The goals of practice are primarily determined by agency policy and the social worker's contribution is to work towards the achievement of those goals. In most circumstances, she could not make that contribution unless it were sanctioned by her employers. Thus any changes that occur in the client are agency-facilitated and possibly agency-determined. On the other hand, the personal style and professional skill of the worker are major components in goal-achievement. Her approach to the job, her relationship with the client, are known to be key factors in securing a positive response and bringing about change. Nevertheless it is erroneous to think of the social worker as having more skills in social engineering than other similar occupational groups: trade union negotiators, school teachers, insurance agents, clergymen all need to achieve excellence in the use of interpersonal relations if they are to be good at their jobs. The social worker differs from them primarily in the identity of her work-base, and it is her work-base – the agency – which, through her, effects changes in the clientele and their circumstances.

What we see, then, is that the social worker is a professional agent of change only as one part of her maintenance role. People are not so malleable nor their social circumstances so amenable to change as to be radically reformed by the mere intervention of a social worker, one who is, moreover, similarly dealing with anything from ten to a hundred other people or problems at the same time. Such changes as the social worker can prompt are best considered as contributing to the maintenance of the client and society – for maintenance in any living system implies continual evolution. Change in social work cannot be miraculous, instant, or magical, and the individual social worker is but a modest participant in a large number of interacting networks involving different clients. Within these, there are models of practice which are thought to be capable of influencing to some degree the attitudes and behaviour of clients and others, and there are models of practice which have been shown to have an impact on social groups and their intrinsic interactions. Although care must be taken never to regard any one of these aspects of practice as *the whole of social work*, they do nevertheless make an important contribution to it.

Eleven strategies for achieving change

The achievement of change can be attempted in a variety of ways, and in the remainder of this chapter I will outline a selection of those strategies regarded as feasible in practice and thought to be effective to some degree, although in many cases their effectiveness is not proven and in some it is subject to serious empirical doubt. The first two strategies are basic to almost all community-based social work: counselling and environmental intervention. The remaining nine are a sample of others thought to be of some importance. They are by no means mutually exclusive, and some overlap significantly with others, but they are sufficiently separate to be regarded as different strategies.

1.   Counselling

There are libraries of books devoted to counselling and there are numerous schools of thought, many of them led by charismatic figures like Carl Rogers. The traditional body of social work knowledge labelled 'casework' is primarily concerned with counselling activities, and almost all studies of social work in practice reveal the dominance of the one-to-one interview. In statutory social work, however, counselling rarely takes a 'classical' or 'in-depth' form. It tends to be brief, often superficial, and geared either to routine maintenance or to the provision of practical help or guidance. Nevertheless most social workers (at least, those engaged in medium- and long-term work) do use a variety of counselling techniques with *some* clients much of the time. Formal counselling is not a preponderant aspect of their working week, but it is a recurring part of regular practice.

There are many hundreds of possible examples of counselling as a medium for change, and, out of them, I will quote just three:

The Denver response to child abuse   In the United Kingdom, pioneering work on child abuse has been centred, not surprisingly, on the National Society for the Prevention of Cruelty to Children. But the NSPCC was itself influenced by a clinic in Denver, Colorado, which trail-blazed a therapeutic response to child abuse, under the leadership of Dr C. H. Kempe.

The Denver unit emphasises the importance of *caring and intimacy* in its programme of therapeutic work with the parents of an abused child. A team of professional therapists and lay workers use a strategy of providing a 'corrective, nurturing experience' with the aim of encouraging the parents to seek their satisfaction from other adults rather than being child-dominated. In the first instance, the children must be removed from home, and efforts made to reduce any financial or other stress on the family. Ideally the therapists then work intensively with both partners. Immense time and energy are needed, and it is usual for the client to become heavily dependent on the therapist – so much so that the therapeutic role has to be played by a lay worker who can become a 'parent aide' with the task of 'befriending and mothering' each abusive parent. The aim is not to give insight, but to provide intensive support with a view to improving basic child-rearing practices.

The Midlands experiment in prisoner counselling   In British prisons, probation officers are available to provide a welfare service as needed, but they do not normally offer a long-term counselling facility. In two prisons in the Midlands it was decided to experiment with the provision of regular interviews for prisoners for six months prior to discharge. Casework techniques were to be employed but no further restrictions on the theoretical approach were imposed. Most men had between 12 and 15 interviews and each one usually lasted for about 40 minutes, although some were considerably longer. The facility was appreciated by the men, and those who had received the counselling service were significantly less likely to be re-convicted during the two-year period following release. 'The findings indicate that as a result of their greater contact with welfare officers, the attitudes and behaviour of the experimental group differed significantly from the control group' (Shaw 1974). Unfortunately it was not possible to pinpoint the true reasons for this result — it could have been due to the content of the counselling sessions, or to the fact that these men simply received more attention from concerned people. Nevertheless the experiment is an important one and perhaps suggests that social work might be important for the way in which it can be used to counteract the damaging effects of imprisonment *per se.* The casework sessions in which the men were treated as people may have been important for improving their morale and so leaving them better prepared to cope with the stresses of society after they left prison.

A foster-care prevention programme in New York State   Almost all state welfare organisations would, other things being equal, prefer not to have to remove children from the care of their own parents, and one experiment in New York State was committed to the objective of trying to keep children at home for as long as possible rather than admitting them to foster care. In order to pursue the experiment, money was made available to provide a 'more intensive service to families than is ordinarily available'. A wide range of provisions were on tap but the researchers concluded that counselling made by far the greatest contribution to progress in the sample. It was the workers' view that, however important the other services, they could not have been provided and would not have been of value, without the counselling relationship. The most important topics discussed between social workers and clients were:

1.   parental functioning,
2.   parental behaviour or emotional adjustment,
3.   the child's functioning in the family, and
4.   the child's behaviour or emotional adjustment.

The experiment was a success and it is claimed that the provision of intensive counselling facilities significantly reduced the number of children who were taken into foster care, and so achieved substantial economies for the states (Jones, Neuman and Shyne 1976).

The time has passed when it was always assumed that counselling had to be non-directive to qualify for the designation. Jones, Neuman and Shyne note that in the foster-care prevention programme, one of the two dominant roles fulfilled by the social worker was to give advice, guidance and direction. And Sainsbury (1975), in his study of Family Service Units, notes that social workers did not hesitate to employ firmness when it seemed to be appropriate: 'Direct instruction and strongly worded advice were employed (for example) to get the house cleaned up, to prevent the abandoning of children, to get the rent or other debts paid and to get a man back to work.' But he emphasises that the ability of the social worker to be directive depends very much on her having established good working relationships with the client family, and it is now widely accepted that Truax *et al.* (1967, 1968) have successfully identified the major characteristics required in a counsellor if she is to work successfully with a client and help bring about improvements in the client's life-setting. The counsellor must have:

(a)   *authenticity:* the conveying of genuineness, of being herself, as distinct from adopting a role in her dealings with clients;
(b)   *non-possessive warmth:* the attitude of caring, conveyed by a friendly and concerned approach to the client;
(c)   *accurate empathy:* the capacity to feel with those who seek help, so that the client feels understood; and
(d)   *persuasiveness:* the giving of strong social reinforcements in a chosen direction.

There are, of course, a great many unresolved problems and issues concerned with counselling. Can the four identified qualities be taught and learnt? And how is it that the demand for and the provision of counselling facilities grows despite the accumulation of empirical doubts about its efficacy? For although I have quoted three fairly positive examples from the literature, the body of evidence overall is much more sceptical. It seems doubtful whether the counsellor is justified in regarding herself as a reliable agent of change under all circumstances, though she can certainly be an agent of reassurance and ventilation.

2.   Environmental intervention

In addition to conversing with clients in interviews, a great deal of a social worker's daily routine involves her in environmental intervention: phoning the job centre or the gas company, visiting a youth club, placating a neighbour, negotiating a grant, meeting a head teacher, discussing treatment with a psychiatrist, arranging a place in a day centre – all with the hope of making some kind of impact on the environment for the client's benefit. It is inconceivable that such functions should ever cease, but the extent to which, under normal conditions, they produce measurable changes in behaviour or circumstances should not be exaggerated. Two studies in the Home Office's probation research series emphasise the need for caution.

In the first (Davies 1974) a retrospective study of routine casework practice found that environmental intervention – for example, helping the client to get a job, finding accommodation for him, mediating in family conflict – tended to take place in response to pressure from the probationer rather than as a planned treatment strategy, and rarely led to any long-term improvement. The author comments on a paradox that continually recurred in the study and that is illustrated by the problem of accommodation:

> Accommodation is a basic need for young men under supervision. Where those young men have sufficient ability to satisfy that need on their own account, the probation officer is only too glad to let them do so, although he will happily give them verbal support or advice if they appear to require it. Where the probationer shows signs of personal or social inadequacy, however, or where his general environmental condition is exceptionally bad, the officer can seldom enable the probationer to settle himself in medium or long-term accommodation; the whole sample (of 463 men) contains no more than six cases in which the probation officer recorded a positive achievement in placing his client in accommodation and in keeping him there for as long as six months.

Later, a specially designed experiment, IMPACT (Folkard 1974, 1976), created the conditions for intensive efforts to be made on behalf of clients in their environment, by reducing caseloads and requiring officers to concentrate on practical needs. The results were wholly negative so far as re-conviction rates were concerned: the increased environmental support strategies did not have the effect of reducing the chances of these probationers re-appearing in court.

One major criticism of IMPACT is that the increase in the intensity of environmental intervention provided for was really quite slight, and that its negative results should not deter the social work services from pursuing developments in the use of groups, sheltered workshops, day centres and specialised accommodation over a lengthy period of time. If the aim is to produce more of a continuum of community care in order to avoid the extreme step of institutionalisation, then the rather haphazard and cursory approach to environmental intervention that has traditionally characterised social work will need to be improved.

For there to be any chance at all of change being effected, two prerequisites must be satisfied: there must be additional resources to which the social worker can turn in order to intervene successfully in what is inevitably a complex and turbulent environment; and the client's full cooperation and involvement must be secured if the strategy is to work. In other words, positive contributions must be expected, not just from the social worker, but out of the wider environment and from the client himself.

As we shall see in Chapter 8, the introduction of a 'patch' philosophy in social work encourages practitioners to adapt their one-to-one counselling skills for use in the wider community, and to develop the use of networks of associates for the benefit of the client. Although Hadley (1984) is careful not to claim too much in the way of environmental gains, there is no doubt that such a strategic approach offers more scope than traditional reliance on the supposedly charismatic influence of the solitary social worker. Cooper and Stacy (1981) illustrate the point by describing how, in Normanton, 18 wardens for the elderly were allocated to patches of about 1 200 population.

They are responsible for organising care for any needy old or handicapped person in their patch and also to encourage the informal networks to help in this process. This should provide an effective early warning system as well as an encouragement of community care at street level. Already the scheme is showing that wardens are offering a contact point to people who would never normally consider they needed help and who have been struggling with serious difficulties.

In this way, the concepts of maintenance, change and prevention merge into one another, something that seems appropriate in the complex field of environmental intervention.

3.   The use of structure and sanctions

The planned use of structure in social work depends on the practitioner's confidence in the validity and viability of her own performance. More, perhaps, than with any other aspect of practice, this confidence comes with training and experience, and fulfils the client's expectation that the social worker 'knows what she is doing'. Often, for example, in the simple business of helping the client to cope with everyday problems, the social worker who is prepared to sit down with him and, putting pen to paper, work out a sensible strategy for tackling them can hope to bring about modest changes in the client's ability to manage his own affairs.

Some aspects of agency practice involve more structure than others, and some clients are more likely than others to have the threat of sanctions held over them. Perhaps the most clearly structured innovation in recent years has been the community service scheme for offenders which is administered by the probation service. Empirical research studies have not been able to prove that community service orders reduce crime rates, but most of the parties involved in it – probation officers, work supervisors and the clients themselves – are enthusiastic about its value in society. Community service can develop sensitivity to self and to others, teach the client to undertake tasks and complete them, and demonstrate that authority can be consistent and insistent without being destructive or cynical.

The critical components in community service orders as social work are:

1.   The orders are explicit contracts, binding on both parties. 'Offenders know precisely what their obligations are, how long they will last, and the nature of the work they must undertake.'
2.   They are legal penalties with a punitive component, but a rehabilitative aim. The use of control and authority are an integral part of the process, but primarily, suggests West (1976), because the social worker can thereby emphasise the centrality of the 'work currency' for the functioning, status and value of the adult male. Thus 'the community itself, rather than any mediating social worker, can *rehabilitate* the offender, re-invest him with dignity and put him on a proper footing in society'.
3.   Because of the explicitness of the contractual and punitive component, there has been a greater tendency for probation officers to return offenders to the court on breaches

of community service orders than is the case with probation orders. Research has shown that breaches of probation are both rare and inconsistent, and, although there may be occasions to justify leniency, all the evidence in child care and behavioural psychology would lead to the conclusion that a social work which threatens sanctions and then never resorts to them is unlikely to gain the respect of those it is trying to help. It is significant that most residential child care workers learn to recognise the value of consistency and structure, if life is to be tolerable for both residents and staff, and if the experience is to be beneficial for children whose earlier lives were themselves all too often characterised by threats and discipline unevenly and illogically distributed.

A different kind of structured setting is to be found in the development by the probation service of motor projects and car offender groups, designed to provide a non-custodial alternative for persistent motor-vehicle offenders – usually so called joy-riders. While subject to a probation order, offenders are engaged in group work intended to make them face up to the responsibilities of legal driving and attaining a full licence.

Programmes run for about six months, during which offenders participate in a mixture of lectures, offending behaviour sessions and perhaps some off-road driving lessons. Groups cover topics such as road safety, the Highway Code, documentation, insurance and other issues surrounding the legal use of cars on the road. Advocates of the approach claim that there will be a reduction of offending as awareness of roadcraft increases and that, once an offender has a licence, he or she is unlikely to want to lose it through disqualification (Whitehead 1993).

4.   Behavioural methods

No social work approach falls so unequivocally into a chapter on 'achieving change' as behaviour modification. Derived from, and still closely linked with, the work of psychologists, behavioural methods have enjoyed varying degrees of popularity in social work over the years.

They involve the application of learning principles to specific behaviours with a view to reducing or eradicating problem behaviours and encouraging or reinforcing desirable behaviours. Clinical psychologists, of course, also use such techniques, but their lure to social workers is understandable both because of client need and because of the virtual impossibility of referring all such problems to specialist professionals.

They have been used in two main settings: mental health and child care. For example, Holbrook (1978) describes the technique as it was applied to a nine-year-old child displaying severe behavioural problems. As described by his mother, a typical day would begin something like this:

> There would be problems over breakfast because Christopher was faddy about food and eating a very restricted diet; most of the time he would eat only pancakes. He refused to use cutlery and his parents tolerated his using his hands to handle food in order to avoid arguments. There

would be a tantrum over his going to school, and he would shout, kick and often have to be carried out of the house.

At school he was quiet but not progressing; he had no friends, and sometimes stole small objects. He tended to pull his hair out and the resultant bald patches 'made him look strange'. As a result of his behaviour, family life had virtually broken down.

Christopher was first admitted to hospital and then returned home. Behavioural methods were used in both settings, with his parents playing a key role on his return home. Casework techniques were employed simultaneously but three important behaviours were tackled behaviourally: the temper tantrums were controlled by 'time out' techniques (that is, by depriving him of pleasurable activities with absolute consistency); the use of cutlery was enforced by removing his plate, without scolding or fuss, the moment he reverted to the use of hands; the hair pulling was reduced by shortening his hair style. The treatment, though exceedingly costly in the use of staff-time, was regarded as highly successful.

Behavioural methods emphasise the importance of structuring a therapeutic approach, of concentrating on achievable elements within it, and of proceeding logically step-by-step towards clearly identified goals. The methods are particularly suited to work with phobics, and they have been employed with patients suffering from a stutter and other speech defects. Aversion therapy with alcoholics, drug addicts and sex offenders is a major area of work, although it is generally carried out under psychiatric direction rather than by social workers on their own initiative.

Behaviourism has been used in residential settings to good effect, but there are often organisational problems because of the need for a consistent approach towards the resident in order to ensure success, and that means involving *all* staff. Behavioural methods enable staff to concentrate on eliminating undesirable behaviours and developing new skills, often by the use of a 'token economy' in which good behaviour is reinforced by tangible rewards.

Vevers (1981) has described how disruptive behaviour in a children's nursery was reduced by rigorously imposing a system of 'time out' and rewards on a single child, and Harris (1981) has recounted ways in which goals can be set for people with learning disabilities with a view to improving behaviour:

1. The client should participate in setting the goals;
2. The client's strengths and needs should be listed;
3. Goals should be reached by a series of small steps;
4. It should be made clear who is doing what, and when.

The advantages of this approach were said to be fourfold: clients' skills did improve; clients benefited because they were given constructive personal attention; staff communication improved; the method related to the business of ordinary day-to-day living, and thus made sense.

There remain some vigorous opponents of behaviourism as a contributory discipline to social work, but its advocates in recent years have adopted a pragmatic, non-doctrinaire approach which has helped to strengthen its position. Its emphasis on objective clarification, evaluation, role clarity and a structured style of working which makes sense to the client are so obviously preferable to the vague virtues of 'doing good by stealth' that its contribution is certainly likely to grow. Sheldon (1981b) puts the case in admirably balanced terms:

> In advocating that social workers should take behaviour modification more seriously, I am not arguing that they should be blinkered by it. Social workers cannot be just therapists – whatever their persuasion. An ability to work together on community projects, a knowledge of welfare rights, and certain personal qualities are among the many other skills and attributes necessary. However, when social workers do find themselves involved in counselling work, or making plans to change someone's behaviour, then there is very considerable evidence in favour of an approach based on behavioural principles.

5. Social skills training

Social skills training is a direct spin-off from behavioural methods: it uses similar underlying theories and requires the same specificity in goal-setting, contract agreement and consistency. It is concerned not so much with restricting undesirable behaviours as with overcoming deficiencies and enabling the client to survive, and even thrive, in his everyday environment. Given the fact that many studies have shown how frequently social and personal inadequacy are core elements in the problems presented by the social worker's clients, it is not surprising that practitioners have been enthusiastic about the possibilities of this approach.

Three examples drawn from the social work literature describe the use of social skills training with a group of sex offenders, with a depressed woman and in a hostel for mentally ill people:

1. Burgess *et al.* (1980) set up a skills training group for six sex offenders held in close confinement (for their own protection) in prison. They were all seen as anxious and inadequate men: 'The basic criterion [for admission to the training group] was social incompetence. Those who appeared overly submissive, who spoke quietly and diffidently, whose posture was withdrawn, who either stared or avoided eye contact, or had difficulty conversing, were given priority.' The skills training programme 'focused on five "micro" components of social behaviours: eye contact, voice, use of hands, posture and facial expression, and on incorporating these into the situational dimension of the social skills.' Three therapists engaged in structured role-plays and modelling in an attempt to improve client performance. The kind of situations tackled in this and similar programmes with other offenders have included:

    (a) how to handle job interviews (including the development of scripts for coping with the inevitable and awkward questions of how to account for missing stamps on an insurance card);

    (b) how to handle aggression without temper-loss;

(c)   how to ask for help from a probation officer;
(d)   how to talk to an unhelpful landlady;
(e)   how to relate to an unknown person of the opposite sex;
(f)   how to resist pressure to engage in crime;
(g)   how to claim your rights at the social security office.

In their study, Burgess *et al.* claim that worker assessments made before and after the programme showed improvements in specific behaviours, but no information was available on whether these were maintained or generalised into other areas of everyday life.

2.   Cree *et al.* (1979) describe a skills programme designed for a 22-year-old woman, Heather, with a psychiatric history and current depression. During the joint worker-client assessment, Heather identified her lack of social relationships and her loss of interest in recreational activities as particular difficulties. It was agreed that she and the worker would concentrate on improving her conversational skills as a first step. Exercises were employed to develop both listening and speaking skills, and interviews were so structured by the social worker that the client was required to take the initiative, so using the occasion to practise the art of conversation. Progress was rapid after initial difficulties, and Heather was then directed to begin to employ the same arts with friends. 'She recounted with delight the first time she found herself alone with a relative stranger when visiting a friend and, although terrified, sustained a ten-minute conversation while her friend made coffee.'

3.   Scott (1982) recounts how he and a colleague set up a social skills group in a hostel for people who had all been diagnosed schizophrenic and who had spent a year or more of their lives in a mental hospital. He claims that the method seemed particularly suitable for them, since chronic schizophrenic clients probably show the most extreme deficiencies in social skills and he argues that, in order to make them acceptable to the community, they need to be adequately prepared in communication skills. The project consisted of nine sessions which included relaxation and trust exercises, but focused chiefly on practising how to initiate a conversation and keep it going. Evaluation of the exercise led to the conclusion that the more intelligent members of the group improved markedly in non-verbal and attending skills, but that complex verbal skills proved elusive. Scott says that, although they provided some assertion training (that is to say, 'being firm when someone has done wrong to you'), the workers felt that the programme would have benefited from more.

Skills training can be carried out in a number of different ways, but Scott's project illustrates a good range of approaches and demonstrates the need for planning and structure.

Index cards summarising the contents of each session were given to group members about an hour beforehand, partly to allay fears. The leader started each session by *modelling* a particular social skill, then indicating how it was in keeping with what was on the index card; then the modelling was *repeated*. One of the group would *role-play* the same scene. *Feedback* was provided on the client's role-play, being as *specific* as possible: for example, 'The questions you asked really showed that you were interested in what she said.'

Feedback included *praise* wherever possible, and poor performance was followed by *constructive advice*: for example, 'How about looking at her during the conversation next time?' Following the feedback, the client *re-enacted* the scene once more.

Homework was given, requiring the client to practise the lesson in real life. They were expected to make a commitment for the coming week: for example, 'I will initiate a conversation with two strangers.' The next session began with a *review* of homework. Later, attempts were made to achieve *transfer* of the learning to the real world by taking the clients out or simulating external reality.

In any spell of social skills training, considerable encouragement, repetition and reinforcement will usually be needed if the new improved behaviours are to become permanent and transferable to different situations. Cree *et al.* are probably being optimistic when they say that the method, which in their case was based on weekly meetings over a period of a year, is little different from normal work in its demands on time and commitment. Indeed, one characteristic of all structured change strategies is that they almost certainly require investments of energy and involvement which are unusual in contemporary practice. If they get the results that are sometimes claimed for them, however, the time might be considered well spent.

6. Task achievement

Task achievement methods again concentrate on specificity of aim, contractual agreements between worker and client and a concentration on achievable goals. The main difference from the social skills training model is that it does not involve the social worker in a training role (although the two approaches are of course entirely compatible with each other and may be used in tandem).

Goldberg *et al.* (1977a) have reported on a small project in Buckinghamshire Social Services Department where a task-centred approach was tested. Clients were invited and helped to carry out problem-alleviating tasks within agreed time-limits. Particular attention was paid to clients' *own* conceptions of their problems, and the method had five phases:

1. Problem exploration, in which the client's problems were identified and placed in rank order.
2. Agreement on the target problem.
3. Agreement on action: What was to be done to alleviate the problem? How were the tasks to be formulated? Agreement was reached on how much time the social worker would devote to working with the client on task achievement.
4. The social worker directed techniques and strategies towards bringing about the achievement of the task by the client. No precise method was specified. Imagination,

spontaneity and creativity were required, but the precise focus had to be maintained, and this could lead to a relatively directive approach.

5.   Because time-limits were set, the time for termination was known throughout. In the last interview, a review of the problem was carried out, and an evaluation made of the effectiveness of the client's efforts.

In the Buckinghamshire study, 23 fully task-centred cases were identified, and tasks were either substantially or completely achieved in 15 cases. Goldberg reports enthusiasm for the method among social workers, although it was found to be applicable in only about one-third of agency referrals. The workers 'felt strongly that the model enhances respect for the client, stresses the client's equality, and helps to demystify social work by clarifying the social worker's role'.

Case example: The partialising process

Mrs I., middle-aged divorcee, was referred by the GP suffering from hypertension and back pains. She admitted to having financial worries. The allowance she received from her ex-husband was too low, but because he was a chronic invalid she felt unable to press for more. Her son paid her only a small sum for bed and breakfast, and she supplemented her income by many hours of dressmaking, for which she charged very little. The task agreed was 'to find ways of improving her general financial position while the social worker would try to meet some specific debts'.

First, Mrs I. was to ask her son for an increased contribution; he willingly agreed. Second, the social worker was to seek a grant from a voluntary agency; this was successfully accomplished. Third, Mrs I. was to seek advice on realistic charges for her work; by the fifth interview she had the information, and raised her prices accordingly. The financial strains were eased, and her health improved. In review, Mrs I. was clear that the partialising process had been invaluable and expressed appreciation of the social worker's understanding role.
(Abridged from Goldberg *et al.* 1977a)

A successfully administered experimental study in Southampton found that a task-centred social work approach could be employed with just over half of a sample of parasuicide clients in a hospital-based department. In controlled comparisons, it was found that the task-centred treatment had positive effects on clients' social and interpersonal problems and led to a reduced dependency on psychiatric services; it was also found that the clients were significantly more satisfied with the service they had received, compared with the 'normal' service. However, on the critical and central question of whether the task-centred approach reduced the likelihood of further suicide attempts, the researcher reported wholly negative findings: there was no difference between the experimental and control groups (Gibbons 1981).

Gibbons, however, is quick to emphasise that the experiment should not be regarded as a reason for abandoning task-centred methods. It strongly suggests, she says, 'that social work intervention can produce encouraging improvement in clients' immediate social situations and morale and is much appreciated by them. "Effective" social work achieves modest (from a social policy perspective) but important (from an individual perspective) objectives.' The important thing is to be clear about one's objectives.

7.   Cognitive therapy

One therapeutic method that has gained ground in social work — especially in work with the large number of women experiencing degrees of depression — is based on cognitive theory. The theory starts from the idea that, although environmental pressures may justify negative feelings in women ('women are depressed because they have much to be depressed about'), the intensity of depression may be a personal response to the way the individual thinks of herself:

> Human emotions are seen as a result of what people think or tell themselves. Depression, specifically, is caused by negative perceptions of oneself, the world and the future. A depressive episode may be externally precipitated, by a loss for example, but it is the individual's perception and appraisal of the event that renders it depression-inducing . . . If internal obstacles could be overcome, women might indeed get more out of life. (Corob 1987)

Cognitive therapy aims to counter the negative and pessimistic thinking about self which is seen as a major cause of depression.

> Cognitive therapy is a pragmatic, active approach, involving client and worker in a collaborative effort to combat depression. A time limit (usually 15–25 sessions) may be set to achieve desired goals, and specific problematic areas, such as social isolation or self-criticism, can be targeted for intervention. The focus of the approach is on the here and now, concerned with conscious, rather than unconscious behaviour. (Corob 1987)

First, the worker will help the client to understand how they 'automatically' interpret external events in such a way as to induce negative feelings in themselves; this learning process might involve the client keeping a record of depressive episodes, and trying to make links between thought, feeling and behaviour. Sometimes this process can be carried out through role-play sessions with the therapist.

The therapeutic sequence proceeds by helping the client to differentiate between her feelings and 'objective reality' — perhaps by keeping a daily record of thoughts and events, so that their relationship can be rationally explored. The worker will help her client to 'identify and challenge distortions in her thinking', and so prepare to face up to depression-inducing events.

Cognitive therapy has proved especially useful for use in association with feminist theory, because it explicitly challenges themes that reflect gender stereotypes, such as 'women should be kind and selfless at all times and never hurt anyone', or 'women can only be successful if they are slim and beautiful'.

Corob says that cognitive therapy should be used sensitively and with flexibility. It can be combined with behavioural methods, such as task assignment or social skills training, and it appears to require a certain amount of verbal sophistication, intelligence and a capacity for introspection. A good relationship between worker and client is essential, with the traditional qualities of empathy, warmth and genuineness seen as paramount.

8. Self-help groups

> Self-help groups are notoriously vulnerable. The typical group is started by one or two energetic, charismatic figures and collapses when they withdraw, exhausted, or move away for work or family reasons. (Crine 1982)

Such is the reaction of many social workers to the idea of self-help groups; others recoil from the untidiness and amateurishness of vulnerable clients struggling to further their own interests without direction from the welfare professionals. Nevertheless it is now generally recognised that self-help groups are not only therapeutically valuable, but represent an important element in the community orientation of social work.

Probably the most common examples of self-help groups have been found in the probation service with prisoners' wives groups, and in local authorities with foster parent groups. In each case, it is normal for the social worker to take the initiative and bring together a number of potentially interested members. Often the groups are primarily talking shops and, although mutually supportive discussion *is* a form of self-help, it has usually proved difficult to encourage them to aspire to more ambitious objectives. Other examples are to be found in community action with social workers being instrumental in encouraging and enabling a variety of self-help initiatives. In south-east London, a 'patch' team in Lewisham has seen a housing estate in Honor Oak take on a wide range of self-help functions with social work encouragement: mothers' and toddlers' groups, women's groups, pensioners' clubs and a community transport scheme.

At first sight there is a logical inconsistency in any *self*-help group being prompted or initiated by a professional social worker. Levy (1976) has defined self-help groups in five ways: their *purpose* is to provide help and support for members; their *origin* rests with the group members themselves and not with some external agency; the *source of help* is to be found in the members' own efforts, skills, knowledge and concern (where professionals do participate, they do so at the pleasure of the group, and only in an ancillary role); the group's *composition* is of members who share a common core of life experiences and problems; the group will be *controlled* by its members, although they may seek professional guidance.

Such a definition would preclude the social worker from launching self-help groups, and the need for caution is further emphasised by the fact that many of those who turn to self-help often claim to have had unhelpful or unpleasant experiences of social work. Alcoholics Anonymous (AA) has claimed that its approach is superior to 'the overtone of parental disapproval and discipline' that it senses in professional helpers, and one of the best British examples of a successful self-help group, Chiswick Women's Aid, says that it came into existence *because of* the failure of social workers to satisfactorily meet the needs of battered women.

Glassner and Freedman (1979) pinpointed the difficulty when they say that 'professionals find it difficult to be "peers", rather than "experts", unless they fit into the focus of the group (as when an alcoholic physician joins AA)'. It is perhaps significant that the founder of Chiswick Women's Aid, Erin Pizzey, though not herself a battered wife, has said that she was powerfully influenced by vivid childhood memories of the atmosphere of violence which pervaded her own home.

To insist on such a clear-cut separation is, however, too restrictive. The social worker needs to employ a high degree of professional sensitivity: where self-help groups already exist, clients can be told about them and encouraged to attend, and, despite Levy's restrictive definition, professional encouragement to a group starting up, if handled with sensitivity and humility, is often of immense value and greatly appreciated. 'She gave us the confidence to believe we could do it,' commented the members of a parents' self-help group about a social worker. And in another instance: 'She gave us moral support at a time of crisis, although she never came to our meetings' (Brimelow and Wilson 1982). Social workers can offer practical resources, information and advice, and they can give groups credibility to help them to cope with opposition from departmental officials.

On the other hand, if the social worker assumes and retains a leading role in the group, then it will be prevented from being or becoming a true self-help group, and its members will be thrust into a dependent role of an inappropriate and perhaps unwanted kind. Brimelow and Wilson (1982) argue that the attitude of the worker is crucial. Those social workers most successful in maintaining the 'sensitive balance between offering constructive support and taking over the group' believed in the intrinsic value of self-help and in the capacity of members to organise their own affairs. Workers expressed this in different ways: 'It's important for people to do things for themselves'; 'A bunch of clients together may be much more effective than a professional'; 'They are the experts about their own problems'.

> The effective workers saw their role as complementary to group members, and described the relationship as one of partnership, in which worker and members had different roles. Even if they played a significant role in starting a group, they saw their role as facilitators, helping to bring people together and provide back-up support. (Brimelow and Wilson 1982: 12–13)

Do self-help groups work? It depends, of course, on what one means by 'work'. To anyone who has observed them in operation, there can be little doubt that they are a key element in the maintenance and improvement of morale and the will to survive. Whether they are therapeutic in a narrower sense is, as always, more problematic. It is generally accepted that the best-known of them, Alcoholics Anonymous, has been more successful in its approach than has any other strategy for the cure of alcoholism. Whether this is due to the 'selfness' of the help or to the rigorous and ruthless use of shaming techniques and group discipline is, however, not clear.

9.   Social advocacy

Strategies of change in social work might sometimes need to be directed, not at the client, but at dysfunctional elements in the client's environment. In her study of an intake unit, Corney (1981) found that the majority of clients coming to a social services department for the first time wanted some form of advocacy from the worker. More often than not this would involve contacts with local authority departments, but the benefits office and voluntary agencies were also involved.

Advocacy in social work can be either personal or structural: that is, it can either focus on the needs of a particular client or it can take up cudgels on behalf of an entire community. In either case, the assumption is that the social worker has skills and qualities or access to resources that are likely to tip the balance in the favour of those whose interests would otherwise be overlooked or overridden. Kahn *et al.* (1972) have identified the qualities that make for a good advocate in social work: she is likely to be a natural leader with a strong personality and expertise in her subject; she will be knowledgeable and have her facts right; she will be politically adept, knowing which are the appropriate leverage points to bring about change; she will be known for her professional integrity; and she will be capable of presenting her client's case forcefully and efficiently. Kahn found that workers needing to have constant recourse to team meetings or to consult with colleagues did not make good advocates: the practitioners of sound advocacy programmes were found to be more self-reliant and autonomous than other social workers.

How might a social worker be drawn into advocacy? Many instances are likely to involve accommodation crises or financial problems: the worker acts on behalf of a harassed mother in a face-to-face confrontation with a housing manager or landlord wanting to evict her and her family for non-payment of rent; or she speaks up for an ex-prisoner whose boss is threatening to sack him because he has found out about his convictions. In each of these cases, the social worker's intervention, if successful, will have a significant impact on the client's welfare – at least in the short term.

Structural advocacy is probably less common in routine social work, but most practitioners are likely to engage in it at some stage of their careers, and many will see it as a major aspect of their agency role. The social worker – probably operating within a group, and drawing on supplementary help, perhaps from students – might carry out a survey in the local community and, using the results obtained, set out to persuade the relevant authority, for example, to provide more play space for youngsters, to improve the quality of its housing stock, or to run a better transport system. Another social worker, because of her intimate knowledge of client-group deprivations, might make an organised and persistent attempt to persuade national charities like MIND or Age Concern to establish or sponsor improved local facilities.

There is some controversy over the extent to which structural advocacy is a legitimate activity for all social workers, and any kind of advocacy can undoubtedly lead to delicate situations because of the statutory social worker's position as an employee of a politically managed local authority. However, although the nature of the boundary between social work and politics will always be imprecise, it is certain that an advocacy role for the social worker will remain valid.

10. Empowerment

A model of change which is exceptionally compatible with maintenance theory is to be found in empowerment social work, an approach to practice which acknowledges the oppressed state of many clients, and offers a service which takes into account their 'self-defined service needs and their inalienable right to remain in control of their own lives' (Holdsworth 1991).

The crucial aspect of the approach lies in the way the worker uses her own power in relation to the client, Those who advocate the method say that all too often social work serves only to compound the client's sense of powerlessness, whereas an avoidance of such 'oppression' will bring real benefits in terms of the client's future performance. Workers must be willing to learn from their clients and to enter into a genuine partnership with them.

Holdsworth argues that empowerment social work is of particular value with physically disabled people. It 'necessitates responding to their needs in a way which enables them to stay in control of, or regain control of their lives, whilst benefiting from the knowledge and skill of professional workers in a non-stigmatising, non-demeaning way'.

A key element in this requires the participation of disabled people themselves both in policy-making and in constructing and managing their own personal packages of care. In parallel, Holdsworth argues, there is a need for an empathetic information and counselling service in social work; this will provide the driving force for the empowerment process, because, of course, knowledge means power (Oliver and Hasler 1987). Without access to information, participation cannot happen.

Empowerment social work entails accepting 'disabled people as knowledgeable partners in the service planning and delivery process, and being prepared to listen to their ideas and to discuss them on an equal basis. This in turn means that social services departments must accept the social model of disability and acknowledge the oppressive nature of able-bodied society, including able-bodied social workers and policy-makers who regularly decide what services should be provided for physically disabled people. One example of the involvement of disabled people in the service planning process is provided in Kirklees, Yorkshire.' The social services department there started in 1988 to consult disabled people about the services provided; a disability reference group was formed to advise on policy, and, from 1990, consumer panels were appointed to comment on existing provision and to make recommendations for the future.

The changes that can be wrought in peoples' lives when they are given the power to help themselves are among the most important therapeutic effects of contemporary social work.

11.   Developmental perspectives in social work

The developmental perspective involves exposing the client or the resident to new, perhaps challenging and even risky experiences. In intermediate treatment (IT), for example, children whose horizons have been limited can be taken on adventure trips to the sea or to the mountains; mental patients with a long history of institutional containment can be placed in domestic situations where they have to learn how to cope with the demands of cooking, budgeting and social cooperation; and old people in residential care can be encouraged to walk out to the shops, go on buses to the town and even play wheelchair sports. The assumption underlying these tactics is that all human beings have innate strengths which not only enable them to cope with limited stress, but which, when encouraged, produce responses that are in themselves beneficial and growth-producing. Although the model is closely associated with a social work philosophy of individualisation, its efficacy has never been effectively tested, and it is known to carry with it some dangers: the child on an exciting IT course in the mountains of North Wales may find the ordeal too threatening for him and so have his feelings of inadequacy confirmed, or he may return to the humdrum world of his urban home disillusioned and embittered by the glimpse of something better; the institutionalised mental patient may break down under the strain of coping with everyday life and have to be re-admitted to hospital; and there is evidence to show that old people in homes which encourage independent activities have a higher incidence of broken limbs and consequent admission to long-term stay in hospital.

The use of developmental models in social work is still at a very early stage but it offers a major field for research and experiment, with a wide range of questions to be explored. For example:

1.   How can developmental perspectives be employed with different client-groups?
2.   When, and under what circumstances, are they inappropriate?
3.   What resources are needed to facilitate them?

Conclusion

Nothing so illustrates the confused state of knowledge in social work as a discussion of the concept of change in practice. There are at least four elements involved in such a review:

1.   *Empirical evidence:* The empirical foundations of social work practice have proved exceedingly difficult to establish. While lip-service has been paid to the importance of research, almost all developments of any significance in the field have been based

more on pragmatism and politics than on positivism. The main contribution of research has been to introduce a sceptical note to counteract managerial or professional enthusiasms; it is a foolish man now who would speak too easily of social work's capacity to achieve radical change, no matter how the task is attempted. Reid and Hanrahan (1982), however, have said that a structured approach to therapeutic aims does have the backing of empirical support.

2. *Practice theory:* Social workers draw on their knowledge of the psychological and social sciences and their experience of similar situations in the past to decide how to act in specific circumstances. They may not always be able to locate the theoretical origins of their actions, but that they do exist is quite clear.

3. *Conventional wisdom:* Very little is known about conventional wisdom in social work – the practice of 'doing things' because that's the way they've always been done – but the suspicion is strong that its effects are powerful. We know, for example, that conventional wisdom varies significantly from one agency, one office, one home to another, and that, although leadership is obviously a factor, the traditions often outlive each generation of participants.

4. *Fond expectations and personal ideals:* The motivations of social workers are important – whether they are salving their consciences in a materialistic society, or rendering themselves capable of surviving the inevitable stress of living in residential settings. Social work has always had its idealists, its visionaries, its prophets and its believers in the millenium: salvation might come through psychoanalysis, revolution or organisational efficiency – but that it *will* come is not by some people doubted.

Whichever framework is adopted – and it might be a combination of any or all of them – there is frequently an underlying assumption that change is a legitimate, even a necessary, objective. The yearning for change is a long-lasting element in man's psyche: the desire for miracles to reverse the inexorable onset of illness and the decline of human faculties, the longing for beneficent influences to counteract evil forces, and the feeling that because life is a rearguard action against death, the ability to 'change' people is a welcome proof of one's own superhuman strengths. Social work is operating in this most emotive of human areas and the temptation to proffer solutions and elixirs is always great.

It is impossible to deny the occasional legitimacy of a change-objective, though to embrace it too enthusiastically must be to invite disappointment and disillusionment. Conventional wisdom is unlikely to offer much reliable guidance. Idealism might inspire a response, and if the goals are relatively modest, lead on occasions to success; it may also be a necessary morale-booster in some spheres of social work. Practice theory is probably more at ease with modest expectations, and despite the setbacks and the shortcomings of research to date, the scientific optimist in me has to conclude that only empirical study and theory development can ultimately hope to improve the performance of social work in respect of achieving change.

However, conventional wisdom and fond expectations can only be discarded, if at all, when empirical research does two things: it must demonstrate the inappropriateness of current practice; and it must suggest – and justify – a viable alternative. Unfortunately, to date, research studies, while drawing a number of conclusions in the first area, have been notoriously weak in the second. Behavioural psychology has contributed a little in highly specialised areas, but sociology – which has been active in undermining present practice (especially in casework and counselling and in all attempts at achieving change) – has been exceedingly disappointing in its prescriptions. The problem for sociology is that its subject matter – the framework of society – is highly complex, unpredictable and yet conservative. Hence strategies of change are necessarily structural/political, and the place of the social worker in them either problematic or irrelevant. Two of sociology's proffered solutions – radical non-intervention and the resort to revolution – are antagonistic to social work *per se*, while a third – the use of networks and community intervention – is relatively undeveloped. It has not been subjected to the same kind of analytical investigation that has been applied to casework over 40 years, and given the vagueness of many change-objectives in the community, empirical evidence would almost certainly be hard to come by.

Significantly it is a social scientist whose entire career has focused on social work who has produced some of the most stimulating research material in the field. Thorpe (1982) has clearly demonstrated that intermediate treatment (IT), intended to be both therapeutic and benevolent in its effects, has more often than not been neither. After its introduction, he argues, the commitment of young delinquents to institutions soared – the very opposite of what was intended. Although the launch of IT was well-intentioned, it led to an immense growth in the target-group for intervention and to a phenomenon of penological drift – offenders being 'sucked into' the institutional system simply because they had become more visible to the critical decision-makers. From there, the future would hold for many of them only a life of crime and punishment, as a direct result of the therapists' preventative intervention.

However, Thorpe, instead of detachedly leaving his critique there (as tends to happen in sociology), goes on to emphasise the importance of social work learning the lessons of his investigations. We must be much more specific about our target-group and about the problems we focus on with a view to bringing about change. Just because a child has committed a minor crime is no reason for subjecting him to the full panoply of welfarist responses – especially if it leads to him being admitted to care on grounds which, *if he had not committed a crime*, would not have justified the making of a care order. The problem with IT, he says, is that it has been decidedly non-specific and non-problem-focused.

To the extent that maintenance is the aim of social work, then it is certainly crucial to ensure that intervention does not lead to deterioration. The achievement of change (*beneficial* change, that is) is seen as an element in the maintenance strategy; but it is only one element and is not a precondition for the profession's existence. Other elements include the provision of effective support, the exercise of responsibility and pro-active intervention in the community. And a full recognition of the range of activities, strategies and emphases in social work facilitates a more sophisticated and valid understanding of what the discipline is all about.

7 Power and responsibility

The trainee manager, school teacher, trade union official and surgeon quickly learn and accept that, both by virtue of their paid position and by their confidence in the use of acquired skills, they are each in positions of power and responsibility. If one of their number seeks to deny this role, if he is confused about its legitimacy, ambivalent about the appropriateness of taking decisions, acting firmly and asserting his ascribed authority, he is unlikely to be a good manager, teacher, workers' leader or surgeon. No firm wants a manager who vacillates; neither school nor children want or respect a teacher who cannot keep order; and a trade union does not want an official who fails to fight for its members' interests.

It is the same in social work. By virtue of her employment, the social worker carries significant power and bears great responsibility. Empowered by legislation, she can affect, for better or worse, the fortunes of all those who come into contact with her. The difference between good practice and bad practice can often be identified by the extent to which the social worker improves or damages the lives of the clients for whom she is responsible.

A generation ago, critics were perturbed at what they sometimes saw: social workers uncertain of their duties, uneasy with their obligations. Hence the depressing conclusion drawn by Stevenson and Parsloe (1978) at the end of their mammoth investigation into the work of social services departments: 'The best endeavours of many individuals to provide good services to those in need are . . . undermined' by, among other factors, 'an overriding lack of clarity about objectives and roles, about the proper functions of the personal social services and of social work in particular'.

Thankfully, the pressure of public opinion has compelled the profession to recognise that social work *can* have no existence independently of the agencies in which it operates. And without any doubt, the two largest employers of social workers in the United Kingdom − the local authorities and probation areas − while recognising and valuing the special contribution of social work as a compassionate and humanising force, nevertheless expect it to operate according to guidelines, some of them laid down by statute, others by administrative decision. Within these boundaries, social workers carry heavy responsibility, and it is the purpose of this chapter to describe briefly the many different ways in which they are expected to fulfil it.

Oversight and containment

'Now, John, I'm going to place you under the supervision of Mrs Bakewell. You'll have to go and see her, and you must do as she tells you. I'm sure she'll help you if she can, and we don't expect to see you back in this court again. Is that clear?'

With words like these, many a probation or supervision order begins, and the new client goes off with his social worker to find out what is expected of him.

Social workers in all agencies are deputed to supervise, to oversee, to keep an eye on a wide variety of clients, young and old, delinquent and distressed, recidivist and 'at risk'. The hope is that the worker can *contain* the situation or, if it deteriorates, take action that will prevent further trouble. We will consider two examples.

Supervising clients in the community

Offenders constitute one major group supervised by social workers in the community. In 1991 almost 100,000 convicted persons in England and Wales were made subject to a variety of supervision orders by the courts, and so passed onto the caseload of a social work agency; 44 per cent of them were adults placed on probation for periods ranging from six months to three years (see Table 7.1). The biggest group were given one-year

Table 7.1
Court orders on convicted persons which required supervision by a social worker (1991)

	Number	%
Adults placed on probation	44 067	44
Youths placed under supervision following criminal proceedings	6 525	7
Suspended sentence supervision orders	2 272	2
Community service orders	41 190	41
Money payment supervision orders	5 674	6
Total	99 728	100

Source: Probation statistics, England and Wales 1991, Home Office, London, February 1993: 5, 60.

orders (44 per cent compared with 29 per cent in 1981), reflecting a steady trend towards shorter probation orders. Seven per cent were youth offenders (that is, aged between 10 and 16 inclusive) and they, like the adults, had mostly been convicted of theft, handling or burglary; one-third of the young criminals were supervised by probation officers, the rest by local authority social workers. About 80 per cent of the orders either ran their full course or were discharged early for good progress, and there is evidence that the older the client the greater the chance of successfully completing supervision.

The community service scheme for offenders was introduced in 1975, and it undoubtedly represents the most radical and far-reaching penal innovation seen in the second half of the 20th century. By the end of 1991, the number of community service orders on the probation service's caseload had reached 30,400 and was still rising steadily.

The scheme involves active cooperation between the probation service and other organisations in the community who provide the setting in which offenders must work for up to 240 hours over a period of weeks or months. It has no explicit therapeutic component, and has the unique distinction of appealing equally to both liberal and conservative wings of the social policy spectrum: to the former because it has been shown to be a viable and positive alternative to imprisonment, and to the latter because it is seen as a real punishment which can be meted out according to the 'just deserts' principle and is therefore preferable to what is often thought of as the 'soft option' of probation.

The Home Office (1992) has introduced tough national standards for community service designed to prevent orders being allowed to 'drift': probation officers are required to get the offender working within ten days of the court order, to aim at a minimum work rate of five hours a week and to take immediate action on any defaults, with breach action being taken after no more than three instances of failure to comply. Thus, a form of quality control has been imposed on probation officers, in order to ensure that similar standards of practice operate throughout the country.

Apart from those 'sentenced to social work' by the courts, there is one other large group of offenders under supervision: those who have been released from penal institutions, including prisoners on parole. In 1991 there were about 46,000 after-care clients on the probation service's caseload. At one extreme were a small number of murderers who had come out on parole and would inevitably be treated with circumspection by a probation officer alive to the political sensitivities of her supervisory responsibility – the entire policy of releasing serious offenders on licence is perpetually poised on a knife-edge of public acquiescence, and any suspicion that the social worker is oblivious to continuing crimes or misdemeanours is always likely to put the policy in jeopardy. At the other extreme were the large number of petty recidivists, of whom it has been said that at least a half ought not to have been in prison at all. They come to the after-care office for immediate help, but their problems of homelessness, unemployment, alcoholism and ill-health are often so chronic that the social worker's contribution is self-evidently inadequate.

Occasionally voices are raised against the use of social workers in surveillance, but the probation officer is 'inescapably an officer of the law', and so too is the local authority

social worker so far as the supervision of juvenile offenders is concerned. If they were to
deny the appropriateness of their responsibility for such offenders and withdraw from a
surveillance role, a new service would have to be created instantly. Moreover the use of
social workers to perform this function has undoubtedly had the important effect of
slowly, if hesitantly, instilling a humane voice into the penal system. The state of prisons
in most countries shows that there is still a long way to go before they are truly civilised,
but there is little doubt that the probation officer has been and remains a moderating
factor in institutions known to be especially resistant to outside influences.

Offenders are not the only clients whom social workers supervise in the community:
ex-mental patients, the physically handicapped and the elderly can also be subject to
oversight, not of course in lieu of punishment, but rather to protect their own interests or
to detect warning signals of impending trouble. The NHS and Community Care Act 1990
is intended to lead to a system of networks, led by the social worker, but also involving
other professionals together with volunteers and neighbours formally deputed to keep an
eye on old people thought likely to be at risk.

Monitoring children at risk

The second example of 'containment' concerns the problem of child abuse. Although
there have been other alleged scandals of child abuse or neglect which have led to
inquiries and published reports, it remains the misfortune of East Sussex Social Services
Department that the case of seven-year-old Maria Colwell should have been the
headline-hitting *cause célèbre* in the emergent phenomenon of non-accidental injury. For
most of her life, Maria had been fostered by her aunt and uncle, and for five years had
been in the care of the county council. In October 1971, she went to live with her mother
and stepfather, the Kepples, whom she had been visiting for some time. The care order
was revoked and a supervision order made; while this arrangement was in force, William
Kepple, Maria's stepfather, killed her, an offence for which he was convicted, first of
murder, and then, on appeal, of manslaughter. The Secretary of State for Health and Social
Services set up a public inquiry which reported in September 1974, and which, more than
any other single event, highlighted the developing pattern of complex and generally
unsympathetic relationships between social work and the public. Shearer (1979) graphi-
cally depicted the pain, the bewilderment and the continuing air of injured innocence that
social workers have expressed whenever the events of 1973–74 are recollected. 'It was
bizarre,' remembers Jeanne Wall (an area director in East Sussex at the time): 'It was so
beyond one's experience to be a sort of pawn or puppet, pushed and pulled.' 'It felt so
totally unreasonable, so totally unjust . . . It [the inquiry] was so unprofessional – Olive
Stevenson apart – and so sensational which was beyond our experience, because until
that time nothing had been more private than social work.'

'Nothing had been more private than social work.' A telling phrase: a phrase that
illustrates the traditional temptation to ignore the public context and communal
responsibility of social work; a phrase that contradicts the Timms's reasonable assertion

(1977) that social work is performed under social auspices; a phrase that evokes the real feelings of people who were caught up in something that had taken them totally by surprise and that they did not know how to handle. Above all, it is a phrase that marks a watershed in the history of social work – before it, social workers really could believe in the private nature of their activities; after it, they would have to get used to media exposure, to the need for public explanations of their actions, and to the idea that never again would society be prepared to assume that the social worker's good intentions would always and necessarily be translated into good deeds. Of course, the abuse hurled at the profession in general, and at the East Sussex department in particular, was exaggerated. The fact that the social worker concerned had to have physical protection as she went in and out of the hearing was outrageous. And, of course, the Colwell case could have happened anywhere in the country, to any social worker. But the strength of feeling provoked by it, and the strong undercurrent of hostility towards social work, could not be, and still cannot be, ignored.

Parton (1979) has argued that social workers were the victims of political prejudice and moral panic, but, although media manipulation certainly contributed to a mood of scapegoating, the social work profession of that time had rather laid itself open to public criticism and ridicule by the way in which many of its practitioners and some of its leaders seemed to claim too much for it: it would repair and strengthen family life, combat juvenile delinquency, ameliorate the conditions of the handicapped, improve on the record of the NSPCC and reduce the incidence of child cruelty. And here, in the case of Maria Colwell, the social worker's fallibility was cruelly exposed.

It became painfully apparent that the Colwell Inquiry was ultimately concerned with the nature of the relationship between the social worker and society, and social work and the state. The public declared its interest in the matter of child safety, and social workers were compelled to accept that their decision-making processes had to become more formalised, more rigorously recorded and more open to investigation and assessment by political superiors.

In the wake of Colwell, we have had to tackle two separate but equally critical issues with regard to the monitoring of children at risk. The first is this: can the social worker operate a surveillance service efficient enough to satisfy the public's desire to reduce the incidence of child abuse? For here society and its representatives are undoubtedly demanding a *policing* function: for example, when a 13-month-old child died of hypothermia after being found by ambulancemen on a urine-soaked mattress covered in sores and suffering from gangrene, the judge commented that the social worker had called 51 times 'but didn't go to the right part of the house'. The slowly accumulating evidence seems to point to the conclusion that social workers have had to adapt themselves to fulfil a policing role of this kind.

The second issue is related to the first and is this: having satisfactorily determined that a child is at risk of significant harm, how can a preventative policy best be pursued? In extreme cases of neglect or abuse, the initial response is fairly straightforward: either the social worker has to negotiate with the parents arrangements which ensure the safety of the child, for example, by his placement with a relative or in accommodation provided by the local authority; or the social worker must obtain a court order authorising her to remove the child against the parents' wishes.

Most reported cases, however, are by no means clear-cut. Whenever a local authority is advised of a case of suspected abuse — no matter what the source — it has a statutory duty to arrange for a social worker to investigate the allegation and to report her findings to a child protection conference. Having taken account of the available evidence, the conference will decide on the level of risk involved and consider whether the child's name should be put on the Child Protection Register. The conference will also appoint a key worker to the case, who will have the job of liaising with each agency in touch with the child and ensuring that information held in different quarters doesn't get lost or ignored.

Pritchard (1992) has suggested that the United Kingdom's child protection policy has significantly reduced the number of infant murders and therefore probably also the incidence of child abuse itself.

Why then do social workers not play safe and engage in much more child removal, even when the risk is marginal? One answer was given by the spokesman for a social services department defending its decision to allow a 15-year-old schoolgirl mother to live with her lover, a few weeks before the couple's baby daughter was murdered by the father. He said that social workers were often forced to take a gamble with children who might be subject to abuse: 'We get 40 child abuse allegations every month and if we play completely safe and put every one of these children into care then our homes would be overflowing. We try to keep families together and in doing that take inevitable risks.'

If removal to care were the policy desired by the community, then the community would have to invest enormous additional sums of money in residential child care. But even if that were to be politically and economically feasible, we still have to confront another dilemma: it is the experience of social workers everywhere that the removal of a child from its own family setting is very often not the better alternative that is widely assumed. If first-class, stable foster care were available to all who needed it, then hooray! — the child at risk could indeed be offered an attractive, long-term alternative. But all the evidence has led to the conclusion that a range of services designed to support the child within his own family is more likely to produce a satisfactory outcome than permanently removing him from home. After carrying out a detailed assessment of the child's needs and the family's capacity for change, the social worker will decide on the kind of services that might be appropriate. These could include providing nursery day care for children, giving help with parenting skills and offering short-term 'respite' accommodation for the child designed to take the pressure off a family in a time of stress.

Because the social worker is committed, whenever possible, to leaving the child with his parents, to work with them intensively, supportively and encouragingly while still keeping a storm-watch-out for future violence . . . because of this we come back, full circle, to the first issue. Can the social worker fulfil the policing role firmly, even aggressively, if she also has to gain the family's confidence, and to convey the personal warmth and genuineness implicit in her professional role? The answer is that it *has* to be done; and the evidence suggests that it is by no means impossible to achieve — provided the social worker is crystal-clear about the nature of her job and the duality of her roles.

Furthermore, there is evidence from client-perspective studies that clients prefer openness, and are neither deceived nor impressed by the social worker who appears to want to deny the importance of such functions as the prevention of child abuse.

Involvement in making critical decisions

Most social workers are frequently required to write reports about clients in which they assess their psychosocial circumstances, describe and comment on aspects of their behaviour and make predictions about the future. Sometimes they are asked to make recommendations for decision; sometimes they have to present a range of possible options with only an implicit indication of their own opinion. The reports are read by the decision-makers – doctors, magistrates, judges, committees – who may have to take into account factors which it was not the business of the social worker to comment on; for example, a judge might be influenced by the need to pass a sentence which incorporates an element of general deterrence.

If the social worker is familiar to the decision-makers, and if there is trust and understanding between them, it is often possible for the social worker to exert a quite radical degree of influence on the eventual outcome. It is known, for example, that forensic psychiatrists will place particular reliance on reports from probation officers known by them to have specialist knowledge of mental health practice.

Pre-sentence reports in criminal cases

Every year the probation service prepares about 200,000 reports on offenders appearing before the courts: almost two-thirds are concerned with adults brought up before the local magistrates, and most of the remainder are for the Crown Courts. In addition, local authority social workers prepare court reports for the Youth Courts.

The prime purpose of a pre-sentence report in criminal cases is to convey relevant information about a convicted person to decision-makers who have the difficult task of deciding what penalty he should pay. The probation officer has to operate within the very clear framework laid down by the criminal justice legislation, and, since 1991, this has demanded a heavy emphasis on the specific nature of the offence and its assessed 'seriousness'.

'A pre-sentence report should be obtained before a custodial sentence is passed to ensure that potential community sentences can first be properly considered, particularly in borderline cases' (Stone 1992). Stone argues that sentencers are in little doubt about what they deem to be a helpful report: 'one which conveys something about the defendant as a person, assesses the likely effect of a particular sentence on the individual offender, suggests what might stem their offending, and notes the extent of family responsibilities or current efforts to address behaviour problems'. He also thinks it appropriate for probation officers to draw to the attention of sentencers a number of other issues: 'for example, the indirect effects of conviction or particular sentence options

(Has prosecution for this offence ended the defendant's marriage? Will imprisonment terminate the defendant's career or accommodation?), or the effect of same upon innocent dependents of the offender (eg the consequences of imprisonment for the defendant's children)'.

The pre-sentence report should offer to the court detailed information about how the offender could be punished in the community and so avoid the known detrimental effects of a prison sentence. This approach has placed on the shoulders of probation officers the requirement to use their imagination and initiative in making maximum use of community options and so contribute towards the reduction of the prison population.

Copies of the report should be given to the defendant, or, if he is under 17, to his parent or guardian, and it should be written in language that he can understand. Horsley (1984), in a disturbing research study, has shown that probation officers more often than not use words and grammar that demand a far higher IQ than average. One officer, instead of saying 'He can tell right from wrong', put down: 'He can differentiate between the correct course of action and the inherent wrongness of his offences.' Such writing may be clever but is not good social work. As much information as possible should be checked, and the report should be kept brisk and brief.

Reports regarding the care of children

Apart from reports prepared on children who have broken the law, social workers also have to assess family circumstances in a variety of other legally defined situations. Local authority workers and guardians *ad litem*, for example, write separate reports on children of all ages who are being considered for adoption.

Since the passing of the Children Act 1989, however, the responsibility previously placed on social workers to make recommendations in court reports about the desirability of removing a child from his home has been abolished. Instead, social workers have to persuade the court through the presentation of detailed evidence if they wish to be allowed to take the drastic step of removing a child from home when the circumstances give rise to concern. It is, perhaps, not surprising that client hostility to the social worker is at its peak. The mother of a child taken into care knows that, although the court sets the seal on it, it is the social worker's evidence that effectively makes the decision possible. The right of the parent to cross-examine the social worker on her evidence is, however, designed to ensure that such decisions are neither arbitrary nor clandestine.

Despite suggestions that the responsibility for all child care enquiries should be transferred to local authority departments, the role of the probation service in England and Wales has, in recent years, grown rather than diminished. As well as remaining responsible for supervising middle-teenage offenders (the prime age group for detected crime), probation officers, acting as court welfare officers, have assumed greater influence in family proceedings. The rise in applications for private law orders under the Children Act 1989 has led to a substantial increase in the number of enquiries concerning questions of the child's residence and contact with parents in dispute.

A probation officer, often one who specialises in the subject or is even attached to a specialist team, will need to interview the children in the case (if they are old enough to be involved), both parties to the divorce and any other relevant persons – grandparents who may be called on to care for the children, potential step-parents who may themselves be involved in the court hearing as co-respondents, and other relatives. The recommendations in such cases (of which there were 29,000 in 1991) are normally unambiguously made, although the balance of reasoning that leads up to them is rarely straightforward. Divorce court and other civil work enquiries involve the probation officer in an arbitration role, in which there is no room for faintheartedness. The clients may be rich or poor; lawyers will be actively involved on both sides and ready to challenge evidence that seems to go against the interests of their client; and, at the end of the day, there usually has to be a winner and a loser, with the probation officer necessarily being identified with the decision. Ninety per cent of probation officers' recommendations are accepted, and if courts do not follow the welfare officer's recommendation without giving a reason, that will constitute grounds for appeal.

Adoption enquiries

'Adoption brings about the virtually complete and irrevocable transfer of a child from one family to another . . . The significance of the change of status means that all procedural requirements have to be meticulously complied with' (Ball 1991: 73). The process is one which social workers take very seriously, and they may find themselves involved in several ways.

When the adoption agency (which is often the local authority social services department) has placed a child with potential adopters, one of its social workers will be asked to prepare for the court a detailed report on the suitability of the applicants and on all other matters relevant to the welfare of the child whose interests are regarded as paramount. Only if the report makes a positive recommendation is it likely that the adoption will be confirmed.

If the prospective adoption has been instigated by someone other than the adoption agency (for example, where a girl of 16 has had a baby, and the girl's mother and father wish to adopt it), then a social worker will be required to investigate the circumstances and prepare a report for the court. Government guidelines lay special emphasis on the importance of the social worker seeing the child and the adoptive applicants together in their home environment (Ball 1991).

There also exists an important panel of independent professionally qualified social workers, the guardians *ad litem* and reporting officers. They play two crucial roles in the adoption process. First, in every case, one of them is appointed as a reporting officer and she has the job of ensuring that birth parents fully understand the consents which they are giving. Second, if the birth parent refuses consent or 'when there are special circumstances and it appears to the court that the welfare of the child requires it', then a guardian *ad litem* will be called on to investigate all aspects of the family situation. Circumstances are not always straightforward:

A Reporting Officer was asked to obtain the consent of a willing birth mother, who turned out to be a woman who had agreed to bear a child for a male friend with an infertile wife. He had apparently returned home one day, carrying a baby, to tell his wife, 'Look, I've had this baby for you.' The surrogate mother was quite happy to sign the consent form, but the Reporting Officer thought there were circumstances which needed looking at for the sake of the child's future welfare, such as how the adoptive mother felt about accepting this child. The court then appointed a Guardian ad Litem to investigate and report back. (Kerr 1990: 103)

In making her report to the court, the guardian *ad litem* will provide a brief chronological history of the case and give details of the child, the birth family and the applicants. She will be expected to indicate the wishes and the feelings of the child where these can be determined, to comment on the work of the adoption agency and to indicate the relevant options available to the court. She should then make an assessment, and conclude with a clear recommendation.

Abortion counselling

The Abortion Act 1967 created a whole field for social work activity: counselling potential applicants for abortion. Independent agencies like the Pregnancy Advisory Service have provided a simple counselling facility in which the worker would have no power of decision-making, although Hildebrand (1977) illustrates how an interview could lead to a change of mind in the applicant:

Mrs I. was a happily married woman of 38; she already had three children all of whom were already at school or working. She wanted termination for financial reasons because another baby would mean less time and material comfort for the remainder of the family. After discussing her real feelings about having a baby as opposed to those the counsellor felt she was projecting on to members of her family, it became evident that it was basically embarrassment at this unplanned pregnancy at her age plus fears that it might be self-indulgent to have another child which had brought her for termination. After further discussion with Mr I. and the counsellor, it became clear to Mrs I. that her husband was prepared to support her through another pregnancy and had only agreed to termination because it appeared to be what she wanted. Mrs I. left smiling. No application for termination was made.

But abortion counselling also takes place in hospital social work departments, and here it is likely to be influenced by the well-documented variations in the exercise of medical discretion in response to abortion requests. In some hospitals the role of the social worker is similar to that in the private agency: to provide a counselling service as a constructive exercise aimed at offering emotional support and practical help and hopefully enabling the client to cope more effectively with the consequences of her decision, whether it is to lose or to keep the baby. But in other hospitals, as well as fulfilling a traditional counselling role, the medical social worker can be asked by the consultant gynaecologist to prepare a report on applicants for abortion, to provide a detailed social history and to express an opinion about the appropriateness or not of a termination (Cheetham and Learner 1972). Where this happens, it is obvious that the social worker is making a significant contribution to the decision-making process, but Cheetham (1980), who closely observed the developing pattern of practice after the passing of the Abortion Act, comments that the role of medical social workers has always been fairly limited numerically: 'In the early '70s they saw only about 6 per cent of women who had abortions in NHS hospitals and about 19 per cent of those who were refused.' Since then, Cheetham believes, the part played by social workers has diminished considerably as doctors have become more experienced in implementing, and more reconciled to, the Act.

Pre-discharge reports

In general hospitals and in mental health, in prisons and in residential child care, social workers play a part in determining whether a particular patient, prisoner or resident is to be allowed to return into the open community or be transferred into specialist accommodation.

With regard to life sentence prisoners, whose eventual release depends on appropriate arrangements being made in the community, the probation officer is most likely to influence the decision-making machinery, not by a simple assertion that the man would be better off out of prison, but by taking active steps to facilitate release. In cases where homelessness is likely to be a problem, for example, the probation officer can often tip the balance of probability by making sophisticated arrangements for supportive accommodation to be available on discharge.

In psychiatric hospitals, the decision to discharge is ultimately in the hands of the medical profession, but in many hospitals the recommendation of a social worker – as of other ancillary personnel – can influence that decision and especially its timing.

Moreover, the implementation of the NHS and Community Care Act 1990 means that care managers in social services departments are responsible for the arrangement of suitable community care facilities in order to enable patients to be discharged. In general hospitals, the active involvement of social workers on the ward has been shown to increase the speed with which patients can be returned to the community (Tibbitt and Connor 1989).

In residential child care, decisions to return children to their homes are generally made by social work personnel, although increasingly machinery has been established for this to be done at a managerial level following the receipt of reports from the residential head of home and the relevant field worker. Some authorities, in the wake of adverse media publicity, have instituted procedures for such decisions to be confirmed by committee members rather than professional staff, but this would still be done on the basis of social work reports containing recommendations and the arguments supporting them.

Resource allocation

Social services is now a major spending department in the local authority, and almost the whole of its money goes, directly or indirectly, on the provision or the purchase of facilities for selected clients. A part of the selection process is determined by legislation, but significant influence is exerted both by management and social worker – and the social worker, of course, is normally the person responsible for conveying the results of decisions to all clients. Thus, both in appearance and in reality, the allocation of resources is another area in which the social worker can wield substantial power.

Admission to service

We shall see in Chapter 9 that the admissions, reception and intake systems in social work can all act as rationing devices. Clients can be deterred from even setting foot in an agency by its inaccessibility, its unattractiveness or by inconvenient or restrictive opening hours. Hostile receptionists and unhelpful telephonists can be effective deterrents to a hesitant enquirer, and both can be encouraged in their behaviour by social workers feeling the need to keep the clients at arm's length. In the intake system, a curt response by the social worker or a departmental policy of priorities which excludes some applicants from all service can be an additional means of administering scarce resources.

The converse of all this is a generous, non-restrictive 'open-door' policy, in which the availability of a service is given maximum publicity, new clients are always welcomed and the organisational structure is constantly adapted in order to respond more efficiently to changing patterns of demand. This was the intention of the Seebohm Committee (1968):

> We can and should encourage those who need help to seek it . . . Information must be simpler and more widely available (and research into need should become a permanent feature of the new service). One single department . . . is an essential first step in making services more easily accessible. The organisational structure of these services should not deter those in need and they should be available to all. There need be no uncertainty about where to turn for help nor any ambiguity about where responsibility for providing assistance lies.

In two respects these hopes have proved rather naive. First, they ignored the intensity of demand especially in the more deprived areas of present-day society; there is almost certainly *no* limit to the facilities that *could* be provided in the absence of formally agreed and clearly defined criteria for service. Second, to an extent that was not envisaged by Seebohm, many of the most pressing problems presented to the social services departments (as to other social work agencies) are often derived from poverty and the inadequacies of accommodation – matters which, in the long term, are not within the social worker's sphere of responsibility. Hence the need for social workers to refer on a surprisingly large number of applicants for help – the very tactic that Seebohm had hoped to discourage.

The allocation of community resources

The bald analysis of how the availability of resources gives social workers power has been most clearly articulated by Handler (1973):

> The social worker has command over goods and services that people need and want. Thus,

there is no problem in recruiting clients to the agency. The creation of power arises out of this command over scarce resources. It is a power relationship because the clients need the resources and the agency has discretion as to how the resources are to be distributed. Many clients are extremely dependent and more than willing to accept administrative conditions as the price of receiving benefits. (Adapted)

The NHS and Community Care Act 1990 requires social services departments to prepare 'community care plans' for all disabled or elderly clients who are deemed to be in need of help. In drawing up the plans, the social worker consults with carers, voluntary organisations and health service agencies. The plan outlines the resources that are needed by the client, and proposes a method of delegating to a voluntary or private agency the responsibility for meeting those needs. In other words, the social worker, having made a professional assessment of need, 'purchases' on behalf of the client a range of services designed to alleviate the client's difficulties: no longer is the local authority the primary provider of services, although it retains full responsibility for maintaining quality, and is expected to carry out inspections to that effect.

Through the 1990s, although there will be a shift towards 'purchasing' services in this way, there will continue to be some resources available in-house.

For disabled people, all departments have available a range of aids and adaptations. There are varying degrees of central control over their allocation, with occupational therapists often playing a more influential part in the decision-making process than social workers. Expensive house adaptations are always centrally controlled, and the procedures for effecting them often ponderous and slow. Free telephones can be provided for those thought to need them but, because of the cost involved, it is common for councillors to play a part in the decision-making.

For elderly people, the main resources available are home helps, meals on wheels and day care. In all cases, the overall provision is effected by the administration, and central directives to restrict meals on wheels to no more than three a week per person or home help to a maximum of two hours a week per person, for example, are policy decisions not at the discretion of fieldwork staff. But, within these boundaries, the allocation or withholding of service is usually either determined by the area team or strongly influenced by it.

The social worker often has access to a second-hand clothes or furniture store, or alternatively can use departmental authority to allow the client to buy necessities under voucher schemes. And her influence can be employed to secure access to residential facilities: the arrangement of either emergency provision in overnight hostels or bedsit space with 'known' landladies, or, most critical and valuable of all, string-pulling influence on the local housing department in an effort to secure accommodation for a homeless family. Most social workers are well aware that, in the majority of cases, the effort will be futile, but, in extreme circumstances, 'it might be worth a try', and it has been known to work.

In one London borough the process of negotiating with the housing department on behalf of clients has been formalised by introducing a system of housing assessments: if a client is seen to be in *prima facie* need of accommodation, the social worker completes a detailed report on family composition and current circumstances, passes it up through the hierarchy via the team leader, area officer, to the assistant director who, if he is in agreement with the assessment, passes it on to the housing department, with a firm recommendation that a sympathetic response be made.

The provision of cash

Social workers have always given money to some clients on some occasions – not infrequently out of their own pockets, when faced with the hopelessness of the real down-and-out. But, undoubtedly, the simple financial transaction has also always presented difficulties – either to the worker, the client or both.

To say that dispensing money gives social workers power over their clients is not necessarily a cause for concern. Power in a human relationship is inevitable and the direction of authority in the social work relationship is clearly defined whether or not the payment of money is a part of it. Social workers, especially inexperienced ones, find it hard to come to terms with the reality of their ascribed role, but to imagine that avoiding the distribution of small sums of money will in some way expiate the sins of power and thereby lead to moral improvement in practice is naive in the extreme.

Of course, there should be campaigns for improved programmes of income mainten-ance; of course, there should be battles to raise the wage-levels of low-paid workers; of course, the social worker's personal contacts with those who experience the degradation of poverty will lead her to lend her support to such campaigns. But there is now, and will almost certainly always be in any society, a need for crisis responses of a discretionary kind. It is an integral part of the social work agency's task to make such responses. Cash should be given on an individualised basis. It should not be used to undermine the client's civil rights or his self-respect; it should not be unfairly withheld or indiscriminately provided; special care should be taken with the provision of loans, because of our knowledge that the relationship between the money-lender and debtor is a difficult one to sustain simultaneously with the social work relationship. Although there should be departmental or agency guidelines, these should stop well short of being seen as a code book intended to cover every eventuality. Councillors and administrators should respect the right and duty of the individual social worker to exercise discretion in her cases; and, at all times, the power which the social worker undoubtedly wields should be used to maintain and extend the self-respect of the client, to avoid further deterioration in the client's circumstances, and, preferably by explicit agreement with the client, to enable and encourage him to become self-sufficient within the laws and conventions of society.

Gatekeeping

Society is full of gatekeepers. In return for money, you can gain entry to a four-star hotel, a football match or a brothel; with money and influential friends, you can join an exclusive club; with ability and effort, you can be admitted to a university; with perseverance, talent and good looks you can make it to the top in show business. But the gates to which social workers hold the key are not opened to applicants with money, influence or talent. They are not for people who are climbing up or seeking pleasure. They are retreat routes, survival strategies, and they offer risky solutions to often intractable problems.

The press and the public, made aware of the plight of the people in desperate situations, might plead: 'Why doesn't someone do something about it? Why don't the authorities move them, take them away, give them a chance?' But, as Stevenson (1976) puts it, 'Those who press for the removal of the vulnerable person are frequently ignorant of the alternative care which will be offered . . . But social workers are uniquely placed to see the consequences of removal in respect of children and, to a lesser extent, old people.' And the consequences are, to say the least, often uncertain.

The social worker's responsibility as a gatekeeper is therefore all the greater because of the very riskiness of the operation, and because of her commitment to a philosophy which accords the vulnerable client rights and respect.

For the onlooker, Stevenson (1976) reminds us again, it is the *removal* of a child or a vulnerable old person or a troublesome disturber of the peace that is the critical event; when the event occurs, a sigh of relief goes up. But 'for the social worker, it is only the beginning' – indeed, it is not even the beginning, for her involvement starts much earlier.

For gatekeeping, the social worker and her agency operate in five stages:

1. *Obtaining resources.* The opening of residential accommodation, the recruitment, selection and preparation of foster parents.
2. *Quality control and maintenance.* Inspection, the provision of adequate funds to maintain standards, the continuing employment of suitable staff.
3. *Preparation of the client for transfer.* Explanation, persuasion, reassurance, ventilation, bargaining.
4. *The act of transfer.* The physical process, transport, acceptance of emotion, the bringing together of the critical parties, the provision of a safety net in the event of rapid breakdown.
5. *The provision of support and supervision* – for the client, and for the new setting. Possible preparation for later moves and another gatekeeping process.

The most critical of all skills is that of being able to achieve maximum organisational efficiency while simultaneously fulfilling the normal obligations of the social worker to establish good rapport with the client and his relatives and good working relationships with other employees in the gatekeeping process. To do that to everyone's satisfaction is the mark of a very good social worker operating in a first-class agency.

We shall consider four gatekeeping processes in social work: fostering, adoption counselling, the admission of an elderly person to Part III accommodation and admission to psychiatric care.

Allocation to foster care

The act of fostering other peoples' children is centuries-old and the allocation of orphans to foster parents was officially authorised by the Poor Law Amendment Act of 1834. The tradition has been maintained and the first child care officers to be appointed following the Children Act 1948 were designated boarding-out officers. Since then the level of enthusiasm for fostering among social work theorists has fluctuated, but the use of foster care remains a major plank in Western child care policy.

The social worker's task in arranging a foster-placement involves liaising with all the various parties: the child, the birth parents, the foster parents, other child-care personnel and colleagues in her own agency. She will have to cope with negative as well as positive reactions, while at the same time acting within the statutory and policy constraints of the agency and working for the best interests of the child.

There are four stages in the foster-care gatekeeping process, in all of which the responsibility on the social worker's shoulders and the power that she exercises are considerable.

1.   The selection of foster parents   The recruitment of foster parents is a complex process in itself, although the frequently seen newspaper advertisements asking for somebody to care for '9-year-old Catherine who is in need of a loving home' may perhaps make it look deceptively straightforward. Even the role of the prospective foster parent is ambiguous: is she an applicant for employment, a volunteer offering a service or a supplicant waiting for a gift? The social worker's position is correspondingly mixed: does she represent a potential employer, the beneficiary of a service or the donor or withholder of a favour?

The first task of the social worker, then, is to discuss the nature of fostering and to explain that all prospective foster parents have to be carefully vetted. The vetting procedure will, 'if completed, comprise several interviews (with the applicants and their own children, if any), a medical reference or examination, personal references, a police enquiry, attendance at group sessions, a report, recommendation and decision' (Crompton 1979). The worker will need to know about the applicants' attitudes, feelings and family relationships, their life style, emotional strengths and weaknesses, and any experiences that they have had that are relevant to fostering. The worker's approach should be 'encouraging and relaxed', enabling the family to reveal their approach to domestic life, and so gauge the likely impact on them of any foster child and vice versa. The worker's professionalism comes from her controlled use of informality in order to get beyond the official questions and the stereotyped answers to the reality of the home climate.

The decision should normally be made as speedily as possible, and, if it is negative, the family should be told so, not unpleasantly, but clearly and without evasion. If the decision is positive, and there is to be a waiting period before the allocation of a child, care should be taken to maintain contact with the family, to explain why there is such a delay and to use the opportunity for further preparation or training – perhaps by drawing them into a foster parent group.

In addition to 'selecting' foster parents, local authorities have an obligation actively to seek potential foster parents from ethnic minorities in order to guarantee the availability of a wide range of cultural perspectives among foster parents so that the wishes and needs of the child, and the expressed opinions of the birth parents, can properly be taken into account.

2.   *The selection of the child*   The assessment of the child – either in his own home or in a residential setting – will be made by one or more social workers, and ideally the decision to place in foster care will be a part of a continuing period of planned supervision. At one time it was thought that foster care was always, and for all children, the preferred alternative. This is now no longer the case, although the Department of Health says that it still is or should be considered the first choice.

Apart from assessing the basic family background of the child, factors of special relevance to a fostering decision include:

(a)   the reason why he is in care, and his perception of his current situation;
(b)   his typical behaviour patterns, hobbies, skills and ambitions;
(c)   mental and physical health;
(d)   his school or work experience and performance;
(e)   previous history while in care: relationships with other foster parents, residential staff and social workers;
(f)   peer-group relationships, and how he is perceived by his friends and contemporaries.

3.   *Matching child with family*   There is no certain key to matching and, in any case, the pool of prospective foster parents is rarely so large that coincidence can be achieved on a wide range of variables. Thought will inevitably be given to the preferences of foster parents for different age-groups: babies, adolescents, and so on. Children with disabilities, disturbed children and children thought likely to present discipline problems will require careful allocation. The Department of Health has identified a number of known predictive factors, of which the following are a selection:

1.   Long-term foster-placements have a high risk of breakdown, especially during the first year and during adolescence. This emphasises 'the importance of social work support and supervision during these periods'.
2.   Placements of children placed before the age of 12 months tend to be more successful than those involving older children.
3.   Contact between the child and his natural family during a foster-placement appears to help.
4.   Three positive factors in the foster family are that (a) the foster mother is an older woman, (b) she has previous experience of fostering, and (c) her own children are significantly older than the foster child.
5.   Childless foster families seem to be particularly successful.

Of course, as with all predictive studies, the conclusions are never absolute. A foster family and a child could present all the negative factors imaginable and still produce a remarkable success story – and vice versa.

4. *Placing the child*   Although the selection and matching processes complete the gatekeeping tasks, the social worker's skills continue to be required with the actual placement. She must provide all the necessary information to the three main parties involved – the child, the birth parents and the foster parents; she must be ready to cope with each party's questions about the placement, and to support it in its early days. There should be adequate preparation for the child with no hint of concealment of what is happening; and wherever and whenever possible the birth parents should be involved in the placement process. Under normal circumstances, there should be preliminary meetings between the child and the foster family before final decisions are made, and the birth parents should be involved in all decision-making during the placement. Clarity should be reached on whether the placement is thought likely to be short-term, long-term or is truly indeterminate.

The so-called 'permanency principle' emphasises the potentially damaging effects of uncertainty in child care.

> The principle of permanency planning is based on the idea of removing the child as soon as possible out of temporary substitute care, and returning him or her to the biological family as the preferred alternative, or to an adoption home as the second priority. (Morris 1984)

This practice principle also has to be set alongside the partnership principle inherent in the Children Act 1989 which requires social workers to discover whether members of the extended family can offer a permanent home to the child; if so, this becomes the most desirable alternative to birth parent care.

Adoption counselling

Under the Adoption Act 1976, social workers acquired the duty of providing a comprehensive counselling service in the field of adoption, and this work has increasingly become an integral part of adoption practice, often requiring highly specialised skills. The service tends to be provided either as post-placement family support for older child placements, or as counselling for adult adopted people or, more recently, for birth parents, many of whom still have powerful emotions about their loss many years after the event (Howe *et al.* 1992).

The Children Act 1975 gave adopted children in England and Wales the right, on reaching the age of 18, to have a copy of their original birth certificate, thus enabling them to go in search of their origins. But the Act also makes it compulsory for any applicant to receive counselling before the information can be divulged. The intention of this clause is to ensure that the information is presented in a helpful and appropriate manner and that the adopted person has considered the effect of any enquiries that he might make both on himself and others – especially, perhaps, on his adoptive and birth parents. The counselling interview, then, is a hurdle which applicants must surmount if they want the information that is theirs by right. The social worker does not have any power to grant or withhold access; a copy of the birth certificate must be given on request once the interview has been held.

A government circular has emphasised that this counselling role requires a high degree of skill and maturity in the worker, as well as experience of work with families and knowledge of adoption practice and procedure. Haimes and Timms (1984) interviewed 46 social workers who had done the job, and report some of the difficulties they face because of the lack of clarity as to the purpose of the interview. Aggressive clients who 'go about their enquiries like a bull in a china shop' particularly worry the workers who prefer to approach the interview in a more discursive fashion. In some cases, the workers act both as enablers and detectives, helping the client to track down not just his birth certificate which is his legal right, but also his birth parents in person, and to offer continuing support during any meetings that take place; in other cases, the workers act more as 'safeguarders', trying to delay giving information in order to protect the sensibilities of the birth parents, and ultimately doing no more than they are legally required to do.

As Haimes and Timms point out, the job of adoption counselling provides a nice example of the 'Who is the client?' conundrum. Is it the adoptee making the request? Or is it an invisible person – the as yet unknown birth parent?

The major weight of counselling applicants under the Act has fallen on social services departments, but only a tiny proportion of adopted people – as little as 1 or 2 per cent – have actually taken advantage of the opportunity provided by the legislation.

Accommodating elderly people

At any one time there are about 100,000 people living in old people's homes run by local authorities, and there are even more in homes owned by the so-called 'independent sector', which combines a large number of commercial operations and rather fewer non-profit voluntary organisations. A significant proportion of residents in private or voluntary homes, estimated at about 50 per cent, have their costs met out of the public purse.

Government policy towards the care of the elderly was radically reformed under the NHS and Community Care Act 1990; it was designed to encourage social workers to make greater use of community care packages in order to reduce the demand for high-cost institutional facilities. But demographic projections tell us that the number of people over the age of 85 will continue to rise well into the 21st century, and it seems similarly likely that the number of infirm and dependent old people in need of residential care will also grow from decade to decade. Indeed, the level of need is likely to be accentuated by changing patterns of family life and possibly by a less willing compliance on the part of those women who have traditionally provided 'care in the community'.

Local authorities are required by law (enacted by the National Assistance Act 1948) to 'provide residential care for all persons who, by reason of age, infirmity or any other circumstance, are in need of care not otherwise available to them', and, under the 1990 Act, the care manager in a social services department (who may be a social worker) is responsible for carrying out the assessment which will determine whether or not an elderly person will be able to enter residential care at public expense. (Anyone who can afford it can of course continue to make their own arrangements for entering a home in the independent sector.)

The assessment process is designed to offer the elderly person a degree of choice, to take into account the interests of carers, and to deliver an imaginative service package, either by involving local authority or health service 'providers' or by drawing on the facilities available in the independent sector.

Phillips (1992a) has shown that the process of admission into residential care is heavily influenced by relatives and by various groups of professionals (for example, the family doctor and the hospital social worker), and, despite the good intentions of the 1990 Act, it is likely that such will remain the case. It should be the aim of the social worker in touch with the assessment process to maximise the rights of the client while simultaneously being realistic in her recognition of the often less-than-perfect arrangements that might have to be made.

Admission to psychiatric care

For 24 years, the Mental Health Act 1959 governed the process of admission to psychiatric hospital, but it came under increasing attack partly because of the way the facility for emergency admissions was abused and partly because of the ambiguous role of the social worker in the process.

The Mental Health Act 1983 was designed to improve matters. It introduced a statutory requirement for 'approved social workers' to be properly trained for the responsible task of being involved in psychiatric admissions, and it placed a strong emphasis on the fact that, in order to fulfil their role, social workers would be required to make a professional assessment of the case.

The passing of the 1983 Act, however, did not bring to an end the debates within social work about the incompatibility of carrying out policies which commit mental patients to forms of institutional treatment sometimes thought to be potentially harmful, and the social worker's duty to defend the client's rights against the possibility of persecution by his family, to work with him in the community and to move towards a more sympathetic view of mental illness as a social phenomenon.

Under the 1983 Act, it is the duty of an approved social worker to make an application for admission to hospital provided she is satisfied that it is proper to do so. The British Association of Social Workers has emphasised that this procedure should only be carried out if the relatives are unable or unwilling to do so themselves, and furthermore that the approved social worker must be strong enough not to be steam-rollered into it either by a doctor or by the local authority (Rashid and Ball 1991). To a large extent, the sectioning process remains unchanged, though the concept of an 'approved social worker' has strengthened the profession's role in mental health.

In the eyes of the patient, however, there may remain some confusion. For the social worker is not only a party to the compulsory order, but may well be the agent by whom he is forcibly conveyed by ambulance to a place of detention. With this role remaining, it is difficult to see how the social worker can simultaneously fulfil the role of a campaigning civil rights worker and still retain credibility in the eyes of both patient and the psychiatric system of which she is inevitably a part.

Sheppard (1990) has shown that disagreements between social workers and psychiatrists in the course of compulsorily admitting mentally ill patients are rare, and he suggests that there is nothing incompatible between the *social work* role of the ASW and the *mental health* role of the doctor.

Following his research into the duties of approved social workers, Sheppard designed an assessment schedule for use during the compulsory admissions process. It allows the social worker to outline 27 possible hazards facing her client and those close to him, requiring her to note, for example, whether he:

– goes out naked or insufficiently dressed to prevent serious personal heat loss;
– is creating a disturbance or nuisance; or
– is behaving in a physically threatening manner.

Sheppard's schedule facilitates an assessment of the level of risk, and of the availability and adequacy of appropriate support in the client's environment. By focusing the social worker's attention in this way, it should be possible to achieve higher levels of reliability between different gatekeepers and to ensure that approved social workers remain alert to their statutory and professional responsibilities.

In addition to the requirement that social workers be 'approved' following post-qualifying training, the 1983 Mental Health Act gave new emphasis to patient rights, and allocated to the Mental Health Review Tribunal and the Mental Health Act Commission the responsibility of scrutinising both psychiatric and social work activity. Moreover, patients were given under the Act a right to statutory after-care following discharge from hospital, with the requirement that such after-care should continue until such time as the authorities concerned are satisfied that it is no longer needed (Rashid and Ball 1991).

Review

It is no accident that the chapter on the powers and responsibilities borne by the social worker is one of the longest in this book. It should be clear from it that the authority of the social worker is considerable. It should also be clear that her discretionary powers are rarely straightforward: sometimes they are enacted in parliamentary legislation, though these are frequently ill-defined; sometimes they are determined by council committees or by departmental management (for example, in one fuel strike, social workers in several departments were delegated with the power to allocate coal coupons to deserving people); sometimes the powers are derived from professional judgment; but most frequently they are defined by agency function and especially by the way in which that function is limited by restricted resources – a ceiling on the number of places in residential care, for example, or on the availability of home helps.

In recent years there has been a steady tightening-up in definitions of social worker powers and duties. The Home Office, for example, has issued national standards for community service and for the supervision of offenders on probation. In local authorities, instructions have been drawn up to indicate what criteria care managers should look for when assessing elderly people for packages of community-based or residential provision; policy guidelines are provided in regard to the preferred ethnic identity of foster parents if the child is, for example, of Afro–Caribbean origin; and the appropriate action is outlined for cases in which notification is received of either a child or a vulnerable adult being at risk of serious injury or neglect.

Departmental practice manuals exist, and the phenomenon is likely to gather pace rather than disappear. The nationally encouraged idea of 'quality assurance' in the public sector will see to that.

Maybe this is not what some people came into social work to do. If not, it is better for them to realise it early in their careers and to depart. For there is no escape from the undeniable fact that the social worker, caught up in the affairs of the state, is necessarily a party to the state's programme of policies and practice in respect of the deprived, the deviant, the underprivileged, the needy and the disabled.

Social work not only has to operate within that framework, it has to ensure that its practitioners fulfil statutory and agency responsibilities to the highest achievable standards of professionalism. In allocating resources, in making recommendations or reaching decisions, in exercising control, and in all gatekeeping functions, the social worker must be just, sensitive to her role of mediation between the interests of the client and the state, and concerned always to act in the way that best achieves the overriding goal of maintenance.

The crucial role of social work is to influence *the way in which* welfare policies are put into operation, *the way in which* power is wielded, and above all, *the way in which* vulnerable people are protected against abuse. It is the responsibility of the social worker to challenge aspects of policy which appear to require her to act in a way that is incompatible with social work's ideals of the importance of the individual. Problems, however, undoubtedly arise if the social worker challenges the *status quo* in the course of her practice – that is to say, if she seeks to effect a change in policy by unilaterally refusing to operate it – and there is necessarily a limit to the frequency with which this can be done. As Hunt (1979) says with regard to the role of the social worker engaged in mental health admissions:

> The social worker is not only presented with an emotionally charged situation, he is also caught up in his own internal conflict and uncertainty about the issues. He doubts whether he would want to be admitted to a mental hospital himself; he may be unsure whether the hospital has much to offer his client; he is aware of the environmental and personal stresses on his client and

suspects that they, rather than his client, need treatment. He also has a deeply held commitment to the basic right of the adult individual to make decisions about the way he will order his life.

At the same time, the client is clearly disturbed, and 'tension is escalated by the fearful social worker, and the likelihood of a clumsily executed emergency admission is increased'. Now, it is clearly the right of every social worker to refuse to participate in any single process against her conscience. But on purely pragmatic grounds, it seems doubtful whether social work *per se* could survive a situation in which large numbers of professional staff were refusing to operate a range of functions across the board. In other words, there is a difference of degree between conscientious objection selectively employed and a total unwillingness to recognise the legitimacy of the role of social work in a statutory setting, and it would be only sensible for employing authorities to ensure that the staff they appoint to social work posts are conscientiously able to reconcile their professional commitment and their humanitarian ideals with the realities of the political economy within which they will be expected to operate – whatever ideological complexion it might have.

What happens, it may then be asked, if and when the social worker in a statutory agency becomes satisfied that the deprivation, the deviance, the disabilities and the lack of privilege in the people with whom she is required to work are all either caused by, or are seriously aggravated by, the state's own approach to social policy, or, even worse, are an integral and inevitable consequence of its political philosophy? Can the social worker continue to operate *as a social worker* with such views? Of course, again, each will respond to the question individually. But my view is unambiguous. If the worker's critique of the state is ideologically rounded and total, then her role as social worker *for* that state can only be pursued clandestinely, dishonestly. For it is a crucial aspect of the model of social work presented in this book that the worker is engaged not *solely* for the benefit of the client as an individual (such a commitment, it should be clear already, is logically unattainable) but for the benefit of achieving a reconciliation between the client and the society of which he is a part. In given societies, there may well be a case for political and revolutionary overthrow, but such activity is not and cannot be synonymous with social work.

On the other hand, it is not a consequence of this position that the social worker should not engage in policy debates and in attempts to change and to improve the climate for practice. But again, though essential to progress in a democracy, such campaigns are not *of themselves* social work. They are paralleled by teachers campaigning for comprehensivisation, textile manufacturers campaigning for import restrictions, and doctors campaigning for improved research facilities or a ban on cigarette advertising. Policy campaigns are an essential component of any area of contemporary practice: hence the need for reforms in the field of mental health, penal policy, the provision of support facilities for disabled housewives, and so on – but at the same time, practice has to continue in each of these areas, and according to current conventions and legislation. Anything less than this, and the whole body of social work practice would be wholly idiosyncratic, answering the needs neither of society nor the client but only, perhaps, of the worker. And although some social workers may think that they know best, the powers which they wield are potentially so far-reaching that they must be and must remain subject to publicly defined and culturally sanctioned limits. The mere fact that social workers claim that their aim is always to 'do good' is no guarantee that they will never, if left to their own devices, do harm.

8 Pro-active involvement in the community

Active involvement in the life of the community is now acknowledged to be a crucial element in the achievement of social work's primary objective of maintenance. Although, as we shall see in this chapter, there have been major developments towards this goal in recent years, the idea itself is not a new one. Some probation officers and social workers have always seen themselves as community managers or social care planners, but the duties involved have tended to be regarded as extra-mural, providing something of a bonus for the client and offering a contribution to social welfare above and beyond the call of duty. That is not the case now, and many social work posts require the practitioner to engage in community activities which are a world apart from the roles of office interviewing, home visiting and maintaining telephone contact with other agencies.

There are two major questions concerning social work's involvement in the community. The first is this: should social workers operating in the community turn their backs on a client-focus? Should they, in other words, be community workers pure and simple, without reference to the client-group for which their agency exists? The profession is nearly unanimous that the answer to this is clearly negative. Social workers are not general-purpose community operators, but are recruited to serve the needs of particular groups, and any community strategy must not lose sight of that fact.

The second question concerns how best to involve oneself in the community – especially bearing in mind the limited time and resources of any social worker and the scale and complexity of any community, for the social worker, as Figure 8.1 illustrates, is necessarily on the outer fringes of her client's network.

For some time now, increasing thought has been given in the social work literature – and in practice, too, of course, – to the implications of networks. Will the probation officer's influence always be negated by a delinquent peer group? What is the effect of the husband on a woman's depression? How is a marriage affected by the demands of a spina bifida child? Can a teenager with learning disabilities be helped into some suitable occupation? Can the social worker join forces with the parents in the use of learning techniques to help a disturbed or deviant child?

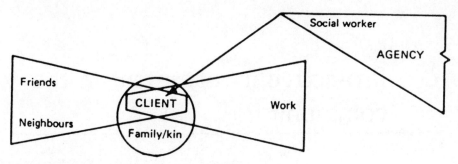

Figure 8.1   The client's social network

There are two distinct, but obviously related, issues. How does the social worker interact with the client's network? And, given that many clients are often rather short of friends, neighbours and relatives, how does the social worker make up for deficiencies in the network? To further complicate the issue, it must always be recalled that social workers are themselves parts of complicated networks which involve their colleagues, other professional groupings, other clients and, not least, their private lives. The remainder of this chapter will outline the various ways in which social workers have sought to make their services available in different community settings.

Outreach and detached work

Projects in which social workers (often from a background in youth and community work) operate in the field rather than from the security of an agency office have a long tradition. Sometimes they involve the creation of a detached social centre providing recreational facilities and other services designed to meet the needs of local residents. Social workers and voluntary assistants are able to work in close proximity to their clients, and to provide help within a natural context. Other projects – most of them tending to concentrate on work with adolescents – have been run from council houses, city-centre walk-in refuges or advice shops. In each case, the aim has been to get closer to natural networks of need than is normally possible. Although there is evidence that this can be achieved, it has also been found that the ambiguity inherent in the detached work relationship is very difficult to overcome: the very act of getting closer to the client, dressing like him, identifying with him, becoming a part of his culture, can lead to confusion on both sides. If the detached worker retains loyalty to her agency, what happens when the client challenges the agency or the standards it upholds? If the worker identifies totally with the client, what happens when the agency by whom she is employed makes demands on her which she finds to be incompatible with the client's interests? Even though most detached work has been done under the auspices of voluntary bodies, such dilemmas are commonly recorded, and the task of reconciling conflicting perspectives in social work does not appear to be made easier by the approach.

Unless the delicate nature of the worker-client relationship is handled well, there is always the risk that clients who had been led to see detached workers as being much closer to them than other social workers in their experience might feel betrayed if the worker's allegiance to them were ever thought to be in doubt.

Increasingly outreach projects are concentrating their efforts on the needs of homeless young people and on ethnic minorities. For example, in Thames Reach, the outreach team make contact with those sleeping on the streets, offer assistance and liaise with their own colleagues involved in resettlement work and the provision of accommodation. In Birmingham, the Nechells Community Project works in a deprived inner-city area, aiming to coordinate community resources and develop self-help initiatives in a multi-racial community. And the Children's Society maintains a network of youth link projects using street work to make contact with young people vulnerable and at risk in city-centre locations; they particularly focus on the needs of runaways from local authority care or from home, and provide an integrated programme of counselling, advocacy and access to a drop-in or advice centre.

Drug users pose particular problems for conventional social work units, and Dorn and South (1984) have described a variety of street agencies sited close to addicts' communities and which make themselves available as necessary. The Hungerford Project in London's Piccadilly area is a detached unit, but operates mainly through an accessible reception desk. Availability is the keynote, as the project's administrator says in an interview:

> Say, a couple of people could come in who had been living homeless, and we know them quite well, off the street, and maybe one of them is slightly stoned and we would suggest that they come back later and they may or may not want referral to emergency accommodation or whatever.
>
> But we do have quite a large group of young people who are not particularly at the moment wanting to stop using drugs, needing some kind of local support and a bit of advice now and again, maybe getting into trouble with the police and needing a bit of advice about that. Sometimes when we get very busy, we get a very wide range of people who come wandering in. Basically we sort of advertise ourselves as seeing anybody about anything to do with drugs. It could be the person themselves, or a relative or friend or whatever ... (Dorn and South 1984: 11)

The interesting thing about such an approach to detached work is that it tends to be limited to counselling and advocacy — and even that role is sometimes restricted by virtue of the anonymity of the agency base. The Hungerford Project is close to the clients, but lacks the authority or the responsibility of a state agency; this can make it feel safer for vulnerable and frightened addicts, but it almost certainly reduces the scale of aid available.

A particularly remarkable exercise in detached work operated in Sheffield, where the probation service opened a unit in Havelock Square, a run-down part of the city. The workers' initial aim was to help drug addicts but later their primary focus switched to work with prostitutes (Morris 1976). The unit was not expected to operate according to conventional probation criteria; but was 'an utter contrast to the usual office setting in which the typical probation officer works. The probation officers lived alongside their clients and offered a 24 hour round-the-clock service', and one of the workers called it 'the ultimate in social work'. The unit had four probation officers, three of whom were living in, and there was a part-time senior in charge. Caseloads were small with an upper limit of ten per worker, and the atmosphere was informal, with clients free to walk in at any time of day or night. The workers said that there were two main planks to the unit's philosophy: first, the honesty between worker and client – 'There are no barriers to hide behind, no secretaries or receptionists; you have to deal with it there and then; you can't say, "I'm knackered, clear off" or get the receptionist to tell the client that you're away'; and second, the residential fact which meant that workers and clients were 'all sharing the same grotty area'.

Morris commented that the unit, though regarded as successful, also threw up the two major problems in detached work: the strain on staff, and the 'whose side am I on?' dilemma. The strain was such that the workers told Morris that a two- to four-year stint was as much as any of them could manage. The unit's originator, Bruce Hugman, left to work on a smallholding in Kent (although he later returned for a time to the probation service); and other workers said that they worried about the effect of their job on their families, or, quite simply, reached the point where they could take no more.

The lack of privacy in detached work is one aspect of the strain, but the absence of the kind of role protection which most social workers enjoy is another:

> Freedom entails risks and this is certainly true of the unit ... Most of the risks hinge upon that delicate line between legality and the role of the probation officer. 'Where does one stand?' asks one of the workers, 'I have been in pubs with drug users where they have openly injected and have known that they got the drugs illegally. I will say that they're being daft but what more should I do?' It is the ancient dilemma at the heart of social work: either the social worker reports the incident to the police and destroys irrevocably the trust he has established with the client or he turns a blind eye and connives in the commission of criminal acts. (Morris 1976)

The Sheffield unit survived for nine years, but eventually a decision was made to close it down on the grounds that its work did not constitute a high enough priority for probation expenditure. Controversy stayed with it to the end: 'respectable' members of the neighbourhood (which had been refurbished and had moved upmarket) attacked it because they said it attracted prostitutes to the square, and others criticised it because it did not fulfil the reformative expectations that they had of the probation service.

Such criticisms are not specific to detached work. They are equally applicable, and often applied, to more conventional settings. But detached work is necessarily more public, more exposed to view; and, because it lacks a structure and reduces role-clarity, its practitioners are more frequently confronted with the inevitable dilemmas and ambiguities of their task. Although the balance of functions might vary, however, detached workers still find themselves operating the triad of social work behaviours – maintenance, change and the fulfilment of responsibility. The only real difference in their work comes in their attempt to get closer to the target population with a view to fulfilling their agency objectives more efficiently and more successfully.

Community networks

The idea of community, though conceptually controversial in sociology, was given a boost by the English school of community studies which examined kinship and neighbourhood relations in a wide variety of locations: in inner London and its outer suburbs, in Liverpool, in the mining-belt of Yorkshire, in rural Wales and in Cumbria. Abrams (1980) has argued that the romantic view of neighbourhood relationships prompted by these studies is misguided and misleading, for the sense of community arises, not out of free choice, but as a defensive response to external threats, economic hardship and restricted opportunities for personal and social growth. It follows from Abrams's thesis that any policy which seeks to emulate the community self-help model is inappropriate in a highly mobile society and, because of that, unlikely to succeed.

Notwithstanding such theoretical doubts, there has been a growing interest in the part that the community might play or ought to play in promoting the welfare of its members. A big fillip to this movement was given by Bayley's (1973) study of the plight of the mentally handicapped in Sheffield which led him to conclude that the 'statutory social services are quite unable to cope with the sheer volume of care and support that is needed' (Bayley 1978). He recognised that the two support networks – one provided by the social services department, the other by the community – could and should co-exist, but that efforts should be made to ensure that their roles complement each other. To characterise this process, he used the term *interweaving*: 'The social services seek to interweave their help so as to use and strengthen the help already given, make good the limitations and meet the needs. It is not a question of the social services plugging the gaps but rather of their working with society to enable society to close the gaps.' It has certainly been established that, so far as people with learning disabilities and the elderly are concerned, relatives play the major role in providing care, and this has led to the cautionary comment that when we refer to 'community care' it is important to recognise that what we are almost always talking about is 'care by the family'. Wilkin (1979), writing six years after Bayley, was much more hesitant about the strength of informal networks operating in support of the families of subnormal children. He concluded that, although the extended family did have some part to play, its contribution was not normally relevant to the day-to-day domestic routines, and that friendship and neighbourhood networks provided even less support: 'The cosy idea of neighbourhood mutual support systems conveyed in the concept of community care did not exist for these families.'

The attractions of looking to the neighbourhood for support services have been eagerly grasped by politicians who have – I suspect, wrongly – seen in the idea a cost-free benefit: if what they think of as 'social work' can be put on tap by friends, neighbours and family, then, lo-and-behold, the need to train and employ growing numbers of professional staff would evaporate.

In 1978, Parker provided a simple guide for the statutory services to adapt to natural helping networks:

1. Workers must begin to identify much more closely with geographical neighbour-hoods, or patches.
2. They should build up contacts with other agents and agencies, especially home helps and street wardens who are likely to have 'an encyclopaedic knowledge of the support given by friends, relatives and neighbours of clients'. This involves working with 'perfectly ordinary people who are not hampered either by the labels that society confers on social workers or that social workers confer on clients'.
3. Social workers might aim to mediate within natural networks when problems arise that weaken the caring pattern.
4. It would be helpful if social workers could build up records of the kind of support which clients receive, thus adding greatly to our knowledge of natural caring systems.

This guide heralded a major conceptual development in British social services practice. 'Patch' systems emerged as a natural evolutionary phenomenon, born of the recognition that social workers alone cannot always achieve maintenance objectives either as solitary operators or even through the medium of their agencies; some system of partnership with the community is essential.

Patch

The emergence of the idea of 'Patch' as a model for service delivery was a major development of the 1980s, and laid the foundations for the interdisciplinary approach to community care. In its simplest form Patch might mean only that a team of social workers (or even a single social worker) is attached to a clearly defined geographical district, but in its most advanced forms, it means that the office buildings are decentralised, that the social worker coordinates teams of colleagues in the patch, that maximum use is made of volunteers, of informal caring networks and of inter-agency liaison, and that the social workers are therefore both more visible and more accessible to the community.

The idea of a social services department adopting an adventurous community perspective was incorporated into the Seebohm Report (1968), but it took over a decade for it to become adapted to political and professional reality. It is, moreover, one of the few developments in British social work which has been prompted from within the profession. It tended to emerge initially in areas staffed by particularly imaginative, energetic and charismatic officers; others followed on, recognising an idea that made sense, and other social services departments implemented the model from the top.

Normanton in West Yorkshire became known as the trendsetter; and descriptions of the way Patch worked there certainly give the feel of the phenomenon.

A small industrial town of about 19,000, Normanton became the laboratory for the community-oriented ideas of its Area Officer, Mike Cooper. He divided the area into three patches. Each patch team included a social worker (as leader), two patch workers (typically a social work assistant and a care worker), perhaps six part-time community wardens and about 25 home helps. 'Staff were encouraged to make themselves readily accessible to users, to respond flexibly and rapidly to the problems they encountered and to collaborate closely with local people in developing community resources' (Hadley and McGrath 1983).

It was reported that there was no real division of labour between the qualified team leaders and the social work assistants except that the patch leaders were required to oversee statutory work like child abuse and to be present during days when the team was on duty for the area as a whole (Sharron 1982). Even the work of the community wardens became less routine: they used to visit 30 old people a day from a prepared list. 'Normanton, in keeping with its philosophy of extending the responsibilities of its untrained staff, allowed them to alter their roles and become the front-line in referring any problems of needs to the patch team.' The community wardens came to use their own discretion as to whom they should visit and for how long; they referred requests for home helps and meals on wheels to the patch social workers who then assessed the needs of the clients; they acted as listening posts and brought problems to the attention of the team; they drafted in volunteers and doubled up as community workers.

Sharron describes the work of one Normanton patch warden, Mabel Betts. She had 40 clients, many of them elderly and with medical complaints such as diabetes, angina or confusion. She lit fires, brought milk or medicine and cooked meals. With one seriously confused octogenarian, Mabel called five times a day — the first call at 8 o'clock — and it was that, she thought, which kept the client cheerful.

Sharron found that Mabel Betts was very well known in the community; it was through her and the other wardens that the patches penetrated to the roots of the people, and a major factor in the success of Patch was thought to be the extensive involvement in the team of local people who already knew, and were known by, a great many of the prospective clients. Whatever else Patch did or did not achieve, it undoubtedly overcame the problem of the social workers, who, because of rapid turnover, spiralling career patterns and detachment from the location they were appointed to serve, dealt with their clients at arm's length, and never thought of them as having complex relationships within the community.

Hadley claims that Patch definitely increases accessibility and serves to reduce the emphasis on crisis management, since, through the network, the team gets early warning of impending domestic or other crises before they reach full fruition. Patch increases the public's awareness of social work services, which could obviously have resource implications, but it does enable steps to be taken to preclude institutional admissions wherever possible.

Mike Cooper, the leader of the Normanton initiative, has spelt out two principles that bring Patch firmly within the framework outlined in *The Essential Social Worker*. He sees the chief aim of Patch as being to 'divert people from institutional care while satisfactorily maintaining them within their families and neighbourhoods'. The model aims, above all, to make home-based care the departmental priority for all clients (Cooper and Denne 1983), and he and Stacy (1981) outline the argument that 'the place of the qualified social worker in this context is to act as an enabling catalyst who may also have expertise to offer in particular fields of work'. This lends emphasis to the community's reservoir of ability, good will and expertise which can be offered in partnership with the statutory services.

There is a suspicion that the exponents of Patch sometimes get carried away in their contrast of its virtues with the shortcomings of traditional approaches. The idea, for example, that the patch worker is accountable both to the agency and the neighbourhood, is not specific to Patch, and Croft and Beresford (1984) have criticised the failure of Patch advocates adequately to gauge client opinion.

Nevertheless, Patch does go further than any of its predecessors in bringing into reality the idea of maintaining the client in ways that both appeal to him and key in with the warp and weft of community life. Politically it is not an especially radical step forward, but it is one that takes the idea of community involvement and makes it into a feasible strategy for a local government department to pursue.

The trained social worker becomes a kind of community manager in the world of Patch; elsewhere, specialists are still required, and decisions involving responsibility, power and social control will always have to be taken. But these functions are easier to accommodate within the tradition and ethos of social work if departments simultaneously accept their role as community and client supporters, as the doctrine of Patch requires.

Community Care

Patch represents an important breakthrough in social services organisation, but as a conceptual element in social work it remains only a part of the full spectrum. It is misleading to imagine that it provides a model upon which the whole of social work can be based. Some critics have, for example, expressed doubts about the extent to which the client population for whom the greater part of the social services budget is allocated is really likely to be helped by a neighbourhood support scheme. A director of social services has put it bluntly:

> Social Services are provided for the most severely frail, vulnerable, and those at the greatest risk of danger or harm to themselves. Although statistically insignificant in the population as a whole, large numbers of people are involved (for example, 880 in Lambeth's old peoples homes, approximately 1550 children in the care of the Council, 1700 meals on wheels delivered weekdays, 2000 meals at weekends). The number over 80 years of age will be substantially more in the future.
>
> The tasks in the form of management and organisation, including staffing, catering, cleaning and transport, require rather more than the enthusiastic efforts of local people and community groups. (Osmond 1980)

Studies in both mental health and the penal system have pointed out that it is usually those with the worst problems who are also the most isolated socially, and in view of the fact that Abrams has suggested that neighbourhood support tends to be given on a reciprocal basis, there is obviously a problem when the giving is all one way – especially if, as is not infrequently the case, the aid offered is not even accepted gratefully by a cantankerous old lady, a disturbed alcoholic or a depressive mental patient.

The role and responsibilities of social work remain distinct from those of the citizen – and even from those of the volunteer or of part-time wardens. That role and those responsibilities require the social worker to put into operation programmes that further the objectives of their department, and it is important that, Patch notwithstanding, a variety of approaches are employed to improve on performance.

A scheme with some similarities to Patch, but one targeted specifically on the elderly infirm with the explicit goal of reducing departmental costs by delaying admission to Part III accommodation, was the Kent Community Care Scheme.

The scheme was wholly client-focused (unlike Patch), and those drawn into the spectrum of the scheme had to be 'otherwise eligible for admission to residential care' by virtue of their frailty, incapacity or confusion. A budgetary allocation was made which represented two-thirds of the marginal cost of a place in Part III, and within that, specially allocated social workers were free to spend resources as they thought fit, normally negotiating a contract for service from an individual or an agency at agreed rates. The aim was to enlist the support of people who would serve the elderly 'more for its intrinsic satisfaction than for material reward', but the fact that there was *some* payment was regarded as critical.

The primary system involved the employment of locally based helpers to perform tasks for clients, usually at relatively small cost. Matching client to helper was regarded as important, and sometimes clients were able to visit the helpers' homes: the social workers became case-coordinators, and the local helpers' activities were dovetailed in with already existing services – especially, of course, home helps and meals on wheels. Challis and Davies (1980) give an example of the investment of effort required:

> Mrs A. is crippled with arthritis, and, since breaking a leg, is virtually immobile. Her home is unsuitable (outside toilet, different floor levels between front room and kitchen), but the package of care has made it possible for her to remain at home against all the odds:
> *Early morning* – Community Care Project (CCP) helper gets her up, dresses her and gives her breakfast; there is a different helper at weekends.
> *Morning* – District nurse helps with washing and dressing her leg.
> *Lunchtime* – Home help provides meal and does other household jobs; a CCP helper does it at weekends.
> *During day* – CCP helper provides tea, social visits and shopping as required; there is also help from friends and neighbours.
> *Night-time* – about 10 p.m. CCP helper assists Mrs A. to bed. (Adapted)

In their evaluation, the research leaders of the Kent scheme claim that it was both of proven viability and able to reduce costs in the department. They quote figures which show that those clients served by the experiment were significantly less likely to be admitted to hospital or residential care during a 12-month period.

Indeed, they claim dramatic results, saying that their implementation of the community care approach halved the probability of death, halved the probability of entering an institution and doubled the probability of the elderly people continuing to live in their own homes. Moreover, not only did it prove cheaper to run than residential care, it 'relieved informal carers of some diswelfares and reduced the cost to them over the period during which the elderly client survived' (Davies and Challis 1986).

Largely as a result of Bleddyn Davies's painstakingly researched pioneering work in Kent, the conceptual model of community care came to be built into the NHS and Community Care Act 1990 and implemented in 1993. It maintained the idea of the social worker (or another person) being responsible for care management and using Kent-style initiatives to devise packages of care likely to maintain an elderly person in the community for longer than would otherwise have been the case. This means that pro-active involvement in the community becomes a main-line activity at the heavy end of statutory practice, and will certainly require new approaches to training, planning and management during the 1990s. Of necessity, it also means that the traditional barriers between health and social services personnel are going to have to be breached if community care packages are to be successfully implemented.

Nationally 100,000 assessments for care will be carried out annually, and although all circumstances will be taken into account, the primary development concerns the role of carers. The debate has moved on from the naive early emphasis on the wider community and has arrived at a recognition that carers are the key figures in the equation. They are officially acknowledged in the NHS and Community Care Act 1990, and they are given the right to make representations to the social services department if they feel that their role is not being properly supported by the social worker. This development means that the social worker is not the only person who can be pro-active: the carers who carry the bulk of the work-burden can speak up on their own behalf and on behalf of the person for whom they are caring. This could emerge as a highly significant shift in political power.

Probation and the community

In its statement of 'national objectives and priorities for the probation service' (April 1984), the Home Office invited the service to engage in 'other work in the community' over and above its role in the courts and with offenders. Certainly for a number of years, tentative steps have been made to encourage community initiatives, and some adventurous areas have gone so far as to make specialist appointments. In a survey of community initiatives, Shaw (1983) says that those officers given a full-time brief to act in a detached fashion succeeded in becoming involved in community-based developments, but suffered from being cut off from their institutional base and hence ran the risk of a lost identity. In other words, they might become good community workers, but as a result they lost their probation identity or found it an encumbrance.

In other areas, where teams of officers were encouraged to operate as a Patch team, the problem was usually one of time and resources, and the evidence of achievements gained was very limited. 'In Hartlepool, for example, the only tangible reward for 18 months input by two workers was a week-long play scheme for residents' children during the school summer holidays' (Barry 1984).

Barry comments that the probation service's attempts at community involvement have suffered from being disparate, isolated and lacking an underlying rationale. There is a feeling that the Home Office's expression of encouragement for action in the area of crime prevention might offer clearer objectives, but even here the boundary between what is appropriate for probation practice and what properly falls within the orbit of the police force is a potential source of confusion.

The significant contrast between the apparently successful introduction of Patch in social services departments and its tentative failure in probation seems to hinge on differences in the availability of resources. Local authority social work starts off with a depth of personnel that the probation service cannot match; moreover, social services have considerable scope for diverting erstwhile institutional funding to community work, and this has led to a much more flexible mode of operation.

In fact, the best developments in community initiative to be found in the probation service are quite different, reflecting greater specificity and hingeing on the availability of external funding. Thus, in a number of settings, the service has drawn on Department of Employment funding to enable it to set up schemes to counteract unemployment among its clients; elsewhere a variety of financial sources have been tapped to provide new or better facilities to house homeless ex-prisoners. Given that the availability of just such accommodation is often the deciding factor in whether or not someone is given parole, it can easily be argued that the probation service will be better engaged in such manoeuvres than in vaguer initiatives of a less offender-orientated kind.

Many offenders — especially recidivists in prison — exemplify a major problem for social workers wanting to adopt a stronger community orientation. These clients frequently have no network, and some are actively not wanted by their neighbourhood, so it is arguably better for the probation officer to ease their way back into the mainstream by striving to create work and housing opportunities.

Conclusion

It has been argued in this book that, for the first time in 25 years, a theoretical framework for social work has begun to emerge clearly.

The overall objective of practitioners in post is the achievement of maintenance: maintenance of the state — which presumes a consensus model of politics, though it certainly does not preclude democratic conflict; and maintenance of those citizens who, for one reason or another, are in need of support discipline, guidance and protection in order to remain within and to co-exist with the community.

The goal of maintenance, although it involves a commitment on the part of practitioners to provide such elements of support and help as they individually and corporately can, also requires them to fulfil a wide and still growing range of statutory and policy-based responsibilities — often concerned with the movement into and out of residential or institutional care — and to engage in such therapeutic activities as seem to be appropriate bearing in mind the needs, the interests and the personal opinions of clients.

And now there is a further dimension to the theory: the pro-active involvement of the social worker in the community, which often carries with it resource implications, and can rarely be carried out by the worker in isolation. Agencies have come to accept this as a legitimate role for their professionals, and committees and government departments have built it into their strategic plans and into legislation, recognising that it is centrally relevant to the goal of maintenance.

These various functions are not necessarily all vested in all social workers. In large departments it is appropriate and natural that there should be a proper division of functions and responsibilities. But, with regard to the community, it seems likely that too many serving social workers have not yet recognised the growing importance of pro-active intervention. This is nicely captured by Black *et al.* (1983) in their study of three social services departments: 'Social workers had a willingness to ignore the community and even in many cases dismiss the relevance of volunteers; to adopt a client specialist approach by design or by stealth and to work in a privatised and *ad hoc* manner in relation to individual cases and other agencies.'

Since Seebohm first mooted, in 1968, the idea of community social work, numerous debates have taken place about the way in which the idea could be activated. Very often these have had a political dimension with the extreme Left arguing that social work could and should move into an activist role – fulfilling an explicitly critical role and striving to influence decisions by militant or collective action. Such an idea, though often attractive to students, normally founders because of its apparent impracticality in a hierarchical organisation which is subject to political authority in its own right and employs a wide range of staff not by any means unanimously at one with a Marxist or radical perspective.

Thomas (1983) identified *service extension* as an equally legitimate community task, and it is clearly this which has now been taken on board by creative social workers. It enables a degree of campaigning, without requiring staff to oppose democratic authority – after all, as Hadley has said, social workers do have their jobs to consider!

Environmental support has long been recognised as something which the social worker ought to be expected to provide, but for many years this only seemed to be possible through the removal of the client from the community – often with stigmatising and destabilising consequences. Many of the most interesting developments of the last decade attempt to achieve the former without recourse to the latter.

Pro-active intervention in the community demands that the social worker accepts a leadership or management role; that she campaigns for resources either within her own department or elsewhere; that she works in full exposure in the local community, making herself accessible and visible; that she attempts to provide facilities on terms that make sense to the client-group; that she utilises indigenous support systems and maximises existing networks; and that she accepts a degree of accountability both to the community and to the agency. The role thus offers a glimpse of social work as maintenance in its most developed form.

Part III

Dimensions of practice

9 First encounter: The client enters an alien world

Social work and probation offices are heavily stigmatised: they are viewed by all except those who work in them with suspicion, perhaps with awe, and frequently with distaste. It is partly the feeling that a small child has outside the headteacher's room, the feeling that comes from knowing that therein is vested considerable power from which it is better to keep well away. But it is also the feeling that such places are strongly identified with poverty, misfortune, crime and deviance, and that higher status is normally accorded to those who have no need of them. Thus to go to a social work agency voluntarily is a sign of having 'given up'; to be compelled to go there is a mark, not only of failure, but of shame.

These feelings are frequently reflected in expressions of client opinion, as in these quotations recorded by Mayer and Timms (1970):

> 'It takes a lot to go to one of those places. You feel very beholden to someone.'
> 'I said to my daughter that I'm almost in two minds whether to go or not. Well, she said, you try them, mum, and see what happens. But I had butterflies in my tummy all the time I was going there and sitting in the waiting room.'
> 'I felt belittled by going there.'
> 'To go for money, to ask them to help you out, seems a right predicament to get into. That was the worst feeling of it.'

Comments such as these lead the authors to conclude that 'clients do not go to social work agencies unless they are sorely troubled'; in another study, 58 per cent of clients admitted that it bothered them 'to be referred' to social work, while one woman said that she had been terrified when she knew that the social worker was coming for the first time: 'I said, "Here is a man coming to see me about the children. What is he going to do?" ' (Rees 1978).

In a society where self-respect is strongly identified with independence and conformity, it is a rare citizen who will approach the enquiry desk in a social work office for the

133

first time with head held high and a jaunty step. That fact should be stamped indelibly on the mind of every social worker and receptionist.

Bombardment

Given a general reluctance, then, to seek out the services of the social worker, what is it that leads an increasing number of people to come into the agency? In a probation office, of course, most of the new arrivals have not *chosen* to be there: they have been directed to attend as a direct consequence of a court hearing. Their relationship with the probation officer is enforceable by law.

But most of the clients of social services departments come for help, not perhaps always entirely of their own volition, but usually because of circumstances in their lives that lead them to believe that a social worker might be of some use.

Who are they? A profile of social services referrals in the East Anglian county of Norfolk and in the Metropolitan Borough of Gateshead in the industrial North-east of England is outlined in Table 9.1.

Table 9.1
Referrals to Norfolk and Gateshead social services departments in March 1992, by client group

	Norfolk %	Gateshead %
Elderly	50	27
Child and family care	18	37
Physical disability	14	14
Blind and partially sighted	3	1
Deaf/hard of hearing	2	2
Mental health	4	3
Physically ill	4	5
Learning disability	3	1
Single persons	0	3
Other	2	6
	N = 3 644	N = 1 779

In each case, unclassified referrals have been ignored: they amounted to 5 per cent in Norfolk, and 11 per cent in Gateshead.

With acknowledgements to Rosy Coles of Norfolk Social Services Research and Planning Office, and to Dave Godfrey of the Gateshead Social Services Department.

At referral, the elderly are the largest single client-group in Norfolk, as in most county areas. This fact provides the clearest possible rebuke to those right-wing critics of social work who persist in believing that social workers are primarily employed coping with deviants and scroungers who 'ought to be out earning their living'. Black *et al.* (1983) studied three area offices in North Wales, East Anglia and Birmingham and found that 53 per cent of all new referrals came from the ranks of the elderly.

The pattern held true in all three areas, although in Metropolitan Birmingham the demand from families and children was significantly greater than it was in the rural districts. This difference can be seen reflected in the Gateshead figures in Table 9.1, with 37 per cent of referrals being of children and families; an inner urban area is always likely to see a significant flow of family casework coming the social worker's way.

Table 9.1 shows that the need for close liaison and active cooperation between the health and social services departments is self-evident from the large number of people with varying kinds of disability who find themselves in a social work office.

Further analysis of the Gateshead statistics provides information about the reasons for referral to a social worker:

	%
Financial	31
Physical disability	18
Behaviour in the community	12
Physical illness	7
Home management	3
Mobility	3
Frailty	2
Behaviour in the home	2
Accommodation	2
Self-care	2
Material needs	2
Transport	2
Mental illness	2

Other reasons given (none of them making up more than 1 per cent of the total) included: emotional disturbance, social isolation, family behaviour problems, suspected neglect or abuse, matrimonial troubles, homelessness, alcohol or drug-related difficulties and adoption counselling.

Four points can be emphasised from these data:

1. Financial and material problems are dominant. This fact has emerged consistently in audits of social work bombardment, but research studies have also shown that they pose particular difficulties for the social worker who rarely feels that she has the resources to respond in a practical or helpful fashion.
2. There is re-emphasis on the significant presence of health-related conditions in the social worker's caseload.

3. Behavioural problems also emerge as a major element in the social services bombardment profile – in the community or in the home.
4. The list is impressive because of its wide-ranging nature. Some headline-catching categories (like child abuse or drug addiction) are small in number, but their presence reflects the need for the reception system to be alert to the need for appropriate prioritisation. Additionally, however, very different kinds of responses are required in different cases, and the clear identification of the three principal categories – family and child care, disability and illness, and behavioural problems – is a good indicator of why social work specialisms have re-emerged in their newly strengthened form.

Gateshead also outlines the nature of the 'task on referral' reported by the social work staff in each case:

	%
Investigate	49
Inform or advise	31
Advocate, liaise or re-refer	7
Mobilise departmental services	7
Report	3
Other	4

Although interpretation of such relatively crude data must be tentative, it has to be said that the initial message conveyed about social work is a rather modest one: in four out of five cases, the client cannot expect instant action, but will either have to await the outcome of an investigation, or make do with information or advice. In only 7 per cent of referrals are services mobilised immediately.

Other studies have shown that those requests most likely to be given a positive response are, not surprisingly, the ones that are the easiest to meet at little or no additional cost. Requests for information, advice and counselling can normally be met in full; indeed they are sometimes provided even where they are not sought. Specific requests for disability aids, occupational therapy or to have a name put onto the Handicap Register will also normally find a positive response. On the other hand, requests for admission to residential care, to adopt a child or to have major housing adaptations provided are more likely to be refused, at least in the first instance.

One of the intriguing analytical problems in social services work that has not received the attention it deserves is to be found in the contrast between the persistent and wide-ranging pattern of bombardment on reception (which can be represented as the 'public face' of social work), and the 'heavy-end' of social services expenditure which involves long-term provision of service for a relatively small number of people in the community or in institutional care. A Kent County Council business plan (1993) provides a profile, not of bombardment, but of long-term provision of service throughout the county. The analysis uses a 'client-week' unit of resource, which facilitates comparisons between client-groups.

In community care (but excluding child and family care), the breakdown of client-week resources committed for 1994 is:

	%
Elderly people	76
Physical disability	12
Learning disability	9
Mental health	7

And in residential care, the client-week breakdown for the same period is:

	%
Elderly people in the county's homes	28
Elderly people in independent homes	26
Physical disability	4
Learning disability in county homes	1
Learning disability in independent homes	12
Learning disability: short stay/respite care	2
Mental health	2
Children in foster care	21
Children in county homes	1
Children in independent homes	2
Children with disabilities	1

Note: the absolute dominance of elder-care in the social service's long-term workload – both in the community and the residential sector; the fact that, in the community, both physical and learning disability client-groups make greater demands on the department's resources than mental health; the role of the independent sector in residential care provision; and the pre-eminence of foster care as a vehicle for the residential care of children.

Social services departments, therefore, have to be geared up to cope with two quite different types of population: short-term applicants with specific needs and long-term clients with both general and specific needs.

The kind of social work practised both with new referrals and in long-term casework is shown to have some remarkable similarities in Black's study (Table 9.2). In particular, there emerges in sharp profile confirmation of the theory of maintenance outlined in Part II of this book. Social workers' single most frequent task is concerned with their responsibility to investigate and to assess – to make decisions for the benefit of the client or according to statutory regulations. Secondly, in respect of both new and long-standing clients, they use their contacts and their expertise to give advice and information; and they move into full maintenance gear with a commitment to mobilise resources and, especially in the longer term, to provide personal support and sustenance for those in need. The actively interventionist roles of advocacy, problem-solving and educating or

Table 9.2
The social work response to referrals and long-term cases

	Work with new referrals %	Work with long-term cases %
Investigating/assessing	74	61
Giving information/advice	48	58
Mobilising resources	40	46
Supporting/sustaining	19	54
Advocacy	8	19
Problem-solving	7	34
Supervising/reviewing	6	34
Providing group activity	2	8
Educating/developing skills	1	14
	N = 1 140	N = 754

Note: The figures have been produced by reprocessing published tables in the volume.
Source: *Social Work in Context*, J Black *et al.* (1983).

skill-training come into operation only with longer-term clients, and only a minority are likely to find themselves referred into a group setting.

This is the shape of what awaits clients once they have put themselves into the social services departmental orbit.

Intake

The function of the intake interview in social work is, first and foremost, *to help the client*, and the overriding thought in the worker's mind must be: 'How can I be of assistance to this person?' A great deal has been made in the literature of filtering and rationing, screening and assessment, decision-making and referral, and, although it is true that all of these somewhat technical processes might be contained within the intake system, if they loom largest in the worker's mind she is likely to have a distant, impersonal and potentially dismissive impact on the client.

Loewenstein (1974) uses a cool, analytical approach to the intake process:

> Whatever form it takes, the initial encounter between client and agency must provide the agency with sufficient information to decide how best to serve this client and to determine if this agency is the best place to provide the needed service. The worker has to ascertain as accurately as possible what the actual problem or enquiry is from the client's point of view, to explore the problem or situation with the client, to evaluate the client's psychological state, to ascertain what coping efforts he might have made, to recommend a course of action, and to

facilitate such a course being undertaken by the client. Not only should an intake system filter out clients who are not considered appropriate for the services the agency offers, but it should also act as a filter in passing on cases to other agencies.

All very true, no doubt. But it is much more important for the intake worker to be smilingly efficient, to help the client feel welcome (even if the eventual outcome is a referral to the housing department) and to demonstrate that social workers are employed to provide a positive service, than to operate a restrictive policy of rationing and refusal.

For work such as this, knowledge, experience and skill are all needed. So, too, are time and immediate access to a social worker. And it is with a view to meeting these needs that many larger social services departments have now established intake teams. Smaller offices and most probation and voluntary agencies continue to rely on a duty-rota system; both methods have advantages and disadvantages, but both should ensure the ready availability of professional personnel to respond to requests by casual callers or telephone enquiries.

Short-term work

Of those who come through the door of the intake worker's interview room, we now know that, in social services departments, a large majority appear to need only a short-term service. Goldberg *et al.* (1977b) found that the aim of an intake team was 'to deal with explicit requests on a short-term basis unless there are clear indications for more intensive and longer-term involvement': 75 per cent of referrals were closed within two months and 88 per cent were never transferred out of the intake team's caseload.

Goldberg's study found that, in intake work, three kinds of activity predominated: exploration and assessment, the provision of information and advice, and the mobilisation of resources. The third of these included the supply of some kind of practical assistance, in which help with applications, usually for welfare benefits, topped the list. In four-fifths of all cases, intake workers were in contact with outside agencies of various kinds, most often health agencies: GPs, health visitors, hospitals and district nurses.

Something not far short of a revolutionary change in social work skills has been required of the profession in the last 20 years. 'One-interview work', from being regarded disparagingly, has come to be seen as a crucial, even dominant, part of the social worker's task and, as Goldberg has suggested, it can need very different skills from the traditional model of long-term care. For the trained professional, there is no excuse for not being able to cope with a steady stream of short-term clients and most social work courses now recognise the need to prepare their students to handle immediate crises and issues like welfare rights. But knowledge of one's own working locality — where the boarding houses are, which other service agencies to draw on, what the potential sources of employment for clients are, and so on — can only be accumulated on the job, and the skills required to handle such knowledge are not fundamentally different from the skills required to undertake any other form of social work.

The idea of rationing

The question of how many referrals an agency should be designed to deal with is impossible to answer because it depends partly on how you define social and economic policy and partly on felt need in the community. In one sense, there need be *no* limit on the services which the social worker might provide, but, in reality, of course, boundaries do exist. It is this realisation that has led policy-makers in recent years to review the balance of supply and demand, and some departments have tried to set down an order of priorities. Nottinghamshire's is quite explicit:

Priority 1: Life or death situations where immediate investigation and action is required. (For example, allegations of non-accidental injury to children, elderly confused clients and clients displaying active depressive psychosis.) And high-risk situations where action is to be taken within 72 hours of the referral being received.

Priority 2: Work with a specific time-span laid down by law or by the department. (For example, court reports, compulsory admission to mental hospital, visits to boarded out children.)

Priority 3: Preventative work with both families and individuals where there is a prospect of their problems being repeated in the next generation. (For example, work with homeless families and handicapped people where there is a perceived risk to the next generation.)

Priority 4: Work with clients who might need residential care or where there is a prospect of rehabilitation from residential care. (For example, the unsupported and isolated elderly.)

Priority 5: Work with all other clients. (For example, clients in residential care with no rehabilitative prospects, work with solitary drug addicts and alcoholics, and so on.)

Within each client-group, wherever they appear in an agency's list of priorities, it ought to be possible to outline the precise steps which social workers should take to meet specific circumstances. For example, Wakefield (1976) has suggested five stages in the preferred intake response to the referral of an elderly person said to be 'at risk', a situation generally acknowledged to take precedence over most other new cases:

1. Clarify exactly what the risk is and what is being asked for. Does the elderly person know of the referral? Wherever possible, the client's consent should be obtained.
2. Collect basic information about what help is already being given. For example, by the family or the community and in the form of domiciliary care.
3. If the risk appears to be connected with health or hypothermia contact the GP, health visitor or district nurse for a medical assessment.
4. If the request seems to be for general support because of loneliness, and so on, and the client himself has called in, consider making a referral to the appropriate voluntary body – Old Peoples' Welfare, clubs, churches, volunteers. In the case of a

third-party referral, either suggest the client calls at the office, or pass to the intake team for an assessment visit.

5. If the request is for residential accommodation, respond as follows:

    (a) Collect basic information: for example, age, address, reason behind request, and consider the need for further investigation by the health visitor or GP.

    (b) Assess the degree of urgency, and the appropriateness of the application. Discuss the alternatives: for example, relatives, friends, neighbours, day care, domiciliary services. Consider providing lists of private and voluntary homes, including the Salvation Army and homes run by the trade unions or occupational welfare groups.

    (c) Establish which domiciliary services are already being provided and consider whether other services might be appropriate and would enable the person to remain in the community. Arrange an assessment visit where necessary and decide how to continue social work contact, for example, where the application for admission to care is accepted but cannot be arranged immediately.

    (d) If the applicant is in hospital, ask for full reports to be sent for consideration.

    (e) If immediate admission is arranged attend to the protection of the client's property – and pets – where appropriate.

    (Adapted from the *Community Care* Supplement on Intake, with acknowledgement.)

As we have seen in Table 9.1, the intake worker has to be prepared to cope with an immense variety of requests, needs and crises, and her responses must be similarly wide-ranging. Most departments now provide operating instructions of one sort or another, and some have developed algorithms to further clarify the process. But although such written guides do seem to be increasingly necessary, especially when there is a rapid turnover of staff, they must be acted on sensitively and in a humane fashion. There will always be a need to aim for and to achieve a nice balance between agency and statutory requirements, the cumulative practice experience of the team and the professional skill and initiative of the individual social worker.

Intake to residential care

If the client feels fearful at the idea of coming to a social work office, how much more apprehensive is he likely to be at the prospect of entering a residential home! It is a giant step to take whether the person involved is a child entering care, a psychiatric patient being admitted to hospital, an offender entering a probation hostel, an elderly person being taken to an old peoples' home or a young woman staying in a mother-and-baby hostel. All of these allocations are, to a greater or lesser extent, subject to the influence of social workers, and inside each institution, too, social workers have an active part to play.

The skilled social worker will always make the process of admission less painful, less stressful than it might otherwise have been. Of course, such moves are often crisis events for which adequate preparation is rarely possible, and no matter what the social worker does, however skilful her efforts, the anguish cannot altogether be assuaged. Entering an old peoples' home, for example, is probably the second most important personal move that many people make in their lives after getting married and setting up an independent household. But even though it is impossible to minimise the pain, or rather, perhaps, especially *because* it is impossible to minimise the pain, the need for a high standard of social work practice is absolute.

The following example reveals a better-than-average model, and one that could be emulated everywhere. It concerns the admission of an old lady to an old people's home, which, as Billis (1973) has shown, often involves complex decisions on the part of the social services organisation, but that, in the client's eyes, is straightforward though far-reaching in its implications:

> Mrs Marchant is in a hospital bed, having been admitted from her own home with pneumonia. Her mobility is restricted, she has no relatives left, and it is thought that she can no longer cope in the house. The medical social worker reports her position to the area fortnightly review meeting where fieldwork representatives, head-of-homes and managers come together. There is a vacancy in St Cecilia's, and the matron, having ascertained that Mrs Marchant is not incontinent, says she will visit her. She does so three days later. Mrs Marchant indicates that, despite many regrets at losing her independence, she will be glad not to have to return to her large cold house, and would like to come to St Cecilia's. Arrangements are made for her to move there from the hospital; she is conveyed by a friendly volunteer, and welcomed, formally by the matron, and informally by the other residents. She will be there for four weeks before the allocation is finalised: this gives Mrs Marchant the chance of expressing her doubts about the move, and the matron of the home the chance of concluding whether or not the arrangement is likely to succeed. The admission is thus made smoothly and with proper concern for the feelings of the new resident, for the interests of the other residents who will have to live with her and for the staff who usually have very clear ideas about the boundaries of suitability for admission to their home.

Conclusion

The successful and sensitive use of intake procedures requires, first, clarity of agency objectives – *why does this social work office exist?* Second, acceptance by the social worker of those objectives – *how can I help my agency to fulfil its obligations?* And, third, a commitment to the use of professional skills of the highest standard attainable. Such skills at intake can be briefly summarised:

1. *Efficiency*, by virtue of the worker's disciplined knowledge of the relevant aspects of practice.
2. Sympathetic *concern* for the client's feelings about his problems and in his relations with the agency.
3. The provision of a positive *service*, and the clear expression of a sense of direction derived from the worker's identification with the aims of her agency and the humanitarian ideals of her profession.
4. *Friendliness* and cheerfulness. The social worker, like the actor or the judge, must

never have an off-day. The crisis in each client's life is unique, and the professional role of the worker demands a reliable and a helpful response.

5. *The ability to handle* distress, anger and depression in the client: these are the emotions naturally associated with the kinds of problems brought to the social worker, and they must be accepted as such.

6. *Acceptance of responsibility* for determining what, if anything, should happen next. The client must have the right to refuse further contact, but he should not be left in any doubt about its availability, or about who − the client or the social worker − is expected to make the next move.

The achievement of a high standard of practice requires the constant reiteration of the central importance of these skills in intake. The agency which ensures that they are practised day in, day out, will know that the first encounter of its clients with social work has been made as smooth, as helpful and as responsive as it can be.

10 Who is the client? Who determines the action?

Despite occasional expressions of unease at the term 'client' in social work ('Clients?! I know what I'd call 'em,' said one Rotary Club stalwart to laughter and applause during the discussion which followed a lunchtime lecture I'd given on social work), it is a word which appears to have successfully made the transition from private, fee-paying counselling to the state welfare sector. The term has stuck and seems likely to be retained.

The idea of 'the client', however, remains fraught with ambiguities, and Pincus and Minahan (1973) performed an important service by pointing out that a distinction has to be drawn between the *client system* and the *target system*. The client system constitutes the person-in-situation who requests a service from the social worker; the target system consists of the person or the situation on which the worker decides her efforts should he concentrated. Thus in a traditional counselling role, where, for example, a matrimonial couple might come jointly for guidance, ventilation and insight, the client system and the target system are one and the same: the clients ask for help and the counsellor provides it by focusing on the husband and wife as interacting individuals. Or, again, a young married woman, her husband in prison, might come to the probation officer and ask her to help her work out a manageable budget on a limited income. The probation officer might do no more than that, in which case, once more, the client and target systems are identical.

However, in the latter case, the probation officer might decide that her client appears to be receiving less than her due deserts from the social security. At this point, having decided with the client to act on her behalf, she will phone, write to or visit the benefit office concerned, and attempt to obtain improved allowances: this will mean that, temporarily, she will be engaged in helping her client by tackling a different target system − the state's income maintenance service. (Pincus and Minahan also identify an 'action system', which would be illustrated in this case if the probation officer were to involve the claimants' union in her client's cause, but this refinement is of no consequence to the problem of defining 'the client'.)

In contemporary social work, there are a great many instances where the client and target systems do not coincide; for example:

1. Mrs Blythe comes to the family casework agency and says she wants the social worker to 'do something about my George' (her impossible husband) or 'our Willie' (her delinquent teenage son). Should the social worker instantly act on Mrs Blythe's behalf, and take up the cudgels for her against those targets that she says are disturbing her peace and quiet? Or should she regard Mrs Blythe as both client and target, and, by patient enquiry, set about discovering whether there is some way in which she could help her to cope with her erring menfolk rather more successfully? Or should she, by virtue of Mrs Blythe's arrival on the agency doorstep, regard the entire family as the client-and-target system, and draw up a programme – modest or ambitious, depending on circumstances – aimed at improving the climate of relationships?

2. In situations where a child is deemed to be at risk of abuse by its parents, the conflicts of responsibility can be severe. At the time of a court hearing the law is quite clear in requiring the social worker to regard the child's interests as paramount. But at the same time, the social worker is expected to work with the parents (who therefore can also be regarded as 'clients' in the traditional sense) even though she may feel their immediate interests to be in conflict with those of her 'true' client, the child. In the event of the child being provided with accommodation by the local authority, the agency's responsibilities require the social worker to concentrate on the parents with the aim of improving their circumstances, their attitudes and their behaviour sufficiently to allow the child to be returned to them: they thus become the target system, while the state – acting on behalf of the child – is in effect the client system.

In a sense, the distinction between 'target' and 'client' systems might be thought to be primarily one of semantics, and the fact that George or Willie Blythe and the parents of a child in need of protection are defined as 'target systems' does not in any way reduce the obligation on the worker to relate to them and engage with them in styles traditionally identified with a social work ideology. In particular, this would include an attempt to negotiate a 'voluntary' relationship or contract incorporating a commitment to cooperation and endeavour on the part of the target system which would effectively convert it into a client system. Pincus and Minahan's major contribution has been to highlight the importance of *clarifying objectives in practice* – of noting the fact that the worker may have different aims depending on *who* made the first approach and *how* the case relates to statutorily defined requirements. Their distinction between clients and targets has been most commonly taken to push the analysis in a radical direction: to show that the welfare of clients might most effectively be served by seeing community change as an appropriate goal and therefore community agencies and facilities (or their absence) as a target system. Less apparent from their own writing, but crystal clear to any reader familiar with a contemporary public welfare system, is an entirely different interpretation of the distinction and one especially pertinent to statutory social work. This represents *society* or *the state* or *the government* or, if your political analysis requires it, *the ruling class* as sometimes the client system, and some statutorily defined consumers of the social services as *targets:* youth custody inmates on compulsory after-care, parolees, persons discharged from special psychiatric hospitals (like Broadmoor) and subject to supervision, youth offenders placed under supervision. These are not people who have sought social work help voluntarily, but people who, by virtue of their past behaviour or present condition, are required by law to enter into a social work relationship. They are referred to as 'clients' and will, no doubt, continue to be so called (indeed, it is strangely difficult to devise a suitable alternative designation); but insofar as the common use of the term *client* seems to imply a degree of freedom to withdraw from the relationship and to exercise unlimited control over it, it is manifestly inappropriate. In such cases, the state is both the employer *and* the client of the social worker, and the legally defined 'clientele' is really a target group.

From this, three things can be concluded. First, that the traditional textbook notion of the social worker's relationship with a homogeneous collection of always voluntary clients is wide of the contemporary mark, and greatly underestimates the complexity of the social worker's pivotal position between the individual and the state. Second, that the power of the state cannot be ignored nor can it be claimed that the social worker is in some sense above its authority. And, third, that, nevertheless, the social worker is delegated to identify and look after the interests of marginal persons who might otherwise be overlooked or penalised unjustly by the state, and this must mean that the social worker is sanctioned to do battle on behalf of designated clients against authority in given circumstances, and to do it in such a way that achieves a measure of satisfaction to all parties.

'The question of 'who is the client?' has traditionally been posed implicitly in debates about the notion of client self-determination. Both Plant (1970) and Whittington (1971) effectively killed off the concept as a prerequisite of social work two decades ago, but the idea has remained a powerful fiction in the minds of practitioners. Whittington lists the following ways in which the social worker exercises direction or control over the client:

1. Her agency function – in probation, child care or mental health, for instance – requires her to use coercion, persuasion or pressure or to have recourse to legal sanctions.
2. Her official position gives her power over the client's life – for example, whether or not to use her influence to persuade the gas or electricity board not to cut off the supply of fuel.
3. The agency setting – in a school or hospital, for example – means that the social worker has to conform to institutional norms and employ social work practices in order to achieve approved goals. If she fails to conform, or if she pursues goals not sanctioned by the agency, she can be regarded as out of step with the team and so become alienated – to the possible detriment of future clients.
4. Within the casework relationship itself, Whittington suggests, the worker exerts influence by virtue of her status and the client's perceptions of her. 'The caseworker, though she may profess commitment to client self-determination, non-directiveness and the client's freedom to choose, finds her therapeutic aims greatly aided by the client's susceptibility to her influence and subtle directiveness.'

Whittington concludes, 'To increase the client's capacity to evaluate choices may be a goal of treatment, and participation may be a technique used to this end, but to maintain that treatment is carried out without directiveness because the latter's skilled and subtle nature has made it less easy to observe, requires nothing short of self-deception.'

If this analysis of practice is accepted, then the picture of clients who always initiate action, social workers who only ever respond to the client's request and target systems which are attacked (or changed) solely for the benefit of the original client is obviously a misrepresentation of social work as it really is.

Of course, social workers do provide a service, but it is a service offered within a fairly precise social context – one in which, in the public sector, they are employed as state functionaries. Even social workers in voluntary organisations are subject to the possibility of sanctions being used by their management committees or the withdrawal of cooperation by sister organisations if it is thought that patterns of practice are departing from consensually defined limits. Moreover, most voluntary social service organisations in the United Kingdom are now heavily dependent on state funds for their survival and growth. Social workers can, must and do defend civil liberties, fight for client rights and criticise abuses of statutory power. But, both in terms of political logic and in the light of actual experience, it is clearly not possible for them to defend the absolute freedom of any one individual nor to embark on a singlehanded assault on the power of the establishment – at least, they *can* attempt to do either or both of these, but their future role and viability in social work may be seriously affected as a result.

A good example of the social worker's feeling of helplessness when confronted with the combined forces of law, community and institutional power is provided by the case of the Robinsons.

Mr and Mrs Robinson and their grown-up daughter, Alice, were all educationally subnormal. In addition, Mr Robinson was stone-deaf and unable to get a job. The family was 'known' to the social services department but rarely demanded attention. Their behaviour, however, was a source of constant irritation to their neighbours who found them aggressive and sometimes offensive. There were no rent arrears, but eventually, because of constant complaints by the neighbours, the district council decided to evict the Robinsons. Social workers who knew the family were aghast because they could see no viable alternative, but their department was powerless to intervene. Attempts were made to mobilise help, but the district council was clearly within its legal rights, and the eviction duly took place. The social worker's role was to arrange transport and storage facilities for the furniture, liaising with the social security office and the local cat and dog shelter. The day before the eviction, a high-level and somewhat reluctant decision was taken in the social services department to support the family financially by providing temporary accommodation in a hotel.

As one of the social workers in the department commented, the case undoubtedly highlights some of the limitations inherent in statutory social work. For such a family as the Robinsons, the primary preventative strategy for social work must be the provision of suitable accommodation. When the council, under pressure from the community, takes that away from them, it is understandable that the social worker should feel that her position is a weak one: 'One of the most vivid memories that remain is the feeling of total powerlessness to make the community care' (Bowman 1978).

The community in this instance was a rejecting, not a caring, community. It may be that the law was a bad law — it has now been amended in such a way that the district council today would not be able to offload the responsibility for housing the Robinsons once it had made them homeless. But the problem in principle remains valid. The social worker has to work within the framework of legislation, and subject to the expression of attitudes on the part of the community: she has no power of veto either over the legislature or the executive, and she cannot claim inherent superiority in her expressions of opinion over members of the general public. The Robinsons' neighbours, for example, could legitimately turn round and say to the social worker: 'You don't live next door to these people. You go home every evening to your suburban semi ten miles away. Who are you to talk about community care in our council estate? We've worked hard to make the street a pleasant place to live, and we're sick of the Mad Robinsons disturbing the peace.'

The social worker cannot be an arbitrary dispenser of justice unique to the needs of one family irrespective of others. She *can* act as an advocate on behalf of the family, but she cannot claim absolute priority for them merely because they are her clients.

All through this book I have argued that the primary function of social work is one of reconciliation: enabling the state and its citizens to live together in relative harmony. On the one hand, the state is prevailed upon to find a significant place in society for handicapped, deviant, deprived, aged and vulnerable people; in this sense, the worker undoubtedly operates on behalf of the underprivileged client. But, on the other hand, those same people are persuaded by the social worker to accept the terms currently offered them by the state. Of course, it remains the social worker's responsibility, not only to get the best terms available now but also — perhaps in unison with client-groups — to press for policy developments that will lead to corporate improvements in the future. This circularity in the social worker's role is critical, and has not always been understood. The social worker owes allegiance to the client, but it is not absolute allegiance; she is employed by the state, but she is not a mere tool of the state. The unique nature of social work can only be grasped by recognising that the two halves belong together, *are* reconcilable, and *are* dynamic in their long-term effects on social policy and practice.

Clients whose interests are not mutually compatible

Yet another complication in dealing with the question, 'Who is the client?', arises when there is more than one client in a single case or situation. The classic example would be in a case of marital conflict, where it has long been recognised that sometimes it is necessary for each partner to be allocated to a different counsellor, at least for part of the time.

But of particular importance in statutory social work has been the question of the vulnerability of a child in a family whose behaviour towards him looks likely to be or has been threatening. It was the death of Maria Colwell which prompted concern about the need to ensure that the best interests of the child were taken fully into account within the welfare system. The report on Maria's death said that 'it would have been of assistance to the court to have had the views of an independent social worker' – that is to say, 'independent' of the local authority and of the child's parents. Since then, step by step, such a system has been put in place. Guardians *ad litem* are social workers given specific functions by the court, and they have the overriding responsibility of protecting the best interests of the child. They belong to panels which, though publicly funded, are not an integral part of any other social work system, and they are required to provide a non-partisan view on a wide range of proceedings in courts which deal with children's welfare. The Department of Health's manual puts it like this:

> The guardian has to safeguard the child's interests, to ensure the most positive outcome possible for the child. The guardian also has to make a judgment between the potentially conflicting demands of children's rights, children's rescue, the autonomy of the family and the duty of the state. (Timms 1992: 3–4)

Under the Children Act 1989, guardians *ad litem* have the job of representing the interests of the child in a wide range of child care procedures. The Act lays special emphasis on the fact that guardians are not 'just another voice' in children's proceedings, but that they are an *independent* voice required to assess the evidence and act as a representative for children in the courts (Timms 1992: 99).

The system of guardians *ad litem* has been put in place because public enquiries into social work practice with children have pinpointed the fact that on at least some occasions it has proved impossible for local authority social workers to serve equally the interests of parents and of their children. Now local authority social workers can be required to carry out their duties in stressful family situations, knowing that guardians *ad litem* have the unambiguous responsibility for safeguarding the well-being of children.

Assessment

Assessment is the key to all good social work, and is a constant element in the practitioner's daily routine. It is a process of *learning about* the newly presented client and *reaching conclusions* about recommended action. What is the client asking for? Is it within the department's power to help – either directly or indirectly? Should he be referred elsewhere? Are there aspects of risk which require legally supported decisions? Is he likely to become a long-term case or will this be the only contact?

Curnock and Hardiker (1979) argue that the assessment process follows, or should follow, a set pattern:

1. The social worker will be involved in a *complex process of interpersonal communication,*

usually within the context of an interview. In order to handle this, she must prepare herself carefully for both the setting and the purpose of the meeting, and try to anticipate how the client will react to the occasion. It isn't just a question of gathering facts; it is more a matter of trying *to make sense of* a particular person's problems or behaviour in relation to his unique social environment – and that demands real skill in the worker.

2. In relating the circumstances of the client's position to his personal and social strengths and stresses, the social worker must be able to individualise the situation and see it in the perspective of her own department. Can she respond to the client's situation, given the reality of her agency base?

3. The most critical stage involves the drawing up of a balance sheet of relevant variables which can be defined as *risk, need and resources.* Will the *risk* of keeping a client in the community be too great? Does the client have *needs* which the department can satisfy from its own *resources*? (If this formula is applied to the Robinson case, it will be recognised that the social worker's frustration derived from the fact that, while living in their own house, the family had their needs satisfied and made few demands on state resources. The social worker's assessment of risk was, however, out of step with that made by the neighbours whose judgment carried greater weight with the district council. After the Robinsons' eviction, the social services department quickly decided that the family had been put at *risk* by being made homeless, had *needs* which the department was authorised to meet, and that, at least in the short run, there were *resources* available to cover the cost.)

4. Having reached a conclusion, the social worker will normally share her findings with the client, and either communicate the assessment to the people who asked for it – a committee, a court, a team leader, a doctor – or decide whether to act herself.

5. When the report has been completed and presented, the assessment process ends. It may or may not lead on to intervention.

The skills required in assessment are slowly acquired through training and experience: some are generic and relate to the process of interviewing, observation and analysis; others are specific to different client-groups.

The assessment of young children

In child care, the Department of Health has accepted the responsibility of laying down specific requirements in the assessment process. In 1988 it published its 'Orange Book' which, for the first time in the United Kingdom, spelt out the information which social workers must obtain as an integral part of forward case planning.

Social workers are required to carry out detailed assessments of children and their family circumstances so that they can make long-term plans designed to protect the child and help the family. The comprehensive assessment must be carried out in a structured and time-limited fashion, and must provide a clear picture of:

- the nature of the cause(s) for concern about the child;
- the child's physical and emotional development, health and personality, highlighting any problems;
- the composition of the family, and its stage in the family life cycle;
- the financial resources and physical environment available to the family;
- each parent's background, personality, attitudes, strengths and problems;
- family interactions, including the couple's relationship with each other and with the child(ren), with particular attention being paid to their ability to meet the child(ren)'s needs;
- the nature of the child's and family's networks of relatives, friends, and links with professional or other organisations;
- the factors which appear to have led to the cause(s) for concern;
- the parents' degree of acceptance of responsibility for the concerns about their child, their wish to bring about change and their ability to do so;
- the help the family will require and the likely time-scale needed for changes to occur. (Department of Health 1988)

When the child is away from home, and in foster care or a residential setting, social workers continue to have a responsibility for monitoring the quality of the care provided and the progress of the child when measured against 'normal' criteria. In 1991, following major research analysis by Professor Roy Parker at the University of Bristol, the Department of Health published detailed outlines of questions to be asked when assessing and planning action in respect of children of different ages. The seven topics listed, with examples given from the schedule designed to be used with children aged 3–4, are:

Health: Are routine immunisations up to date?

Education: Can the child's speech be understood by people outside the immediate family?

Identity: Does the child have contact with other adults or children who come from the same ethnic background?

Family and social relationships: Does the principal carer show physical affection to the child?

Social presentation: Is the child appropriately dressed?

Emotional and behavioural development: Does the child suffer from eating problems?

Self-care skills: Can the child dress/undress itself?

Of course, such an assessment requires special skills in communicating with children of all ages, and these qualities indicate the need for specialist practitioners. The Department of Health (1988) emphasises the importance of planning sessions beforehand; of being scrupulously honest and not giving the child false assurances about the future; and of using activities appropriate to the child's age: books, dolls, puppets and drawing materials.

The assessment of older people for community care

Under the NHS and Community Care Act 1990, accurate and effective assessment is seen as the key to the provision of an efficient system of care for older people in need. Social services departments are required to provide up-to-date information on how people can obtain a service and to tell them how to complain if they are dissatisfied with the process or its outcome.

A care manager (who may be a social worker) is required to carry out an assessment in every case. The assessment procedures are based on the needs of the client, and they take account of the wishes both of the user and the carer. The outcome of the assessment must be shared with all those concerned in it.

Smale and Tuson (1993) have suggested that users and carers can best be empowered by an assessment process which is based on a system of 'exchange' between them and the worker. They argue that this is preferable to a more traditional 'questioning' approach in which the professional is assumed to be the expert in identifying need. In the exchange model, it is assumed that the professional, the user and the carer all have equally valid perceptions of the problems facing the client and can contribute significantly to their solution, and hence to the assessment.

Smale and Tuson's exchange model of community care assessment means that the professional and the service users share information: the professional explains all the service options and the department's procedures; the service users explain their situation and their perceptions of the problems and suggest possible solutions. Eventually, all three parties arrive at a mutual understanding of the situation and of what might be done to advance it in a helpful direction.

Smale and Tuson's exchange model assumes that people are experts in themselves; it is based on the idea that the worker has expertise in the process of problem-solving; and it aims to arrive at an optimum outcome within the constraints of available resources and the willingness of all parties to contribute.

The 1990 Act introduced no new services, and, once an assessment is made, the care manager, the user and the carer will turn their attention to the next steps. These may involve admission to residential care, the preparation of a comprehensive community care plan, or more modest usage of the home help scheme, meals on wheels or attendance at a day centre. In any case, the care manager who has made the assessment will not be responsible for the provision of the service, for one of the principal consequences of the 1990 Act is that assessment and service provision have been irredeemably separated – with the local authority distinguishing clearly between its 'purchasing' role and the 'provision' of the service. The service may well be provided by the voluntary or private sector, though local authority 'provider' departments continue to operate alongside the independent agencies.

Objectives

Traditionally social workers have operated with relatively vague, even grandiose, objectives: 'to improve social functioning in the client's family', 'to show him that crime doesn't pay', 'to improve her self-image'. Following criticisms of such imprecise good intentions from both inside and outside the profession, the current tendency is to move towards greater specificity of goals. For example, Sheldon (1977) argues that it is not sufficient simply to run a group because of a vague interest in doing so: you have to have some idea of what the group is intended to achieve for its members, and how best to set about achieving it with maximum efficiency. Of course, it is easier to make such an assertion than to pursue it, and much depends on whether and how social work's objectives in general are clarified. They may, for example, quite legitimately include a broad commitment to provide a form of oversight or continuing care which might, under agreed circumstances, not merely justify but require the provision of relatively unstructured visits or interviews.

A research overview (Reid and Hanrahan 1982) confirms the position. The most successful social work interventions occur when the practice structure is clearly defined, when there is a specific problem-focus, when personal behaviour patterns or social skills are identified as targets for attention, and above all when behavioural contracting is used at the heart of the relationship. The best results are likely to be achieved when precise goals are set. For example, a behavioural contracting approach proved highly effective with the families of children who had been removed into foster care: the children came home sooner, and family interaction problems were alleviated.

Contracts

Although Smale and Tuson's (1993) exchange model of assessment is an attempt to empower the service user, the traditional notion of *assessment* is generally taken to emphasise inequality in the social work relationship: the social worker has the responsibility of sitting in judgment upon the client, who may not always even know, let alone agree with, the social worker's arguments and conclusions. All too often the identification of objectives has also been carried out unilaterally by the social worker, even to the extent of indulging in *goal displacement*. Sheldon (1977) talks of this as 'an occupational hazard of some importance', and illustrates it by referring to the woman client who didn't know she had a marital problem when she came to ask about a telephone for her disabled husband. The social worker, unable to supply any telephone, was nevertheless willing and eager to engage in a therapeutic relationship with the client, and so focused on the next most relevant topic – the difficulties of living with a handicapped partner. 'This is all right providing we are sure that we have a real problem in hand; one more pressing than some of the others on the caseload, more urgent than the task of joining in the effort to provide more resources – such as telephones.'

But its 'all rightness' also depends upon the agreement of the woman that it is a legitimate area for discussion, something which, if only to achieve ventilation, she is happy to talk about. If such agreement is not obtained, we are back in the world of *clashed perspectives*, in which the social worker's endeavours may be not only irrelevant to the client but also seen as an intrusive impertinence.

It is largely with a view to avoiding this error that recent years have seen the emergence of enthusiastic support for contracts in social work: the idea that worker and client shall make an explicit agreement to work towards clearly defined goals. As Corden (1980) points out, the presence of a contractual element in social work practice is not new. 'Hamilton (1951) emphasised the responsibility of the worker to make explicit the conditions and terms upon which help could be made available, and Perlman (1957) wrote that "it is the business of forming a pact that is the basis of an ongoing productive partnership between the client and the agency".' Many probation officers have, for decades, required their new probationers to sign the probation order indicating their understanding of its terms and their willingness to conform to the objectives outlined.

The new dimension derives from the emphasis on reciprocity in the contractual relationship between social worker and client, although as we have already seen and shall see again, such reciprocity is not without its problems and its ambiguities. The best summary of contracts is provided by Reid and Epstein (1972);

> The major function of the contract is to ensure that the practitioner and client have a shared understanding of the purposes and content of treatment. The contract is formed at the beginning of service and, unless both parties agree to changing it, serves to guide the course of service. ... Use of contracts helps to avoid certain perennial problems in social work practice: misunderstandings between worker and client as to the nature of the former's intentions and the latter's difficulty; lack of clarity on the part of both as to what they are to do together; drift and scatter in the focus of treatment. ... If a client is unsure of what he wants from the social worker, then perhaps the first order of business should be to assist him in achieving some sense of direction in using help. Most important, use of contracts with the unmotivated or uncertain client provides some assurance that he will not be treated 'behind his back' for conditions that have not been made clear to him.

There are three special attractions of a contractual approach in social work: it encourages honesty in the working relationship; it encourages the explicit identification of some focus for action; and it encourages an element of reciprocity in the exchanges between worker and client.

Honesty   Rees (1974) recounts an appalling case in which the social worker, without the explicit agreement of her client, Mr S. – a single father of a family of three, out at work each day for 12 hours from six o'clock in the morning – placed in his house a young 'housekeeper' with two children of her own. The client disagreed with the proposal, but 'not forcefully'. Mr S.'s mother, who rarely saw her son, told the social worker she thought it was a good idea. There were problems of overcrowding and money; the children fought, and the housekeeper's husband came round wanting his children back. 'In spite of the social worker's clarity about her goals and the amount of time she put into the case, she seldom saw Mr S. let alone discussed with him the rationale for her actions.' This case, in which the social worker surely used her powers of discretion wholly inappropriately, could not have followed such a course if the client's written agreement had been required, and if the respective contributions from the various participants had been more carefully spelt out.

Focus   Although precision is not essential in contracts – there is nothing to prevent agreements being drawn up in general terms – there is little doubt that the use of a contractual approach is likely to encourage greater specificity in identifying objectives. Indeed, the use of contracts in the context of task-centred work requires as much.

Reciprocity   It is in the area of reciprocity that the emergence of contracts is both most exciting and yet also most problematic. Take, for example, the case quoted by Salmon in Reid and Epstein (1972):

> In respect of a single mother, whose children were taken into care, a contractual agreement was drawn up between her and the social worker. The mother agreed to:
>
> 1.   secure a stable job;
> 2.   secure and maintain a flat suitable for her and the children;
> 3.   visit the children (in foster care) regularly;
> 4.   set aside some money each month to be used for the children's needs on their return home. (This condition replaced one which required the mother to contribute to their keep in the council's care.)
> 5.   keep the agency abreast of any change in her situation.
>
> The worker agreed to:
> 1.   regularly discuss and evaluate progress in achieving tasks;
> 2.   recommend return of custody to the mother if tasks were achieved and maintained for six months;
> 3.   arrange visiting schedules with children in the foster home.

The case ended successfully, and the client said that she especially appreciated the openness and honesty of the system: 'This was the first time she'd known what the agency expected her to do before she got her children back.' But supposing, in the course of the six months, that the mother had set up a marital association in the flat with a man thought to be wholly unsuitable as a stepfather (perhaps with recent convictions for child molesting, for example)?-The terms of the contract would not have allowed the social worker to take this into account; she would have had to renege on the agreement and the client would have had no means of enforcing it. Corden (1980) comments that 'the justification for a contractual model must be grounded in values rather than in claims about its therapeutic effects', and those values are based on the notion of self-determination for the client and the humane tradition of the social work profession. But we have already seen that self-determination is something of an illusion. If contracts are to become a daily part of the social work scene, then their wording must never go beyond what the social worker knows she can deliver, and machinery must be set up which would enable clients to seek recompense in the event of the worker failing to fulfil her part of the bargain. If this were not to be done, social work contracts would be rapidly seen as another example of fine intentions with no substance.

The contractual approach must begin from an explicit recognition of the inequality that is inherent in the social work relationship. Corden suggests that many clients would welcome an element of reciprocity, and it seems likely that they would not be unrealistic in their expectations of the social worker. Rather than promising to make certain decisions in what must always be an unknowable future, it would probably be wiser practice for the social worker's share of the contract to restrict itself to a commitment of specified forms of help in the immediate future – with further commitments to be renegotiated as time goes by and the relationship develops. In this way, a contract can take due account of the client's preference for short-term concrete services and the worker can avoid becoming overcommitted to long-term service deliveries that may be rendered unobtainable by unforeseen events in the environment.

Who then determines the action?

Clients are not by any means totally powerless. The residents of a residential home, for instance, can have important effects on the lives of staff and the atmosphere of an institution. Any client in the community can influence the nature of the interactions that occur between him and the social worker by the style and intensity of his response. And just occasionally, a client can make a lasting impact on the social worker by his strength of personality, his courage in the face of adversity or even his friendship. But the trend of evidence is otherwise undeniable: the social work relationship is an unequal relationship, it is necessarily and irreversibly so. The client is the petitioner or the recipient; the social worker is the potential or actual giver or restrainer. The client is the object of the social worker's attentions, the social worker the subject of the client's hopes or fears.

It is because of this inequality in the relationship that the obligations carried by the social worker are an essential part of her professional identity: the social worker *must* involve the client in his own self-development as much as possible; she *must* make her own objectives explicit; she *must* be honest in explaining to the client how she is assessing him and his situation; she *must* be frank about the nature of the responsibilities implicit in the social work role. One of the major attractions in the idea of contract work is that it compels just such honesty; it demonstrates to the client that he is not a non-person, an object to be used, a recipient of aid only according to the worker's whim or the agency's arbitrary powers of discretion.

Problems can undoubtedly arise, however, when the client is both vulnerable and difficult – especially in the case of a child or an adult who is essentially unlikeable and dependent. The story of Graham Gaskin (MacVeigh 1982) highlights the abuses that can still be inflicted on people like him – brutality in foster care, regimentation and fear in residential care, the facelessness of professionals, homosexual exploitation by a voluntary social worker and rejection by the social services department at the age of 16. True, he was full of violence and hatred from an early age, but the statutory child care system must be designed to cope with such characteristics without presuming the inevitability of failure. If it is not doing so, then constant efforts must be made to improve it. In view of this, the development of children's rights' groups can only be good for the system, and — albeit perhaps painfully — good for social work. At least they serve to remind us all that, because of our privileged position, we are under a permanent obligation always to strive for the highest possible standards of professional performance.

In conclusion, then, the social worker determines the action, but in doing so strives for a negotiated relationship between all parties, and, above all, aims to reach some kind of balance between the client and the state. In that sense the role of the worker is that of an arbiter and can only be sustained if she retains the confidence of both sides — and other interested parties. Such a role allows for maximum flexibility in regard to many different types of client and many different styles of supervision: in this way the label 'social work' can satisfactorily be applied both to the exercise of restrictive control over a high-risk parolee and to the encouragement of a radical self-help group among single mothers. In each, the goal of maintenance is sustainable.

11 Speech: The social worker's basic tool

Where does social work take place? The only accurate answer is 'anywhere': in an old peoples' home; beside a hospital bed; in the client's kitchen or bedsit; in a prison cell; in a child guidance clinic playroom; in an office – sometimes warm and comfortable, often not. In all such settings the social worker has to strive for professionalism and maximum effectiveness. So she does, too, in detached or transitory locations: a children's play area, a park bench or coffee-bar, a pub or youth club, the streets of a housing estate or the 18th-floor balcony of a high-rise apartment block, travelling in a car (taking a child to a children's home, for example, or a woman to visit her husband in prison) or working with a group of young people on an adventure trip.

No matter what the setting, no matter what the focus, the greater part of social work hinges on the nature and quality of relationships between workers and clients; and the basic tool in such relationships, particularly in the initial stages, consists of verbal contributions by the worker and verbally expressed reactions by her to the client. Group work and community work have ostensibly broadened the range of social work settings beyond the traditional twosome or dyad of the therapeutic interview, but even they make considerable use of verbal exchanges: 'You spend so much time just talking to people,' says one community worker.

Hence the continuing importance of the interview. The interview, rather like religion, has traditionally been subjected to eulogy or obloquy, depending upon the perspective of the critic, but, despite doubts about its effectiveness as a mode of bringing about behavioural change, it seems likely always to remain an integral and essential part of social work practice. Its value only comes into question at times when theorists argue or practitioners act on the assumption that the interview is *an end in itself*. In medicine, interviewing is an aid to diagnosis; in personnel management, an aid to recruitment; in commerce, an aid to selling. The social work interview is not normally different from these, although we have recognised that relief from tension can be achieved through counselling.

The interview can take a great many forms and the social worker is likely to have as many verbal exchanges with non-clients as with clients. (Indeed, as we saw in the last chapter, the question of *who* the client is, is not as straightforward as is usually assumed.) Telephone calls and visits to landladies, to social security offices, to employers or potential employers, to debt-collecting agencies and hire-purchase firms, to the police and to doctors or psychiatrists: all are usually made in an attempt to persuade the interviewee to adopt a sympathetic attitude towards the social worker's client, to moderate a punitive response, to consider giving help, to provide necessary information, or to delay threatening action. Such occasions are, thus, in a very real sense, 'conversations with a purpose', which is the traditional definition of an interview. They have a beginning, a middle and an end, and the social worker must approach them with professional seriousness. All interviews can be subjected to review as Banaka (1971) has suggested:

1. What was the *input*? What questions were raised? What answers were given?
2. How should the input be *analysed*? What inferences could one make about the input – including non-verbal behaviour – during the interview?
3. What is the *output*? What is the end product? What are the conclusions to be drawn at the end of the interview?

It is a worthwhile principle to adopt in social work that no meeting should take place, no interview be held, unless an output is intended. The hoped-for end product may not always be achieved, of course; but, if it is not, some thought should always be given to the reasons for the failure (Redford and Goodenough 1979).

Social work interviews are by no means always plain sailing, and although the apprehensions of those new to the job are sometimes exaggerated, the practitioner certainly has to know how to react to and cope with verbal aggression, threats of violence, tears, total silence or more bizarre behaviour. The necessary skills for dealing with difficult clients and situations can only be properly learnt by simulation or role-play, by observation of the interviewing process through video or a one-way screen, and ultimately through personal experience. But fundamentally the rules are:

1. To combine flexibility in relations with the client with a clear understanding of the agency's goal.
2. To be honest about the boundaries of reality: if, for example, a child has been taken into care against the parents' wishes and on your recommendation, the only realistic strategy is to be frank but sympathetic, and to attempt to persuade the family to look forward to and plan for a happier future.
3. To recognise that, in difficult situations, the agency expects you to retain control of the interview and the professional identity demands that you do so with real sensitivity to the client's feelings. Angry people will not always stay angry; utter desolation can lead to suicide, but it can also be reversed; psychotic extremes are deeply disturbing, but treatment is often possible and relief can usually be given; tears can be distressing but they may be the key to an honest discussion about underlying problems.

Difficult interviews, then, cannot be avoided in social work. They demand adaptability, gentle strength and resilience in the worker, and these are the characteristics of professional expertise.

The skills of the interviewer

The art of interviewing, like the art of acting, of public speaking or of tactical politics, is dependent on the development of a personal style. No Hamlet, St Joan or Willy Loman is ever quite the same as any other; and the stalwart clients on any agency caseload are similarly aware that every social worker is different – sometimes very different – from all the others. Age, sex, ethnic identity and personality: all are inevitably a part of the interviewer's style. But there are nevertheless a number of established principles which should only be varied as experience brings with it the confidence to employ more idiosyncratic, more risky methods – and even then this should never be done without good reason.

Jamieson (1978) has listed ten principles of interviewing which provide the new social worker with useful guidelines for practice. They are not absolute assertions of what is right or wrong, but they have evolved over the years, and have been passed on by word of mouth and the written page from experienced interviewers to newcomers. The following is an abbreviated and amended version of Jamieson's principles:

1. Try to tell the interviewee how much time is available for the interview. 'No specific time is optimum, though five minutes is probably too short and over an hour too long.'
2. Start where the client is. Explain to him why he is being seen, or, if he asked to see you, ask him why.
3. Try to have sympathy for the client, however unsympathetic a person he may be. The aim must be to make the client relaxed and unafraid.
4. Try to have empathy with the client – to see things through his eyes.
5. Do not be judgmental or condemnatory. Try to show acceptance and tolerance.
6. Smile on first acquaintance. This may help the client to communicate more freely.
7. Do not ask questions that can be answered simply 'yes' or 'no'.
8. Do not put answers into the client's mouth. 'I don't suppose you've ever hurt your child, have you?' is a forcing prompt that clearly reflects the interviewer's perspective and that would make it almost impossible for the interviewee to talk about his feelings, let alone his actions. Ask neutral open-ended questions.
9. On the other hand, it is inappropriate to probe too deeply too quickly in an interviewing relationship, and it is wrong to probe deeply at all unless there is a clear purpose in doing so. Even then, the interviewer should only do so if she has the requisite skill to cope with the responses, and if there is sufficient time to return the client to a normal level of conversational reality afterwards.

10. Don't be afraid of silences when the client is thinking his way forward. But don't prolong silences when to do so would be felt as an uncomfortable and even aggressive act on the part of the interviewer.

Interviews are free-flowing, open events: their direction is never wholly predictable, and the interviewer's contribution can never be accurately programmed. An American psychiatrist, Richard Bealka, has demonstrated how many variations there can be in the counsellor's response to even the most common statement of fact or feeling. He uses a hypothetical situation in which a young client says, I don't get along with my parents', and suggests that there are numerous responses that can be made by the worker, all equally suitable and all fulfilling the two important requirements of a successful interview: they allow the client to express his feelings, and they help the counsellor to direct the interview. Bealka's suggested responses are these:

- You don't get along with your parents.
- Your parents?
- What do you mean when you say ...
- I don't understand what you mean when you say ...
- Help me understand what you mean ...
- Give me an example of how you ..
- Tell me more about it.
- Mmm – and? – For instance? – Go on.
- Oh? – but ... I see.
- When did you first notice that ...
- How do you feel about it? (Perhaps the most important question one could ask.)
- What are some of the things you and your parents disagree about?
- What are some problems young people like you have – not just you but all young people in general?
- What are your parents like? What is your dad like? What is your mum like? (General questions.)
- You seem to be very upset about this.
- You look worried. You look unhappy.
- You say you have trouble getting along with your parents. What are some of your troubles?
- Perhaps you could share some of your ideas about what has caused these problems. (It probably never helps to ask the question 'why'. If they knew why they were having trouble with their parents, they wouldn't be seeing you.)
- Maybe it would help to talk about it.
- Compared with you, what type of people are your parents?
- If your parents were here, what would they say about the problem?

(Reproduced, by permission, with minor amendments from material developed by Dr Richard J. Bealka, psychiatrist, Mental Health Institute, Independence, Iowa, USA; and published in Beulah R. Compton and Burt Galaway, *Social Work Processes*, Dorsey, Illinois, 1975.)

Contexts for interviewing

There are three prime contexts for interviewing clients in social work which can be characterised as a meeting of strangers, structured approaches and long-term relationships.

The meeting of strangers

The single interview as an event in itself, or a single interview followed by a strictly limited number of additional meetings but not leading to a developing relationship between client and worker, is what concerns us here.

As we saw in chapter 9, all social services departments are now accustomed to handling a large number of callers every day: many have never been before, and many will never come again. Some have suggested that social workers are not as geared up as they need to be to deal with this persistent bombardment of enquirers and advice-seekers, but most agencies have gradually come to terms with the demand. It is certainly important that they *should* do so, because of the continuing need for a walk-in service where clients are guaranteed a friendly response to the myriad problems they come up against in their dealings with statutory authorities, welfare organisations and the wider community. Whether such a facility is ideally located in a local authority department, which is itself one of the parties most frequently complained about by clients, is a moot point. But that was certainly the intention of the Seebohm Report, it is the way it has worked out, and whether the staff are paid or voluntary, social workers or ancillaries, Jamieson's principles of interviewing apply with full force. In addition, three single-interview principles can be added:

1. Have a full range of relevant information to hand – a knowledge of welfare rights, of local resources and of the law directly relevant to social work. Be efficient.
2. Know and be known by your referral routes. If the client would *definitely* be better off somewhere else – in the housing department, at the social security or unemployment office, at a solicitor's or the probation office – tell him so, make an introductory phone call, and perhaps send a letter of accompaniment.
3. Whenever possible, *do* something. A friendly deed, an indication of your concern, a recognition of the client's vulnerability: these are worth far more than *just* a smile – and a referral on.

The structured approach

Coincidentally with the creation and growth of large-scale social services departments in the United Kingdom, a major development in social work theory has taken place: the recognition that social work needs structure if it is to be realistically implemented. The origins of this realisation can be plotted historically in the casework literature and are well summarised by Smalley (1970): in social work practice 'too little form or absence of form can waste effort and lead to purposelessness, disorganisation, confusion, amorphousness, or outright chaos'. This view represents a reaction against the time-consuming and often meandering work of psychoanalytically inclined caseworkers of an earlier generation, and it emerged initially in two ways.

First, it was argued that structure should be determined by the nature of the agency within which social work was practised, and that indeed social work could not be divorced from the requirements and expectations of that agency. Second, Perlman (1970) developed the idea of social work as *problem-solving*, in which an important first step was to *partialise* the goals and the areas for emphasis.

> The idea of partialisation is simply cutting a dilemma down to its size ... Particularly in work with those who today are central to social work's concern – the economically and educationally deprived, the hard-to-reach, the nonintrospective, long-and-chronically deprived persons, the crisis-prone and crisis-ridden – a nearby, reachable, easily imagined goal is the only one that has reality. And though the goal may be as material as getting and using money aid, or as practical as gaining re-entry into school for the drop-out, the rudimentary steps of problem-solving may be involved and taken by client and caseworker. (Perlman 1970)

From these beginnings, three forms of structured intervention have emerged – each demanding of the interviewer a technically correct approach to the client and his situation.

1.   Crisis intervention   Crisis intervention techniques grew up independently of casework theory in the field of psychiatry, but they were eagerly taken up by social workers who saw their applicability to the client in a distressed state. The goals of crisis intervention are to counteract the effects of a crisis, to relieve the symptoms of emotional pain, and to restore the client to a state of being able to function normally. One of the many areas in which crisis intervention has been employed is in counselling the bereaved, and Lindemann has argued persuasively that the crisis of bereavement can best be overcome if the worker helps the client to do his 'grief work': 'to emancipate himself from the bondage of the deceased, to make a readjustment to the environment in which the deceased is missing, and to form new relationships and patterns of interaction that bring rewards and satisfactions' (Rapaport 1970). Such a problem-focused approach is said to be likely to achieve a healthy resolution of the crisis.

In recent years, local authority social workers have found themselves, from time to time, drawn into the aftermath of major disasters, and Brook (1990) has argued that the theory of crisis intervention is especially appropriate to such situations. It has three components. 'The first is listening – taking account of the need victims will have to express feelings and recount their experience. The second is to find practical ways of helping victims accept what has happened to them. Accompanying them to the scene of the event, as was done after the Bradford and Hillsborough [football ground] disasters, is a useful experience; as is encouraging the bereaved, if they are able, to view the bodies of their loved ones, as happened after the Zeebrugge Ferry sinking. Thirdly, in view of the limitations of the social worker's other role, help may be needed in making contact with other resources such as voluntary agencies or support groups.'

2. *Task-centred casework* Due primarily to the influence of William J. Reid, task-centred approaches have found a ready audience since they emerged out of an experiment which showed that a structured form of short-term service in a voluntary agency secured superior results when compared with conventional open-ended casework (Reid and Shyne 1969). The attractions of these unusually positive research findings and an apparently more economical approach to social work were, not surprisingly, too much for many agencies to resist.

> Task-centred casework is a structured approach to the process of working with clients. The essential elements of the structuring are the use of a short time limit, the selection of a target problem from the problems presented, the use of tasks to work towards the alleviation of the target problem, and the negotiation between client and social worker on the time limit, target problem and tasks. (Butler et at. 1978)

The definition of *problems* can be, and often is, as broad as 'the marital relationship', but *tasks* have to be selected which are highly specific. For example, to improve communications between husband and wife:

(a)   to spend ten minutes alone each evening talking about the children;
(b)   using hands to communicate feelings;
(c)   using more physical contact, with no expectation of sexual intercourse;
(d)   Mr H. to try and take Mrs H. out;
(e)   Mrs H. to moderate her aggressive tone.
(Butler et al., 1978)

The task-centred approach has, to some extent, suffered from social work's tendency to become too ambitious in its objectives. Task-centred studies have shown that the technique brings focus to the worker's approach, and, if properly contracted, is appreciated by the client: it makes sense, it is practical and it demonstrates a degree of professional expertise that is valued by the recipient of the service. Goldberg and Connelly (1981) put it this way: 'We have proceeded from vague and global objectives, such as more adequate social functioning or greater ego strength, to more specific, operationally definable behaviours or feelings. So far, so good.' But, bearing in mind the failure of task-centred experiments in the United Kingdom to achieve major behavioural changes, they acknowledge that 'when the aim is the achievement of more complex behavioural changes, such as non-repetition of self-poisoning or decrease in delinquent behaviour, then the results remain disappointing'.

Nonetheless, task-centred practice has gained ground in British social work, and its advocates argue that it 'is a doing model where learning will be as likely to occur by demonstration as by discussion. It is a participative model, where the client should be as fully informed and as fully involved as possible.' Moreover, it is presented as a politically correct approach to practice: 'It promotes a partnership between the workers and the user of the service ...; it makes explicit issues of power in social work relationships and, as Coulshed (1988) writes, the task-centred approach is the one most favoured by those who are trying to devise models for ethnic-sensitive practice. By confronting issues of power directly and by coming clean about the use of professional authority, in a modest way it promotes anti-oppressive practice' (Doel and Marsh 1992).

3.   *Behaviour modification*   Again with their origins outside social work – this time in psychology – behaviourist methods have been employed by a small number of practising social workers, more especially in the fields of mental health and residential child care where behaviourism's particular contribution has been to emphasise the importance of consistency and reliability in rewarding good behaviour and punishing bad. Hudson (1978) and Holbrook (1978) have described experiments in which the parents of child patients in the community have been involved in behaviourally determined programmes of rehabilitation. The results, though mixed, are sufficiently encouraging to make the model worth pursuing. One problem is that the approach can be quite expensive in the use of staff time in the community, but the frequently quoted advantage is that it is totally subject to evaluation. The objective is spelt out clearly; the method pre-defined, and the end product always measurable.

The principles have been specially utilised in 'portage' schemes in which the parents of mentally handicapped children are trained by social workers and health visitors to employ structured methods in order to further their child's development. 'The programme is based on an analysis of the steps in child development and uses a behaviour modification model. ... [The social worker] regularly visits the family, provides activity charts in those areas where the child is more retarded and helps the parents to plot their child's progress ... The centre of attention is on the achievement of carefully defined and clearly understood goals.' Hanvey (1981: 40) concludes that the approach 'provides a model of social work which seeks to work *with* rather than *for* those for whom help is sought'.

The present and future of structured approaches   'In the midst of vagueness, there is precision; in a turbulent world, there is form.' That is the creed which makes the use of structure potentially so attractive to some social workers. However, in her study of contemporary practice Browne (1978) records that very few use any of these approaches on a day-to-day basis. Even when they do so, the terminology is often not understood, the theories not employed and the structure imprecise. ' "Crisis work" was often used to describe a crisis for the worker or the agency,' she says – not at all what Caplan, Lindemann or Rapaport had in mind!

Structured models, or others derived from them, not only require the worker to understand the methods and to be explicit in her aims. They depend for their success on a stable work-setting in which the practitioner is sufficiently trusted by her superiors to operate both according to agency guidelines and in the client's best interests; they require the ready availability of adequate resources of space and time, energy and initiative, and they also depend on the suitability of the clients presenting for help. One conclusion of Butler's is reminiscent of an earlier research finding: 'The social worker is best able to make a good relationship with those who appear to need least help' (Davies 1969). Butler *et al.* (1978) says:

> At times the [task-centred casework] structure was not adhered to through lack of practice of the practitioner, at other times this was because of the nature of the client's situation. The method seems easier to apply in situations where the presenting problems are fewer in number and where the client is in a secure situation from the point of view of relationships and accommodation, and where the client is a relatively stable person.

Those who have sought to summarise research findings in social work have, however, reinforced the significance of structure as a key to success.

> Time-limited, problem-specific approaches emerge as desirable in many areas ... It may become increasingly difficult to justify practice approaches of a long-term nature, given the attitude of many organisations towards cost-effectiveness. Each social work practitioner must resist the temptation to be 'all things to all men' ... If the objective of social work intervention is to produce the greatest change for the client, then it appears that workers who develop time-limited approaches that are planned and applied to specific problems have an advantage. (Thomlinson 1984)

In the United Kingdom, social workers remain somewhat sceptical of these encouraging noises. On the one hand, it is by no means clear whether structured approaches can ever constitute more than a small part of the total 'maintenance model' of statutory practice; on the other, the theoretical vacuum of recent years has meant that little has been done to prepare practitioners for structured methods. In any end-of-term report, their use in statutory settings still deserves to be regarded as 'promising' rather then 'convincing', and their eventual successful employment depends on greater clarity about their place in the scheme of things and on the development of more sophisticated practitioner skills. Whether they will ever completely replace long-term work with all clients seems much more doubtful than is claimed by those American writers used to concentrating on therapy rather than maintenance − although Thorpe's (1982) damaging claims about the potential for harm in compensatory facilities like intermediate treatment have reinforced the argument for structure, specificity and a focus on limited problem-solving.

The long-term relationship

Traditionally the principles of interviewing and the use of structured techniques are primarily employed with short-term clients. But all social workers − or at least all social work agencies − have responsibility for clients who are in contact with them for periods of time extending from three months up to a virtually unlimited number of years. The family service unit works with families over generations. Probation officers frequently supervise offenders for two or three years and work with recidivists through probation orders, young offender after-care licences, and thence into prison and beyond – such a client may know far more about penal system social work than many a newly trained recruit to the service; local authorities, as well as sometimes taking on FSU-type families, also carry extended obligations to the handicapped, the elderly-at-risk, children in care and others. In the residential sector, Miller and Gwynne (1972) point out how, in a hostel for the chronically sick and disabled, the residents – or some of them – stay on 'for ever' while the staff come and go on a semi-temporary basis.

In such situations, the relevance of any one interview can be muted (although Sainsbury (1975) remarks on how FSU clients always seem to remember their *first* ever contact). What is of far greater force in long-term cases is the overall relationship between client and worker, or between client and agency. And each such relationship is undeniably unique. Consider two examples.

1.   Arthur and Jenny and the mounting debts   Arthur Silsden was 19 and on probation. Two years before his court appearance he had married Jenny, hugely pregnant and very nervous. Arthur found the responsibilities of being a husband and father all too much. He had made one suicide attempt in the face of increasing debts, and, when things got on top of him, he took to drink or his bed or both. Jenny, at the time of Arthur's court appearance, was also on probation and was living 20 miles away in a mother-and-baby home, called Sun-View, with a view to learning housecraft and domestic skills.

Mr Rowland, the probation officer, hoped that he might get Arthur to recognise and accept his marital responsibilities, and he spent a lot of time talking with him about this. He also tried to help him budget his finances, and combatted an attempt by the housing department to gain possession of the council house for non-payment of rent.

After three months, Mrs Forbes-Willoughby, the matron of Sun-View, telephoned Mr Rowland and complained that Arthur, instead of sending money to pay for Jenny's keep, was spending it in the betting shop; she said that she'd asked Arthur to stay away from Sun-View for a while because she thought he was a bad influence on his wife. Three days later Arthur phoned Jenny to say that he thought it would be better if they separated, and at this Jenny became very upset. Later that day, Arthur turned up at Sun-View drunk and 'looking rather shaken'. He'd had an accident in a 'borrowed' car, for which he hadn't been licensed or insured; the police intended to prosecute.

Six weeks later Arthur was back in court for non-payment of fines, and Mr Rowland told the bench that he was trying to get Arthur into a job so that he could pay his debts which were now considerable. He hoped that things might get better as Jenny was home again having completed her condition of residence at Sun-View. However, whatever else she'd learnt there, she had not mastered the art of resisting doorstep hire-purchase temptations, a persistent weakness of hers. The Silsdens plunged deeper and deeper into money trouble. Arthur, though, seemed happier, and Mr Rowland felt optimistic. He had had almost daily contact with one or other member of the family for over six months, and he felt he was winning.

The next week, however, the housing department rang Mr Rowland up and told him that the Silsdens were only paying their weekly rent once a fortnight, and that, as a result, arrears were mounting steadily. Mr Rowland went round to the house, and found the rent man there threatening to evict Arthur and Jenny. A day or two later, Mr Rowland, looking down the morning's court-list, saw that Arthur was 'up' again for breaking into the electric meter. When he saw him, he asked him why he hadn't come to discuss the matter with him or even told him that he had broken into the meter, but Arthur just shrugged his shoulders.

2. Marge and Jill and the friendly relationship Margery Hollick describes herself as a suicidal destructive person. At the time of her first contact with the social worker, Jill Ford, she and her husband Reg had three children aged 19, 17 and 14. The youngest had been referred to the child guidance clinic because of problems at school. Mrs Hollick had made attempts at suicide and had been in and out of the local psychiatric hospitals many times, usually discharging herself. She had known numerous psychiatrists, social workers, casualty nurses and other helping persons, and was critical of many of them.

But for the next three years Marge and Jill forged a relationship that became a classical amalgam of friendship and professionalism:

> Without a genuine liking and respect we would never have got off the ground. Unless these had deepened to love and trust we would never have seen it through. On the other hand, we could never have achieved what we did if we had not both been quite clear that I was her social worker and she was my client. ... She knew she had the right to burden me, to make demands on me, because she could trust me to be clear about where the bounds lay.

Marge brought her tensions to the social worker. She came and talked, and they met approximately once a week for three years.

> There were long periods when she came to see me by appointment and we looked at her past and her present and how they connected and what it could mean for her future – both her very immediate future (how she would get through another day) and for the long term. There were other periods when I visited her, also by appointment, for the same purpose.

Jill got to know Margery's family, especially Reg. Sometimes things seemed to be getting worse rather than better, and then both worker and client sensed the value of 'the uniquely personal and the necessity for unwavering professionalism'. Margery came to know that she could take her wrist-slashing fears directly to the worker; she could share her desperation and terror; and the worker could respond to 'the lost child crying within'.

Ford was concerned how she could manage such a commitment of time, and she describes one critical occasion when she had come into the office early one Monday morning in order to clear her desk before a first appointment at 11.30. Her plans were upset when Marge's neighbour phoned saying that they needed the worker's help. 'I did not feel like going ... But I had to go.' The worker carefully considered her feelings, the fact that she had made an open commitment to the client, and the fact that she had to be honest – with both Marge and herself. 'Having sorted it out and made my decision I felt light at heart and optimistic as I drove round to her house ... But the quality of the decision was vital. Unless I could wholly "will", that part of me which did not "will" would be sure to make itself felt.'

An important aspect of the case lay in the worker's implicit faith in the client: 'I always felt we would make headway, that Marge had within her the capacity to move forward, to grow. I also felt she had the will to do so in spite of the despair which overwhelmed, at times, her sense of having the will.'

The case extended the worker's feeling and thinking capacities to the limit. The first helped her to be aware of Margery's depression and despair; the second to make sense of her thoughts and feelings about the past and the present. These capacities enabled Jill, on one occasion when all seemed lost, to find the reserves of spirit and energy to convince the client that a part of her, an important part, did not want to commit suicide. Why otherwise had the client telephoned at the crucial moment?

The relationship continued until the worker left the district, and even then Marge and Jill remained in touch by letter and occasional meetings. 'There were good times,' writes Marge, 'not all was bad, was it? I'm standing on my own feet now, so say a little prayer for me, as I've forgotten how, but that will come in time. All my love, Marge' (Ford and Hollick 1979).

These two cases, each unique, but neither untypical of the contrasting patterns to he found in long-term social work, amply demonstrate the way in which the primacy of the individual interview is submerged in the totality of the relationship. In the case of Arthur and Jenny, the wider systems in which client and worker operated assumed major significance. All the interviews were dominated and gradually swamped by the chaotic turbulence of the clients' life-style and the formal and informal responses which it provoked in those around them. In the case of Marge, the ups and downs were no less marked, and Ford identifies critical events and meetings in the three-year period, but the crucial aspects of the case are to be found in the recurring evidence of trust, empathy, honesty and courage that characterised the working relationship.

Long-term social work covers the spectrum of client types from multi-problem families living in a turbulent field into which the social worker is almost inexorably drawn, to men and women who survive on their own but who, in a civilised society, have a right to expect a degree of continuous support from the community.

The evolution of policy and practice following the implementation of the NHS and Community Care Act 1990 will see a major resource commitment to the provision of long-term care for people with disabilities and their carers. But its approach is intended to be overwhelmingly practical, and the opportunity for extended counselling work within it will be limited.

Curriculum development

Social workers are always interested in new ideas for practice, although many may be sceptical of their efficacy – often rightly so. The achievement of innovation is not hindered by any lack of worker-motivation, but depends on the development of practice models which represent improvements on present routines, are appropriate and ethically acceptable, and are capable of being absorbed by existing settings. A shortage of adequate resources is often a handicap to the introduction of new practices, and it is significant that innovations like intermediate treatment, community service orders and day centres have all been made as a result of administrative and political decisions which ensured the availability of sufficient funds to meet capital and running costs.

Ideas such as sculpting and role-play (both of which require the social worker to persuade clients to play-act personal experiences or fantasies – for example, in respect of marital conflict, child abuse or going for a job interview) and social skills training (which uses behavioural techniques to help clients improve their ordinary social functioning, such as talking to the foreman, overcoming chronic shyness or controlling a bad temper) are emerging as having considerable promise for social work. But significantly, it has always seemed to be easier to employ them in a residential or institutional setting than in the community.

One area for development in community practice that deserves more attention is the writing of *scripts*. Most experienced social workers develop relatively standardised responses to meet recurring needs and informally these are often passed on to younger colleagues: what answers to give to anxious adoptive parents at different stages of the adoption cycle; what approach to use with a man who has just been sentenced to a long term of imprisonment, and how to tell his wife; what to say to a child to reassure him about his forthcoming foster-placement. Obviously every situation *is* unique and every good social worker will develop her own repertoire of intuitive repartee, but there *are* good, bad and dreadful ways of putting things, and it is surprising that social work, which relies so heavily on the spoken word both for its impact and its justification, should not have recognised the value of explicitly making considered judgments on the best ways of coping with frequently repeated themes and queries.

The idea of curriculum development is barely recognised as legitimate in social work, and yet with the investment of increasing resources, not only in team social work, but in group work, day centres and community intervention, it is becoming economically essential for the accumulated experience and wisdom of the profession to be recorded and passed on to each new generation, so that its growth can be cumulative and each new social worker not have to start entirely from scratch.

12 The social worker's use of self

Social workers have almost certainly done their profession a disservice in the eyes of the public by their apparent inability to reach agreement among themselves on the kind and complexity of skills required to do their job well. The problem has, of course, been exacerbated by the continuing willingness of employers to fill social work posts with untrained personnel, a practice which naturally undermines the case that two (or even three) years' training is needed to produce a good practitioner. It is the argument of this book that, although some facets of social work are in need of de-mystification, it nevertheless remains an extremely demanding professional occupation requiring a wide range of roles and functions. I have defined the central task facing social workers in the statutory sector as one of maintenance, but it is also clear that the key to the profession's identity lies in the recognition that what makes something social work is not *what* is done but *how* it is done. *The way in which* individuals are maintained, *the way in which* their interests are represented in society, *the way in which* society's sanctions, restrictions and powers are conveyed to, and imposed upon, individuals are different if carried out according to social work principles. The good social worker must be carefully prepared for every aspect of her normal duties; she must persistently update the knowledge and skill required for their execution; she must employ real sensitivity in all social relationships, and retain an absolute respect for human life in all its forms; she must espouse a fundamentally optimistic view of human nature; and she must always be ready to use the self to reconcile the often conflicting interests of marginal individuals and the state.

American textbooks down the years have all recognised either implicitly or explicitly that the social worker is potentially her own greatest asset (or liability). Perlman (1970), for instance, says that the style of the helper has increasingly come to be recognised as a potent factor in the therapeutic relationship.

> Ideally this 'style' – this spontaneous, honest expression of the self in the role of the professional helper – flows out from the caseworker's real concern and respect for the client, out of his being unafraid, either of the person or his problem, and out of his deep wish to be of maximal help ...

Style – the helper's ways of relating, of drawing out feelings, of responding empathically, of stimulating and guiding thought, of accrediting and affirming, of presenting reality – is utilised not in a free-form, any-sort-of-dialogue-goes-as-long-as-it's-lively way. Rather, it is contained within the structure provided by both the purpose and the process of problem-solving. (Perlman 1970)

Social work is the structure *and* the person, the agency and the worker: without one or the other, it ceases to exist. The self, then, is crucial, and ironically that assertion can be illustrated as well in the work of an untrained family aide as it has traditionally been demonstrated by highly qualified casework intervention.

Grace Batey describes her work with Leslie Wright, a man with learning disabilities in his late 50s, with whom she has been working for three years: 'I was visiting for six hours every week, with the aim of guiding him into patterns of self-help, as far as possible, and with little real knowledge of how to approach mental handicap.' Gradually the family aide became aware of his capabilities and limitations: she showed an interest in the model-kits which he never finished; she coped with his moods, and developed a sensitivity to his apparently irrational reactions to instructions which went beyond his understanding; she accepted his devotion to ritual, and adapted her approach accordingly; she took him shopping, and learnt the importance of his participation in decision-making. He has recurring and painful attacks of haemorrhoids 'which leave him very low. He has an abhorrence of using either suppositories or healing cream. In the beginning he suffered agonies rather than face the embarrassment of bringing it to my notice, but as trust between us grew, he was able to explain that the blood-stained underpants were what worried him most of all. So in order to relieve this anxiety, I took the underwear and washed it myself. Today he has the confidence to let his home help attend to his laundry.' Grace Batey initiated his attendance at a day centre, and got him a bus pass 'which opened up new avenues through travel'. His neighbours care, she says, 'but keep a discreet distance'. He watches television, buys and talks about his uncompleted model kits, and hoards. 'He leans close to the one-to-one relationship, and places great faith in those entrusted with the responsibility of nurturing his growth and development. He responds to kindness with feelings of kindliness ... He is far removed from the Leslie to whom I was introduced three years ago and has struggled hard for his place in the community. Each experience whets his appetite for the next.' (Adapted from Batey 1979.)

Batey makes no claims for her professional skill; on the contrary, she emphasises that she was learning as she went by responding to the client's situation and to his own reactions as they occurred. To wash the client's underpants may not be everyone's idea of a social work tactic, but it was practical, it was tangible and it relieved anxiety. More than that, though, it demonstrated the worker's willingness and ability to understand and empathise with the mundane but stressful realities of a simple man's existence.

There are two sides to the use of self. On the one hand, there is the client's need to recognise an identifiable person, to know her idiosyncrasies, her name, perhaps in psychoanalytic terms to experience a mild transference through seeing in the worker a family figure of some significance, or, as in residential care, to relate to *one key worker* who will remain in evidence despite uprootings from placement to placement and during movement through the system. On the other hand, there is the worker's own acknowledgement of her strengths and weaknesses – her height, her age, her sex, her ethnic origins, her temper, her energy, her prejudices – these are the qualities she has to work with, for better or worse.

Is it possible to specify and agree on those qualities that make for a good practitioner? Compton and Galaway (1975) make a brave attempt, although they sensibly preface their effort by acknowledging that 'it is difficult to discuss "the helping person" because there are almost as many kinds of helpers as there are people who need help ... There is probably no one person who is an ideal helping person, so that each of us will probably lack some of the qualities a helping person should have.' Nevertheless, Compton and Galaway list six qualities which they see as central to effective social work functioning:

1. The enjoyment of being alive: *maturing*, living, growing, developing. The acceptance of change: seeing all people, including oneself, as being involved in problem-solving.
2. Being a nonconformist, *creative*, intellectually open, receptive. Recognising that most solutions to the problems of life are tentative.
3. *Self-awareness*, genuineness: self-knowledge, self-respect, self-confidence.
4. A *desire* to increase peoples' freedom of choice and control over their own lives.
5. The *courage* to confront clients with the reality of their problems, the courage to risk failure in pursuing social work objectives, the courage to cope with unpredictable situations, the courage to face criticism and blame for one's actions.
6. *Sensitivity* to the client's feelings, doubts, fears and movement.

Conversely, they quote Alan Keith-Lucas's claim (1972) that there are four kinds of people who do *not* make good helpers:

1. Those who are interested in knowing about people rather than in serving them (coldly objective students of humanity).
2. Those who are impelled by strong personal needs to control, to feel superior, to be liked.
3. Those who have solved problems similar to those experienced by the people in need of help but who have forgotten what it cost them to do so.
4. Those who are primarily interested in retributive justice and moralising.

How is one to react to what are in effect moral imperatives, or at least subjective assertions about the boundaries of personality-type suitable for social work? Certainly to anyone who has herself practised, who knows other practitioners, who sifts through applications for social work training and then teaches and assesses the chosen few, there is no doubt that some people make better social workers than others. I am happier with Keith-Lucas's negatives than with Compton and Galaway's positives. It is not that the qualities sought are inappropriate, but that, taken together, they add up to a sort of catechism of virtue more suitable for a Comtean sect than for an occupational group employed primarily in the public sector. They outline ideals that are normally unattainable, and it is difficult for such a list to avoid the appearance of prissiness, to the extent that it appears to claim that social workers need to be morally superior to other people – a risky, not to say unrealistic, suggestion that can easily be counterproductive. It might be viewed as arrogant, not only by the general public, but more particularly perhaps by closely related occupational groups – the police, nurses, schoolteachers, the clergy – who, while willing to recognise the special nature of social workers' skills and activities, might be understandably reluctant to view Jo Helper in quite the halo-justifying light that Compton and Galaway's six qualities imply. An unfortunate side-effect of social work's good intentions is that its practitioners can sometimes fall into the trap of thinking that they have a monopoly of virtue – an error quite as characteristic of the politically aware younger generation as it was once of an earlier gathering of ladies bountiful. The truth is that if you walk into an average probation office or social services department, you do not instantly get an impression of high moral virtue – nor indeed would most social workers want you to. All the evidence is that the best social workers, whatever they might have in common with others, do not necessarily have much in common with each other. Some are clinically correct, in the best textbook tradition; some are highly deviant, ploughing a lone furrow but respected for their independence by colleagues and clients alike; some are permissive; some are firm in the use of authority.

The argument for an open-minded approach to social work style, though (I would have thought) self-evidently desirable in a multicultural context, runs counter to the powerful modern trend of demanding a politically correct approach to practice. Led (not to say, brow-beaten and belaboured) by the UK social work training council CCETSW, an anti-discriminatory (or anti-oppressive) emphasis has been made a mandatory requirement of the curriculum in the new Diploma in Social Work courses introduced from 1990. Concern about this requirement has been expressed, not because of doubts about the good intentions of its progenitors, nor because of doubts about the need for social workers always to be alert to the power imbalance in their clients' lives.

The dogmatic insistence on an anti-discriminatory approach to social work has exactly the same flaws as earlier insistences on the 'political correctness' of Freudian theory or of a Marxist analysis: they all fail to take into account the unique need for social work to respond in ways specifically appropriate to each case, each context, each community, and above all in ways that maximise the personal style and the positive qualities of the worker.

There is a strong suspicion that the initiators of each new fashionable wave of 'politically correct' practice, reflecting as most of them do a particular value system or ideology, do not themselves have long personal experience of social work practice. Often they have their career roots in social policy, sociology or psychiatry; and, although they might argue that those disciplines can give them a breadth of vision legitimising their perspective, I believe that none of them can match the effect of real-world social work practice: professional experience always brings the realisation that a doctrinaire approach to the client is rarely appropriate, but that the sensitive and creative use of self – responding to the unique circumstances of each new situation – provides the best hope of bringing about an improvement in peoples' lives.

In the end, it is impossible to be dogmatic about worker-style in social work. But although those with long experience or special ability can afford to employ creative virtuosity in their practice, for all trainees and for the majority of serving social workers, there are basic essentials that have to be aspired to and achieved:

1. First, it must be said again, come Truax and Carkhuff's (1967) recommended qualities for counsellors: genuineness, empathy and warmth – plus persuasiveness. These are both personality traits and strategies which the would-be social worker can develop under tuition and perfect. In other words, they almost certainly come more easily to some than to others, but they are skills that anyone can improve with practice. They are not, of course, unique to social work, but they do appear to be broadly essential to *good* social work.

2. A growing amount of evidence suggests that an interest in and a willingness to undertake practical activities are of advantage in social work, and may even be essential in the cementing of a useful relationship. The emotionally and intellectually aloof person is not likely to be welcomed either by her agency or her clients.

3. I have argued that social work is primarily concerned with the goal of maintenance, and it follows that the first-class practitioner must be efficient and knowledgeable in those elements that contribute to its achievement: the exercise of responsibility, the pursuit of change strategies and pro-active intervention in the community. In particular, the good social worker must fulfil the client's expectation of her as an expert both in terms of the *facts* that she knows and of the *tactics* that she pursues in the face of the facts.

4. The qualities of awareness and sensitivity are prerequisites for good practice, and that must mean that young adults from a sheltered suburban home background, on the one hand, or the sort of people covered by Keith-Lucas's negatives on the other, are probably unsuitable for social work. The first group need to see something of the seamier side of life before beginning social work training – perhaps at least to have a glimpse of what it means to raise a family on state benefits, or to be out of work for a year or to live in a dingy urban environment. The second group need to be excluded altogether unless they can prove the assessment of their personality erroneous.

In summary, then, the qualities required in a social worker can be reduced to a mnemonic: WE SPEAK PG.

W warmth
E efficiency

S sensitivity
P persuasiveness
E empathy
A awareness
K knowledge

P practicality
G genuineness

Beyond these qualities, the injunction to 'be yourself' is now recognised as sound advice. Self-revelation, so long as it does not intrude on the client's problems or dominate the working relationship, can often be helpful. Each social worker is a unique being, and, since the use of self is one crucial part of her function it follows that the development of self-confidence is an appropriate ambition in its own right. Social work *is* a creative job and the artistry of the practitioner is a vital component once the other qualities have been mastered.

13 Beyond the use of self

In his critique of organised social work, Hugman (1977) argues that 'the business of being a good helper is essentially bound up with being a good person, that is to say, thoughtful, generous, sensitive, relatively unselfish, relatively accepting of self, liberated in spirit, tolerant, reliable, acquainted with weakness and inconsistency, caring, committed, purposeful, capable of joy and sadness, and faithful to a belief in the creative humanity of all people'. His injunction is to *'Act natural'* and to avoid the pretensions of professionalism. There is of course a romantic attraction – in the Rousseauian sense – in such an approach, and it is valuable in its attempt to counteract the conservative and bureaucratic forces that are inherent in large-scale organisations, and that will, if left unrecognised, undermine the creative individuality essential to first-class practice. But bearing in mind the central thesis of this book – that social work is of necessity a socially sanctioned activity – it follows that the creative role of the social worker *must* be reconcilable and reconciled with formal and often large-scale structures. I do not disagree with Hugman that the self is of crucial importance – as it is indeed in many service occupations – but I do not think that social work is solely and always about the influence of one person on another, nor do I think that the resources of social work are or ought to be limited to the use of self. The social worker is the front-line agent through which the agency exercises control, fulfils its responsibilities, offers resources for change and development, maintains the individual in society and enables the client's interests to be represented in relation to the state and its citizens. I have argued that the personality of that agent is not irrelevant, that the personal nature of the relationship between helper and helped is a significant part of the process, and I would further conclude that some occupational stability is therefore of value in achieving agency objectives. Similarly it is in the agency's interests to capitalise on the variations of individual style and ability among its employees and to provide a professional framework which maximises initiative and originality.

However, one major area in which initiatives and originality are likely to vary lies in the extent to which social workers are able to go beyond the use of self in their work with clients. Casework with individuals and families remains the dominant pattern of practice

Table 13.1
Expenditure on preventative child care services

Annual expenditure on day nurseries, intermediate treatment and other preventative support services in selected local authorities, 1991–92:		
Local authority	Net expenditure	Sum per head of population
	£	£
Wandsworth	4 341 000	16.78
Manchester	6 063 000	14.02
Leicestershire	5 141 000	5.77
Cornwall	145 000	0.31
Sunderland	47 000	0.16
Norfolk	84 000	0.11
Source: Chartered Institute of Public Finance and Accountancy 1993.		

in both local authority and probation settings, and much more could still be done by social workers in going beyond the use of self and employing more broadly based resources. However, policy-making in agencies largely determines the style of social work practice in any one area, and the investment of social services departments in, for example, preventative service, varies enormously (see Table 13.1). The level of investment will certainly have a powerful influence on the extent to which social workers are able to call up facilities, such as intermediate treatment for their clients, and so go beyond the standard pattern of a one-to-one working relationship; Table 13.1 suggests that the nature of social work practice in Manchester or Wandsworth would be likely to be very different from that in Cornwall or Norfolk, so far as the worker's access to preventative resources is concerned.

Of course, there are huge variations in levels of social need between different authorities, but, even allowing for that, there are also variations in the extent to which policy-makers and politicians make available to social workers the kind of material aids that can strengthen the package of support available to different client-groups. Some departments, for example, are able to provide for the installation and maintenance of a telephone in the home of isolated disabled people who could not otherwise afford such a means of communication with the outside world; other departments do not budget for such a facility.

The provision of meals on wheels — either to elderly or disabled people in their own homes or in luncheon clubs or day centres — shows similar variations when you compare the amount of money which different local authorities devote to the service (Table 13.2).

The London Borough of Brent spends almost eight times as much on meals on wheels as the London Borough of Bromley; and Nottinghamshire's expenditure, per head of population, is nearly 40 times that in Warwickshire. Whatever the demographic variables which distinguish these areas, the availability of the meals service to the social worker is significantly less in some areas than others.

Table 13.2
Expenditure on meals on wheels 1991–92

Local authority	Net expenditure	Sum per head of population
	£	£
Brent	1 110 000	4.49
Waltham Forest	729 000	3.37
Nottinghamshire	1 992 000	1.96
Bromley	171 000	0.58
Gwynedd	86 000	0.36
Dorset	82 000	0.12
Warwickshire	26 000	0.05

Source: Chartered Institute of Public Finance and Accountancy 1993.

Additionally, social workers themselves vary in the degree to which they make use of available facilities; for example, even with a statutory provision like community service orders, some probation officers are more likely to offer it as an option in their pre-sentence reports than others, with a likely differential effect on sentences passed. The same applies to the use of day centres as conditions of the probation order; those probation officers who are reluctant to make such recommendations may sometimes not do so because of qualms about the propriety of 'sentencing the offender to social work'; unfortunately such squeamishness can have the damaging side-effect of leading to a sentence of imprisonment instead (Wright 1984).

Because of the varying levels of provision and because of the seeming reluctance of some social workers to make adequate use of even those facilities that are provided, there would seem to be a need for innovation and evaluation in the whole sphere of practice beyond the use of self. There needs to be a much more organised approach to the recording and analysis of imaginative developments in community or group care. Despite a few tentative efforts, the idea of a partnership between practice and research with a view to encouraging the emergence of new and more useful strategies for action has not yet found much favour, although the pioneering work carried out in Kent has had an unprecedented impact on parliamentary legislation.

Research, practice and management should combine in such a way that innovations can be monitored, feedback provided, and further development stimulated. In too many spheres of social work research has been unimaginative, and too many practice developments have taken place in isolation for growth to occur in any dynamic sense.

Teamwork

Teamwork, as Harman (1978) says, 'seems almost to have achieved the status of being fashionable'. And, in view of the slightly disarming tendency of some social workers to fall recklessly in love with passing fads and fancies, it is necessary to regard it with some caution. The idea of teamwork can, indeed, mean anything or nothing. At one extreme the mere fact of calling a working group of social workers a 'team' — as happens fairly generally anyway — can lead to the assumption that whatever they do is *ipso facto* 'teamwork'. What seems usually to be meant in the literature, however, is the abandonment of rigid boundaries between each worker's functions, an increase in staff communication (including, perhaps, the more democratic participation of clerical staff and ancillaries), shared assessment and allocation, some shared cases and a guarantee of adequate coverage during the absence of any staff member. Some teamwork schemes have involved attempts at breaking down the hierarchy of responsibility in an office, with all decision-making being devolved to the group, but such an interpretation does not appear to be inherent in teamwork as such, although there may be other reasons for adopting it.

In one sense the idea of teamwork might mean little more than 'good colleagueship': a working environment in which co-workers share each other's burdens, stand in for each other when necessary, discuss problems together and cooperate closely in the course of a working day. Such a model in social work would mean that senior colleagues would come to the aid of a raw beginner if she was faced with a particularly difficult case, or any worker could look to her partners for advice on factual matters — where to find accommodation for a needy client, for example. Another model of teamwork is primarily applicable where the working group have uniform objectives — to galvanise a community into self-help or, more commonly, in the context of an intake team where the daily pressures of an urban environment are better shared. More ambitious is the idea of allocating specialist functions to each member of staff, so capitalising on their respective strengths — rather in the style of a football team in which each player has a slightly different role to play although flexibility is expected as circumstances change. In social work this leads to a form of specialisation, but it also means that many clients are expected to relate to the agency as a whole, and so lose the chance of identifying with one key worker.

An investigation of three social services area teams in Birmingham, Norfolk and North Wales prompted considerable scepticism about the viability of teamwork in the field of routine service delivery. Social workers expressed fears of reduced job satisfaction (because they prized their personalised caseload most highly), and they expressed doubts concerning the extent to which the resource-controllers in the higher echelons of the department would be willing to delegate sufficient powers to render teamwork effective (Black *et al.* 1983). What seems to have happened is that the notion of 'teamwork' became mixed up with linked questions of community work, the use of informal caring networks through interweaving and the place of specialists in social work. In other words, the very problem of fashionableness trapped many of the contributing arguments, and the objectives of teamwork *per se* (and even its shape, structure and place within the organisation) were left distressingly imprecise.

During the 1980s, a nationwide network of multidisciplinary teams was set up to work in the field of learning disabilities. It was planned that the 'community mental handicap teams' in each area would bring together a social worker, a nurse, occupational-physio- and speech therapists, a psychologist and a health visitor for regular meetings. Sadly, most of the teams ended up with just a nurse and a social worker (Plank 1982).

The intention was that people with learning disabilities would be referred to the team, and then allocated to one of the team members, often depending on whether their needs were deemed to be primarily health-related or primarily social. The person would become the key worker in the case, with easy access to other specialists if and when the need arose. Team meetings could keep the needs of each client under review.

The CMHTs were deemed to have been most successful when the nurse and the social worker were in regular contact with each other and especially where they shared the same premises. The multidisciplinary team system, though patchy in its achievements during the 1980s, is in a strong position to evolve further under community care policy, with care management assuming major importance.

Group work

There is a large and still growing literature on group work and general agreement that it could and should make a significant contribution to social work practice, but there is almost certainly a discrepancy between the emphasis placed on groups in social work teaching and the reality of fieldwork outside. Part of the difficulty arises from the structure of practice.

In institutional settings, there is a ready-made framework for groups: natural groups exist anyway, and the captive nature of the population makes it relatively easy for selected artificial groups to be brought together by staff. In fieldwork, there has to be a definite initiative, the social worker has to have the time, the space, the energy and sufficient confidence that the effort involved will be worthwhile to maintain both her own and the clients' motivation. All too often, one or more of these essential ingredients is missing, but although it appears that specialist group work personnel are uncommon, enough social workers run at least one group in their working lives to ensure that the momentum is maintained. Significantly, the greatest impetus to groups was given by the provision in the Children and Young Persons Act 1969 for intermediate treatment for juveniles who had either offended against the law or were thought to be at some risk of doing so. Such statutory backing persuaded most local authorities to allocate resources to the task, with the result that specialist staff were appointed, funds made available and premises provided. With such material support, group work for teenagers became viable.

It was always a fallacy to see group work as a cheap option — a way of seeing eight reporting probationers at once, for example; and although it is doubtful whether anyone ever really believed such a myth, it has taken a long time for there to be official recognition that group work is not usually feasible without careful planning and without due consideration to the resource implications. Even now the sophistication of the approach to IT in many areas falls far short of standards normally regarded as minimally acceptable in special education – a field which has much in common with the practice of group work with adolescents but which has a far longer and richer tradition of curriculum development.

Other examples of group work can be found in:

1. Activity work with adult offenders – motor-cycle maintenance, craft workshops, literacy classes, physical training.
2. Discussion groups in day care settings – for psychiatric patients or elderly people, for example.
3. Parent-groups in child and family guidance clinics – involving the sharing of mutually experienced problems, role-play, or the simple relief of anxiety and tension.
4. Groups for would-be foster parents – partly for training purposes, partly to cope with apprehensions and doubts, and, occasionally, perhaps, to complete the vetting process.
5. Groups for similar clients: prisoners' wives, alcoholics, the parents of children in care, women who have been the victims of violent assaults by their husbands, ex-psychiatric patients.

Sometimes groups struggle for survival, sometimes they thrive, and occasionally they exercise their own initiative and grow into self-help groups with an existence and a will all their own.

Techniques in group work are limitless, and can be either verbal or action-based, or a mixture of the two. Ambitious leaders with the necessary facilities can make imaginative use of video, audio-tapes, role-play or sculpting; or the group can be community-directed, towards some mutually agreed goal of bringing about a desired local development – creating a children's playground, for example. At this point group work merges imperceptibly into community work.

There has to be a good reason for starting a group, but it doesn't have to be highfalutin'. The simple exchange of views and feelings by people suffering from stress is a perfectly valid justification, as is the provision of a place in which the isolated can find company. Reasons don't have to have a curative, therapeutic or transcendental base to justify the social worker's effort. Indeed, the need for groups will often emerge naturally, and requires only a sensitive, alert and committed social worker to pick up the cue, and a facilitating agency to provide the means.

The real beauty of group work lies in the scope it offers for the social worker to operate in a creative fashion, while at the same time responding to client interests and needs in a way that wholly characterises the social work ideal. Three examples illustrate the point.

1. Working with agoraphobics Two final year students aimed to set up a programme to meet an apparent need to help agoraphobics in Bristol. Their first idea was to take the clients out into panic-inducing situations, but this was vetoed by the would-be participants who also overruled the social workers' view that membership of the group should be tightly limited. Meetings were held, and those who came did so because they wanted to make contact with fellow-sufferers. Attendance over eight meetings varied from 6 to 17, with a considerable turnover. The workers had a clear therapeutic goal, despite scepticism on the part of some of the attenders.

Since everyone would have had a personal struggle even to arrive at the meeting, a welcoming atmosphere was deliberately created. The schedule, although planned, was not rigidly adhered to, the first two meetings being taken up with members talking about their agoraphobic condition. In the next three weeks, paper exercises, discussions and encouragement by the workers to venture out led to discussions about risk, dependency and the members' feelings of resentment about their condition. Session six focused on achievements with the lighthearted use of 'gold stars' for anything that deserved a special accolade. This positive emphasis was valuable because of the group's frequent tendency to dwell on setbacks. At this stage, the idea of continuing the enterprise through self-help groups was mooted by the workers, and the last two sessions were used partly to plan these and partly to share feedback about the group experience.

The members valued the opportunity of sharing experiences, and liked the relaxed atmosphere and the encouragement to meet phobic situations. Improvements in behaviour were reported, and two self-help groups were established as a result of the initiative. The role of group members in reinforcing for each other the importance of personal effort seemed to justify the approach (Hutchen 1984).

2.   A telephone group   Gibbons (1984) developed an imaginative technique for using the telephone as a primary treatment resource, and formed Telelink groups, using British Telecom's ability to provide conference facilities through telephone link-ups.

She selected a group of six or seven people, who were usually blind to a significant degree, and arranged for telephone links to be established at a specific time each week. The groups normally ran for between 45 and 60 minutes. The technique involved members imagining a clockface, choosing a number with which to identify him or herself and then, initially, allowing the worker to coordinate conversations. The groups normally met for eight weeks, and developed from the first week when the leader went round the group clockwise engaging in conversation until, later, the members developed group skills and were able to respond spontaneously and freely as if they were face-to-face. In one case, the group developed to a stage where the members actively sought problem-solving work and education; they had guest speakers and listened to articles on specific subjects as a basis for discussion.

Members did not normally meet each other, but some afterwards enjoyed one-to-one telephone contact. The technique was particularly suitable for visually impaired clients, because it minimised the difference between them and the sighted leader.

Group membership was warmly regarded by the members, and they could and did move into further groups after the eight weeks were over. Some groups later met without the leader.

3.   Feminist social work with a women's group   Donnelly (1985) describes a three-year programme of group work amongst women living and working on a run-down Leicester council estate. The social workers drew on tenets central to the women's movement, with a particular focus on their shared experience of oppression, and a belief in the principle that 'the personal is the political'.

Initially two social workers ran four separate time-limited sequences of women-only groups, each of ten sessions. Their aims were 'educative and therapeutic':

- To combat isolation ... by building up friendship and support networks.
- To develop an awareness of women's oppression.
- To build up self-confidence and self-esteem.
- To enable women to gain greater control over their own lives.
- To enable them to articulate their feelings.
- To increase self-awareness.

Because a small core of women had attended regularly, the opportunity was taken to create a more stable group. Fairly quickly, in fact, there emerged two parallel weekly meetings with some overlapping membership; on Tuesdays, there was a chance for safe and confidential sharing of experiences ('the confidential group') and on Thursdays 'an action group' aimed to tackle and overcome the lack of facilities and basic services on the estate.

One of the group members, Cathy, describes some of the work done on Tuesdays: 'We're talking about health problems that particularly affect women, which range not only from menstrual difficulties and child-birth and post-natal depression, but just general depression and anxiety, which more and more of us are realising now that it's not a particular weakness in women but it's to do with the situation women are in.'

The action group tackled lorries driving through the estate, relations with the social security office and the lack of a GP on the estate. Cathy again: '... it's magic really that it's the women's group that are actually breaking through that sort of blanket of depression on the estate ... that they're actually standing up and saying, "No, we don't have to take things lying down – we can fight them." '

The use of volunteers

> Volunteering is as essential to humane social services as highly-trained professionalism, and the professional who disregards this ... is liable to make the most cruel mistakes. (Crossman 1976)

That may be so, but it is also true that the use of volunteers requires not only skill but some imagination, for the addition of a volunteer can further complicate the already delicate balance between the social worker, her agency and the client. One survey (Hatch 1978) found that 15 per cent of the general population had done voluntary work of one kind or another 'in the past year', and the social worker is in a key position to make sure that those who give their time freely are used to maximum effectiveness.

What might volunteers do? One answer is 'almost anything', and certainly the range of their activities is likely to grow. One study in the probation service identified the following as some of the main tasks which volunteers undertook:

> Prison visiting; groupwork with prisoners during their sentence; looking after children during their mother's visit to prison; providing transport to prisons; running canteens at prisons for visiting families; teaching art, craft and literacy to offenders; helping offenders find work; support and advice to offenders and their families; helping the homeless; running hostels; baby-sitting; helping families to budget; practical work (collecting luggage, repairing and decorating a client's home); writing letters to lonely prisoners; participating in pressure groups for penal reform; supervising offenders ordered to do community service; providing holidays for mothers and children; organising a clothing store at the probation office. (Clark 1975)

Volunteers in social services departments can be employed in similar ways but considerable attention has been paid in recent years to the possibility of using them as *good neighbours* in the community: to carry out the job of providing an immediate point of contact for those in need, to keep an eye on those at risk, and generally to supplement the resources of the social services departments at grass-roots level. Some authorities have started paying 'street wardens' token amounts of money because of their belief in the importance of the job and their recognition of the responsibility that it carries.

Finally, the role of volunteers, operating in a variety of capacities, is central to community care and 'Patch' developments, using, as they do, Bayley's notion of interweaving. Gone is the idea of the volunteer as a marginal figure in caring, and in its place have come schemes in which the social worker may conduct, coordinate and mastermind operations, but volunteers act out the central roles. Furthermore, as they become more experienced in the function, the scope for them to take leading initiatives is not denied.

The more traditional arrangement which still holds sway in many probation and social services departments is for one or more volunteers to be 'attached' to social workers – sometimes to specially designated liaison officers but more commonly to ordinary fieldworkers who may or may not have been adequately prepared for the task of supervising them. For example, a volunteer might be allocated to an old peoples' home and come under the wing of the warden. I have seen this work successfully, with an imaginative volunteer visiting the home regularly during afternoons, working with some of the residents to produce a weekly news-sheet, using a tape-recorder to engage residents in an oral history project about their childhood in an industrial town, playing board-games or just chatting and listening.

Recruitment can stretch from insertions in parish newsletters to negotiating access to nationwide or regional television for a phone-in programme. In between come the use of informal networks, posters in schools, offices, libraries, advertising in the newspaper and the issuing of press releases. If the work has a strong community focus, it is essential to recruit indigenous neighbourhood workers.

There is some disagreement over the extent to which volunteers should be trained for their task, and much will depend on the nature of their work. If they are expected to give precise advice about welfare rights, for example, they are going to need a detailed briefing; but in most cases the art of successful volunteering requires more modest qualities. One apparently successful project was praised by its volunteers because:

1.   It had clear objectives, which they could understand and aim to achieve.
2.   They had some discretion to make their own decisions.
3.   There was reasonably rapid feedback from clients.
4.   There was good teamwork between the volunteers and the professionals.
5.   They enjoyed good leadership, with a volunteer as the coordinator.
6.   They had professional support and recognition.
7.   The work was varied.
8.   There was a limit to the commitment demanded of the volunteers, because of a pairing and rota system.
     (Hare 1977)

Projects, of course, are not designed primarily to satisfy the needs of the volunteers but, at the same time, there is now a lot of evidence to show that volunteer-satisfaction is a prerequisite of service for the client. And volunteer-satisfaction will often depend on the skill and commitment of the professional social worker.

Community work

Some social services departments employ community workers but Stevenson and Parsloe (1978) found that their activities tended to be carried out independently of the mainstream social workers, and although there is disagreement over the extent to which the community work role is legitimately one for the local authority and even whether community work is a form of social work at all, there is no doubt that the activities of most social workers often make them aware of the need for community action and community development, and sometimes prompt them to become involved themselves. The worker, for example, might see the deprivations suffered by young children and poor families in an urban environment and, despairing of any foreseeable improvement in their conditions, encourage them, or even lead them, into becoming more vociferous in their demands for fair treatment. Such a role is understandable and defensible but there is evidence that many social workers find it difficult to reconcile it with their more normal duties. As Black *et al.* (1983) say of their area team social workers, 'they wanted to be involved in the community but did not see it as their job to do community work'.

The Barclay Report's insistence on talking about *community social work* as a preferred model has, in some ways, only fudged the issue. It is clear from the emphasis of *The Essential Social Worker* that contemporary practice requires the professional to operate within, and in direct contact with, the community, but I remain quite satisfied that community work as such benefits from being conceptually distinct from most of the tasks which contemporary social workers are expected to fulfil. In the sense that both have a role to play, it is unnecessary to debate whether social work is a more worthy or more necessary activity than community work, or vice versa. Problems undoubtedly arise, however, because of discrepancies in funding, with community work in the UK being very much the poor relation. Until some way is found of pumping public money into programmes which encourage community development, it is always likely that the relatively well-off statutory sector in social work will find itself envied and attacked by those who see community work as a preferable strategy of social concern.

Although community work takes many forms, the most common approach is to work with community groups – either those that already and naturally exist, or those that are prompted into being by the injection of funds or the allocation of staff. The worker's aims can be many and varied, though they are usually concentrated on developing local facilities, campaigning for additional resources, or making explicit the views of ordinary citizens and pressure groups on significant issues concerned with human welfare.

Briscoe (1977) argues that the community approach can co-exist with service delivery, the essential difference being that service delivery is externally determined, with new developments depending on the sensitivity of workers, management and politicians to local needs, while the community approach maximises the involvement of the recipients of aid, both in the way in which it is distributed and in the development of an overall service strategy.

Hence, the community work perspective brings us back to the client's voice, but strengthens it by force of numbers, and sometimes by bypassing the social worker and exercising direct influence on politicians and managerial decision-makers. Herein lies the as yet unresolved dilemma for those who would like to see community work as an integral part of statutory social work – and there are good reasons for thinking it incapable of resolution. If community work leads inexorably in the direction of political confrontation, as it often appears to, the community worker employed by the political authority is inevitably in an ambiguous position – and the ambiguity is double-edged. There may well be limits in the extent to which she can take on her employers on behalf of the community she serves; and she will always be vulnerable to the suspicion that her employers are clandestinely exerting influence on her to moderate the views of her community group. In this sense of being on the boundaries of society, there are similarities between her role and that of the social worker. But whereas the social worker's role is primarily one of reconciliation, the community worker's model is almost inherently conflict-orientated, and that means that the critical question, 'Whose side are you on?' is always being posed. And for the worker to be on the side of a community *against* the political authority demands a degree of independence that is not normally found in a statutory social worker. Hence, despite the pressures in that direction, the conclusion has to be drawn that social workers can never ultimately make good community workers unless contracts are drawn up by their employers which guarantee them a degree of freedom that they would not normally expect.

Coping with unemployment

Unemployment has become almost endemic in parts of the United Kingdom (see Table 13.3), and, inevitably, the competition for jobs has led to a situation in which the clients of the probation and social services are often among the hardest hit. There are offices in parts of Northern Ireland and on Tyneside where unemployment in the client-group varies between 80 and 100 per cent. The requirement on probationers that they should 'lead an industrious life', which has traditionally been interpreted to mean that they should obtain and hold down a job, is no longer enforceable; parole release which initially depended to a very large extent on the ex-prisoner being sure of having somewhere to live and somewhere to work is now regularly granted irrespective of the man's employment chances. How, indeed, could it be otherwise? If skilled, able-bodied, law-abiding men cannot get work, what chance has the recidivist, the psychiatric convalescent or the untrained adolescent drop-out?

The social worker sees the pain and the disillusionment of unemployment close at hand, but traditionally there has been only a limited amount of active help that she was willing or able to give. To some extent this reluctance reflected the psychopathological view that unemployment was merely a symptom of other personal problems that the

Table 13.3
Unemployment trends in the United Kingdom

	Number of unemployed claimants (thousands)	Unemployment rate %
1961	292	1.3
1971	751	3.3
1976	1 302	5.5
1981	2 520	10.2
1986	3 289	11.8
1987	2 953	10.6
1988	2 370	8.4
1989	1 799	6.3
1990	1 664	5.8
1991	2 292	8.1
1992	2 779	9.9
1993 (November)	2 769	9.9

Note: In November 1993, regional rates varied from 7.9 per cent in East Anglia, to 11.9 per cent in the North and 13.4 per cent in Northern Ireland.
Source: Department of Employment.

worker had to deal with. Now, however, it is based on what the workers would see as a 'realistic' perspective on economic circumstances: 'There are so few jobs around that to become involved in clients' employment problems would be a losing battle,' said one.

Since Campling (1980) explored the attitudes of social workers towards unemployment as a focus for intervention, the structural situation has continued to deteriorate, and social workers risk losing their credibility if they seek to deny the uncomfortable fact that most of their clients have no hope at all of getting a permanent job. The dole queue, the pool tables, the street corner and the loss of any sense of meaning in adult life – these are the psychological forces impinging on the client, and the worker has to start by recognising this fact.

Gradually, attempts have been made to get beyond the now outmoded strategy of ringing the job centre or contacting a friendly employer, and these nearly all require major commitment on the part of the agency and a willingness to negotiate working links with voluntary organisations or government-sponsored job creation schemes. For some time, the probation service has administered special workshops almost on a kind of prison industries model: undertaking wood and metal crafts, seeking contracts in light industry assembly work and packing. The centres tend to be staging-posts for long-term unemployed probationers or for others coming out of prison with nothing else to look forward to.

The same type of approach has been developed for people with learning disabilities, but there is some disagreement about whether it is best to provide sheltered workshops or to arrange outside work experience. There are examples of both types:

1. At Oakfield in Bromley, the aim is to prepare the clients for work by providing opportunities in carpentry, packing, printing and clerical work, light engineering or domestic and kitchen work.
2. At Birkbeck in Waltham Forest, by contrast, the aim is to leave behind the old image of intensive contract labour. The supervisor has 'found no limits to clients' ability to work, given the right opportunity. He has been getting people out one, two or three days a week into jobs in restaurants, hairdressers, cleaning cars, gardening, basic car maintenance, industrial work, painting and decorating, furniture removals and leaflet distribution'.
(Crine 1983a)

The Department of Employment and its subsidiary agencies responsible for training have proved willing to cooperate with social work initiatives in different parts of the country. In Norfolk, largely as the result of one probation officer's extra-mural commitment, a community programme enabled 14 offenders and others to spend up to a year in environmental work and in building new premises for a community centre. In a research analysis of the experience, Gosling (1984) has emphasised the feasibility of the approach, but also draws attention to its disadvantages. Social work agencies are not normally geared up to cope with the problems of personnel management, budgeting and development that are associated with industrial operations; the officer's commitment can be seen, at best, as a spare-time bonus for the service's benefit, and, at worst, as an intrusion on his normal duties, with consequential costs for his colleagues. The short-term nature of contract jobs also puts maximum emphasis on the search for work and funds, and allows little scope for the project getting into a cruising gear.

What seems to have happened is that, faced with the enormity of the problem of unemployment, a small number of creative social workers and agencies have taken the initiative and sought to develop work opportunities within the organisation; made possible by the availability of pump-priming funds, there is as yet no sense that the development is more than a marginal element in professional practice. The business of getting a job remains the responsibility of the individual, and the business of creating an economic framework within which jobs are available remains the responsibility of the government. The social worker, responsible for the welfare of designated clients, can only go so far in her role of mediation, but for the client who benefits, any distance is better than none.

The provision of intensive care

It is only relatively recently that it has been recognised that contact between social worker and client is, in quantitative terms, quite severely restricted. Probation research has shown that routine supervision after the first three months of a court order is likely to involve no more than 20 minutes a fortnight; and even the IMPACT experiment (Folkard 1976), which was intended to provide a more intensive facility, failed to increase worker-client contact beyond an hour a week. One of the reasons for this might be an economic one. The marginal costs of using a social worker are now around £8.00 per hour and real costs at least £14.00 per hour. But a more cogent reason is because intensive use of professional staff time conflicts with the normal role of a social worker and the client's expectations of it. Routine duties are many and various but they determine the shape of the social worker's day, and often there are difficulties in reconciling these with the client's most pressing needs. Of course, social workers *can* exercise some control over the use of their time, but the outer limits are surprisingly constricted. The worker may decide to spend two or three hours working one day intensively with a family; the commitment may extend to a whole day or to a repeat performance the next day or the following week; she may even embark on a short programme of planned contacts using behavioural methods or task-centred casework over a period of seven or eight weeks. But such options, on the face of it rather attractive, are rarely taken up and, at best, demand a restricted focus on one or two selected clients. Moderately intensive work may thus depend on the worker being allowed to carry a specialist caseload or being relieved of routine duties, and even then there is a risk of other clients getting short shrift in order to enable the worker to carve out space for strategic involvement with the privileged minority.

It is, however, increasingly recognised that the provision of intensive care must normally mean going beyond the use of the field social worker. Although it is sometimes suggested that the range of available resources can be seen as lying along a continuum, and that they should be employed in direct proportion to client need, the reality is rather less neat and tidy – not least because there is confusion bordering on chaos regarding the status and consequent financial value of different agents employed to provide intensive care. Indeed one of the least logical aspects of the social services field today is that many of those used most intensively have traditionally been lower paid than those operating in the fieldwork front line or in administration. There is a full range of domiciliary care staff – home helps, social work aides, providers of meals on wheels; there are day centres for elderly people, for psychiatric outpatients and for offenders on probation; there are child minders and playgroups; and, above all, there is residential provision for every client-group imaginable. Most recently there has emerged a tendency to employ 'volunteers' to provide a degree of regular daily contact with a client which would be quite impossible for the social worker to contemplate: for example, a 'trackers scheme' uses young Community Service Volunteers to attach themselves almost full-time to young people thought likely to get into some sort of trouble if left to their own resources.

Clients for whom such intensive facilities are made available must inevitably begin to see their original social worker as marginal to their needs and circumstances; and the future relationship between the fieldworker, whose function is largely one of processing, decision-making and facilitating, and the panoply of additional provisions is, to say the least, problematic. Should the social worker have high status, low status or equal status *vis-à-vis* those who are engaged in a full-time caring role with the client? Such a question, of obvious importance for all staff, their trade unions and their clients, arises because of the piecemeal way in which social service provisions have grown, and because of the way they have been brought into ever more complex relationships with each other. The conundrum is aggravated by the fact that client-need for intensive involvement by the state also tends to bring in services outside the range of the social work system – especially the health service and the penal system. At what point, for example, does a disabled old person need hospitalisation rather than residential provision? And at what point does the potential responsibility of the probation service end and the role of the prison service begin? Such 'boundary disputes' are both critical to agency efficiency and inevitable in a complex organisational structure.

A whole range of developments – 'Patch', community care schemes, intermediate treatment, day care, probation centres – have emerged because of the need for an approach that increases the intensity of impact without requiring either the cost or the potentially stigmatising effect of residential care. In each case, the social worker is involved in an essentially managerial capacity with a team of other workers to fulfil specialist functions or to assume a particular attachment to one client.

The NHS and Community Care Act 1990 takes this state of affairs to a logical conclusion with the identification of a care manager in respect of each identified client. The care manager, who may be a social worker but may also be another professional (an occupational therapist, for example), will have responsibility for putting together a package of care which may involve the employment of ancillary staff who will be given specific functions to perform. At least so far as community care is concerned, the fact that intensive care will become the norm rather than the exception will probably mean that social workers as care managers, having carried out their statutory assessments of need, will depute all aspects of practice to others. If that is the case, we shall see that the practice of social work with elderly people and other adults in need of help will emerge as an inherently managerial task, while the face-to-face contact required will be in the hands of non-social workers.

Day-time provision

Almost all social work clients might now find themselves having access to (or even being required to attend) facilities which go far beyond the traditional office interview but which fall short of residential admission. There are probation centres for offenders, attendance at which can be required as a condition of a probation order; there are family resource centres which provide play activity for children, tuition in parenting skills and support groups for isolated mothers; there are day centres for disabled people which have been described as having four main functions – occupation and leisure, work preparation, training or treatment, and education; and there are, in almost all health areas, psychiatric day centres which represent a major part of the government's plan to switch from hospital care to community care for the mentally ill.

Although day centres vary in their emphases, their common aim is to provide somewhere for people to go who, for whatever reason, cannot or ought not to be left at home all day and cannot or will not go to school or work. Day centres for elderly people range from luncheon clubs in church halls to purpose-built establishments with a wide range of activities available. Some research studies have suggested that day centres for elderly people all too often do not provide enough for the attenders to do, and those located in old peoples' homes seem to be particularly lacking in activities (Edwards and Sinclair 1980).

At the other extreme, Crine (1983b) has described the highly organised timetable of the Vale Centre, a Leeds project for psychiatric day care. The centre runs on therapeutic lines with splendid facilities for relaxation, craftwork, cooking, art therapy and group-work. The groups include therapeutic role-playing, creative writing, drama and educational groups. The centre operates in close liaison with local group homes and hostels, and it claims a good record in helping its clients into employment schemes.

Although client studies reveal some ambiguity in the feelings of those who attend, the fact remains that people do use day centres, and almost always voluntarily. A critical note is sounded, however, by Michael Bender (1983), who faults many day centres for the poor quality of their performance and for being insufficiently responsive to the clients' own preferences. He says that they lack clear objectives, run the risk of institutionalising those who attend them and are ineffective with regard to their apparent aims. He thinks that where there is a training or therapeutic function to be done, this should be based on a specific short-term contract and specified goals and, where – as in most cases – the aim is simply to occupy the clients, then this should be done in a way that takes into account the consumers' interests: bingo, films, craft and hobby equipment, a bar and coffee room. Such facilities could well be provided, not by the social services department, but by the local authority or by the independent sector without the consequent risk of stigmatisation.

Bender's critique raises vigorously the question of where social work ends. Certainly, there is a case for arguing that its inclination to extend too far will dissipate its value. Maybe the role of social workers is to advocate the growth of day care and community-based facilities, but then to normalise them as far as possible, by involving the mainstream departments of health or education in their administration or by contracting them out to non-government agencies.

Liaison with other agencies

The social work department's work with the client, even though it does have a certain uniqueness, does not exist in a vacuum, and one prerequisite of service is the development of good working links with other agencies – with school teachers and doctors, in particular. The emergence of child protection conferences has formalised some of these associations, though not always to everyone's mutual satisfaction.

Inter-agency links would be better for spontaneity and flexibility. Intermediate treatment has led to much closer cooperation between schools and social workers, and the development of juvenile liaison panels has meant that probation officers, social workers and police officers meet regularly to monitor their mutual interest in children thought to be at risk.

One sphere where, from tentative beginnings, we now see frequent advances is in respect of social worker attachment to medical practices. Following experiments in south London, there has been a steady increase in the extent to which social workers hold sessions in surgeries or, more adventurously, take a full-time office base there. Close working relationships between the doctor, the health visitor, district nurse and social worker usually follow, although attachment schemes have not been a universal success story. Marshall and Hargreaves (1979) have spelt out some of the pitfalls of attachment schemes: professional isolation, problems of accountability, inadequate interviewing facilities and a failure of the GP to understand the social worker's role or capabilities.

Rushton and Davies (1984) acknowledge that the doctor's attitude is crucial, but say that other factors which lead to successful attachment schemes are careful planning, the existence of a group practice in the surgery, and the self-reliance and adaptability of the social worker. The main advantages of attachment are thought to be the ease of referral of patients who might not otherwise find their way to the social worker, the fact that a significant proportion of GP patients are suffering from forms of depression and might benefit from counselling, and an apparent increase in job satisfaction for the social worker. Rushton and Davies conclude:

> The informality of work carried out in a health setting has great advantages for social work. It is possible that the out-posting of social workers to work with other disciplines may become more

common rather than less so in the future. The same thinking applies to collaborative as to patch thinking, taking social workers out of offices to where people are. (Rushton and Davies 1984)

There are barely any spheres where closer collaboration is inappropriate: workers who know each other are more likely to trust each other and so work together for the client's benefit – hence the functional importance of superficially marginal occasions like local luncheon clubs where workers can talk informally about matters (and cases) of mutual concern.

One especially important area for liaison occurs within the social worker's own department: the quality of cooperation between fieldworkers and residential care staff is often criticised – either because fieldworkers are said to lose interest in their clients once they are admitted or because residential staff resent their intrusion and fail to pay sufficient attention to the importance of their residents maintaining their associations with home and the outside world. Money is a major factor here, as travel costs in large county areas can be prohibitive, although letter-writing is better than nothing. But the separate identity of residential and fieldwork staff can also hinder good relations. One solution is for each person in care to be allocated a *key worker* who then retains contact with and responsibility for him throughout his moves in and out of the residential care system.

In the probation service there have been improvements in communication between officers and the staff of probation hostels since wardens were designated as senior staff and were slotted into the organisational hierarchy. Greater problems, however, continue to be experienced in the probation service's working relationships with prisons, where a sense of alienation between custodial goals and the social work approach has generally prevented the development of liaison and integration. In 1982, a new sentence of 'youth custody' was introduced with the intention of involving probation officers much more actively during the time of sentence. Again, though, resistance on the part of the prison service and reluctance on the part of many probation officers appears to have made progress difficult. In Essex, Foad (1984) found that attempts to encourage supervising officers to visit clients sentenced to youth custody were unsuccessful in nearly 50 per cent of the cases; she discovered that the most successful approach to inter-agency work involved the designation of specialist staff not only to liaise with youth custody centres but to become responsible for specialist supervision.

Conclusion

We have reviewed, too briefly, a range of caring agents beyond the social worker's self. The impression gained is of a system still in a relatively early stage of evolution but developing rapidly, albeit in no clearly identifiable direction. The common thread is that of the environment – the setting in which the client lives and the community upon which the social worker draws for support and supplementation.

Possibly the most important caring agent of all is, in many instances, the client's own family 'carer'. Elderly people who are disabled, confused and incontinent may still live at home and be looked after night and day by a relative – usually a daughter who may herself be in her 60s; children and adults with learning disabilities place a permanent burden of caring on their parents; and patients with serious psychiatric problems – depression or schizophrenia, for instance – may, under medication, be expected to live at home with their spouses, parents or children.

Feminist theory has been influential in emphasising that the great majority of carers are women, and that the practice of social work must take into account their needs as women, as well as the contribution that they make to the welfare of their dependents. Good social work practice will recognise the primacy of the carer's role, and will seek to handle the inevitable conflicts between cared-for and carer with sensitivity and understanding. Supportive groups for carers might be organised; respite care made freely available to take the pressure off the carer; and the interests of the carer be taken into account when the community care assessment is drawn up and put into operation.

Social work 'beyond the use of self' necessarily tends to involve the allocation of resources, often on a major scale, and to follow the making of policy-decisions either in management teams or in committees of councillors or civil servants. Developments like 'Patch', family centres, day care and the payment of volunteers raise issues that go beyond professional skill or worker accountability. They require the design of organisational structures; job definitions and wage differentials mean active union interest; and the allocation of significant budget funds leads to demands for tight monitoring of effectiveness and efficiency. The one-to-one social work relationship was undoubtedly much simpler, but these developments came about in recognition of client interests, and the trend is likely to continue.

In many cases, now, the social worker's use of self is no more than a beginning, a mere passing element in a relationship that takes in the provision of accommodation, group support and community involvement on a large scale. As the welfare services evolve, as the need for provisions 'beyond the use of self' becomes more insistent, both administrators and practitioners will have much to do to improve their methods and to allocate their resources to maximum effect. The professional worker is likely to assume increasingly a grass-roots managerial role in this situation, and to move beyond the traditional counselling and home visiting functions where it all began.

Part IV

In conclusion

14 Skills, knowledge and qualities in the essential social worker

For social workers to be considered essential to society, they do not have to prove themselves *more* essential than anyone else. Theirs may not be the most critical of all occupations: they are not primary producers, nor are they directly concerned with public or private health. But neither is social work the most easily dispensable job in a civilised community.

There are politicians who like to think that social work *is* superfluous, but two facts from recent history are salutary. The first concerns the United Kingdom. Throughout the long period of Conservative rule in Britain, during the 1980s and into the last decade of the century, senior ministers in the Department of Health and the Home Office (responsible for local authority social services and probation policy respectively) have presided over unprecedented growth in social work staff and budgets. Whatever their personal or political preconceptions when in their constituencies or in the Commons, they have found that public concern about child abuse, about the demographic explosion in the number of old people in the community, and about rising levels of crime has forced them to acknowledge the primacy of the social work role in a society which lays claim to being civilised but which finds itself with social problems to manage and to respond to. Even in the lower-profile spheres of mental health and learning disability, media awareness of family stress and public sensitivity to the apparent link between these conditions and the growing number of homeless people on the streets has added to the pressure on ministers to recognise the essential nature of social work practice in the contemporary world.

The second piece of history concerns Romania. Through the power of television, the world reeled with shock at the sight of piteous children in the poverty-stricken, ill-equipped and badly-run orphanages that were exposed for all to see after the fall of the Iron Curtain in 1989. A groundswell of concern led to widespread generosity and commitment from the West; and UNICEF, normally operating only in the Third World, committed itself to reversing an obviously dis-welfare regime. What had happened became clear when Western experts visited the country. The dictator, President

201

Ceausescu, in 1969 had decreed that because under his rule there could, by definition, be no social problems, there was obviously no need for social workers. QED. He closed down the well-established training courses in the universities, and all casework and community work ceased. Unwittingly, Ceausescu had set up a laboratory experiment capable of demonstrating what happens in an urban nation when social work is demolished.

Social workers bring a humanising force, a caring component into the increasingly large-scale welfare setting – a setting which, though created for the best of reasons, can so easily slide into heartlessness and become alienated from the compassionate intentions that fired its originators. The social work tradition that has evolved over a hundred years decrees that welfare functions in respect of elderly, disabled, deviant and deprived people shall be fulfilled in a manner that respects the individuality of those involved, that always recognises potential for survival and growth and that reflects an absolute commitment to care. Society could survive without social work, but it would be a society with a very different attitude towards its marginal citizens: one which shut its eyes to suffering, disposed of its offenders (as by transportation), bricked away the mentally ill, created vast impersonal orphanages and workhouses and ultimately resorted to the convenience and economy of the gas-ovens.

We need to continually remind ourselves of how often in the past communities *have* built walls around the unwanted – the riff-raff, the scroungers, the throw-outs, the has-beens, the spastics, the undeserving – all those people to whom fate and the neighbours have not been kind. Social work is politically sanctioned to devise, administer and run systems which seek to make more humane provision for those unable to cope alone, and, to that extent, social work is best understood as having a function in society just like any other job.

Social workers are essential because of the frailties of human genetics and the ageing body, because of aberrations of human behaviour, because plans go wrong and people die, because all political and economic systems produce victims and point the finger at deviants and wrong-doers, because human nature and human life are occasionally vicious, and because people – especially people in families – sometimes fight with and hurt each other. Social work has emerged as one of the 20th century's attempts to cope with such problems as best it can.

Social work copes with them, I have argued in this book, not by giving absolute priority to client self-determination, but by emphasising the right of the client to a say in his own destiny and his right to enter into dialogue with the state on matters that affect his freedom and his welfare. Partnership between worker and client has become the keystone of good practice in the 1990s.

The essence of social work is maintenance: maintaining a stable, though not a static, society, and maintaining the rights of and providing opportunities for those who in an unplanned, uncontrolled community would go to the wall. The profession of social work is living testimony to a political commitment to safeguard and further the welfare of all citizens. The agencies within which social workers operate employ them in order to comply with society's desire to so manage affairs that scarce resources are distributed fairly and humanely, that critical decisions are arrived at with due regard for the needs and feelings of all parties involved and that provisions for disadvantaged people are made in such a way as to ensure maximum scope for personal and communal development. Such functions need to be carried out in any modern urban society, but the *way* in which they are carried out is of importance to the state of civilisation – and it is the aim and the claim of social work that its principles of humanity and concern can and should raise the standards of welfare practice to the highest levels attainable.

Not all kinds of social work require the same skills, knowledge and qualities. Even within the probation service, for example, there are differences between the kind of work carried out by an officer based in a prison, a specialist court officer and the officer responsible for running the community service scheme. And within a local authority department, the provision of community care for adult clients requires a different approach from that required in working with children.

Nevertheless, it is now possible, in the light of empirical research, to identify skills, knowledge and qualities which together lay the foundations for good practice.

Skills

1.   Interpersonal skills   Social workers have to be able to relate (talking, listening, sharing, giving, receiving, tolerating, understanding, empathising, inspiring trust), not just to clients and their networks, but to all those with whom they have dealings, especially to close colleagues, including those from a different disciplinary or professional background. Social work requires cooperation and collaboration, and the social worker must be capable of developing an effective style within her working team. Whereas interpersonal skills may be said to be advantageous in many occupations, social workers say that their job is utterly dependent upon them – that, quite literally, you cannot be a social worker unless you can relate to other people in a fruitful and personal manner.

With clients, interpersonal skills are developed in such a way that they allow the social worker to communicate through counselling (including the art of listening); through more directive interviewing (advising); in groups; and through the use of specialised techniques such as family therapy or behaviour modification.

The art of communicating directly with children has come to be recognised as a pre-requisite, not of excellence, but of minimally acceptable competence in almost all family social work.

Interpersonal skills of a different kind are needed when the social worker is required to use a more controlling, disciplined or even correctional style of case management, or when formal action has to be taken following the breakdown of a case.

Some specialist duties (especially in residential or day care) involve the social worker in team leadership or management roles, and other duties may require skills in the formal arts of communication, such as public speaking or media relations.

2.   Assessment skills   All social workers have to review the social and psychological aspects of each case, and then prepare assessments in the light of their enquiries. Probation officers do it for courts and the parole board, social workers in local authorities do it in child protection cases and under the terms of the NHS and Community Care Act 1990.

The task of assessment requires social workers to be perceptive, to use judgment and to reach decisions in the light of accumulated evidence. The quality of their performance may have incalculable consequences, for good or ill, on the subjects of their attention.

3.   Writing skills   Most assessments have to be presented in written form, and that, together with the frequent need to communicate with other agencies and decision-makers, has led to social workers' emphasising the crucial importance of writing skills in the work-setting. Such skills include gathering relevant information, keeping it in note form, then turning it into a convincing and professionally impressive document that (often) incorporates an appropriate and persuasive recommendation. Such work demands literacy skills of a high order.

4.   Workload management skills   Social workers have to handle complex pressures from a variety of conflicting directions, and they must have the skills to cope with them in an organised fashion.

Knowledge

Recent studies of social work in practice have contradicted the idea of the activity as an applied social science. Social workers emphasise practical areas of knowledge as being of the greatest importance to their professional performance.

1.   Knowledge of the law   Perhaps the most radical shift in social work attitudes during the 1980s derived from the growing recognition of how much social work practice interacts with and depends upon legal statutes. In criminal justice, in child protection and, most recently, in community care, the law not only draws the boundaries but increasingly demands positive behaviour from the social work profession. Competent practice depends on the social worker knowing the details of relevant legislation, and constantly updating her knowledge in the light of emergent case law and new statutory instruments.

2.   Knowledge of local resources   No matter how well a social work student has been trained, the critical knowledge of local resources can only be acquired when she takes up her post in an agency. And every time she changes her job, even if it is within the same city, she must begin afresh the task of getting to know her neighbourhood, its social and demographic structure and the availability of helping agencies.

The professionally efficient social worker will always have a working network, and it will gain in cumulative importance over the years, for the increasing benefit of her clients.

The network will vary depending on the social worker's own specialist interests but it may well include: specialist workers within her own agency, the social security system, voluntary agencies in the vicinity, self-help groups, psychiatric services, general medical practitioners, the job centre, the court system, schools, and available accommodation in lodgings and hostels.

3.   Knowledge of human behaviour and its social context   A social worker is neither a psychologist nor an applied sociologist. But if she is to make appropriate assessments quickly and accurately, and if she is to achieve professional competence in counselling and in other spheres of interpersonal relations, then she needs an amalgam of experience, personality and accumulated knowledge, including some coverage of relevant psychology and sociology. Her knowledge of human behaviour and its social context, however, are likely to be gained at least as much from supervised practice and personal experience as from critical or detached book-learning.

Sociology has made social workers aware of stigmas, discrimination, and gender and race issues; psychology has taught us about family relationships, child development and interpersonal conflict. These all have a place in social work training, and there is evidence that there is a particularly strongly felt need for post-qualifying courses in psychology as social workers move into more professionally demanding roles as they gain experience.

4.   Knowledge of welfare rights   Most people agree that society ought to provide a welfare rights facility, but there is also an awareness that mainstream social workers rarely have the detailed and up-to-date knowledge that the task requires. Moreover, in an increasing number of instances, the client's rights may need to be represented *against* the social worker's own employer, the social services department.

The argument that all social workers can and should provide an institutionalised welfare rights service has come to seem unrealistic, when set alongside the multifarious other duties heaped on their shoulders. However, it is not unreasonable to demand that all social workers should have a basic sensitivity to welfare rights issues, that they should know where to refer clients who need advice and that they should be prepared to act in an advocacy role whenever necessary and appropriate. Moreover, the trend for social services departments to make specialist internal appointments of welfare rights officers who can then act as a wide-ranging resource available to all staff is a useful compromise.

Qualities

Although some people speak of 'values' as representing the third category of elements which, together with skills and knowledge, go to make up the social worker's toolkit, the broader notion of 'qualities' provides a more accurate picture of what social workers themselves say about their professional profile.

Moore (1992) has provided a list of 'skills' necessary for high-quality child protection social work but most of them are more to do with the personality and style – or the qualities – of the social worker than with learnt skills. She emphasises, for example, the need for:

- perseverance;
- skill in confrontation and the use of authority;
- ability to create action;
- assertiveness and being appropriately self-confident;
- ability to work with hostility;
- skill in working within time-limits;
- ability to work in stressful situations.

These are tough-minded qualities, qualities which reflect resilience and an ability to maintain focus, and they illustrate why child protection social work demands great personal strength and clarity of perspective.

Probation, too, is said to require resilience in its officers; and the serious offences committed by many probation clients mean that social workers in the criminal justice system have to be, above all else, streetwise.

A major research study into the opinions of serving probation officers concluded: 'Some of the qualities said to be valued are those that any employer would seek in a member of staff: punctuality, flexibility and a sense of humour. But probation officers also need to be patient and optimistic because of the nature of their client-group; they need to be tolerant of deviant behaviour; they need to be non-judgmental, and, because of the growing proportion of black offenders, they must be sensitive to issues of race and racism; they must be emotionally secure because theirs is a job which brings them face to face with life's more serious crises; they should have a degree of self-awareness and be reasonably confident of their own ability to perform appropriately in a professional setting' (Davies 1989).

Pastoral pluralism

The practice of social work can be seen as a form of pastoral care in a secular society. Like the mediaeval church, contemporary state welfare agencies have a variety of functions – punitive, protective, compensatory, watchful – and, like priests, social workers are at their best when their attention is focused on the needs of individuals or small communities; it is then that they act to represent the interests of ordinary men and women to the state and vice versa. Social workers exist because of the pastoral commitment of the modern welfare state. But such a commitment is neither simple, nor unified, nor unchanging. The maintenance task carried out by the social worker must inevitably at times lead to debate and even to conflict between the various parties – hence the need for a strong welfare rights role in contemporary practice, and hence the inevitability of social work challenging some traditional perspectives in institutional settings like prisons and hospitals. But social work *per se* is not about revolution. Neither, of course, is it about the uncompromising, relentless and naked imposition of state power. Social work operates within, and represents the interests of, the state by which it is sponsored; it asserts the primacy of the individual and to that extent is a product of the evolution of social democracy in the 20th century. The social worker is jointly accountable both to her client and to the agency, and, because of this duality, social work must inevitably reflect a degree of tension and ambiguity, and be increasingly ill-at-ease and eventually untenable in any society under absolute rule or in a state of anarchy.

Some critics might reject such a pluralist interpretation of what social work is about. I can only argue that this theoretical representation seems to me to best fit the empirical evidence of how and why social workers are employed, of what their agencies and clients expect of them, and of how the vast majority of workers respond to those expectations.

Social work is essential in two ways. First, because we know that, in a complex urban world, there are certain tasks that need to be carried out if we are to maintain an acceptable level of humane social management; if social workers did not carry out these tasks, they would not get done – and vulnerable people would suffer even more than they do now.

And second, social work is essential because of the professional standards that it has espoused and which it brings to bear on the tasks allocated to it. They reflect democratic and humanist values, and they epitomise the state's aspiration to accommodate a caring community and to respect the absolute right of every man, woman and child to an independent life.

Of course the state and its employees fall short of this ideal, but that is no reason to abandon it or to deride the efforts made to achieve it. Social work will continue to evolve as we enter the 21st century, but the foundations laid by its pioneers over one hundred years are sound and enduring. The century now nearing its end has seen many improvements in the way that basic welfare functions are carried out, and there is every reason to be confident of future developments.

Bibliography

Abbreviations: BJSW – British Journal of Social Work
CC – Community Care
SWT – Social Work Today

Abbott, P. and Sapsford, R. (1988) Community Care for Mentally Handicapped Children, Open University Press.

Abrams, Philip (1978) 'Community Care: Some Research Problems and Priorities', in Barnes and Connelly (1978), 78–79.

Abrams, Philip (1980) 'Social Change, Social Networks and Neighbourhood Care', Social Work Service, 22, February, 12–23.

Adams, R. (1990) Self-Help, Social Work and Empowerment, Macmillan.

Anderson, D. (1982) Social Work and Mental Handicap, Macmillan.

All-Wales Working Party (1983) Services for Mentally Handicapped People, Welsh Office.

Armitage, Mary (1979) 'The Cost of Caring for the Elderly', SWT, 10 (38), 5 June, 15–16.

Ashton, G. and Ward, A. (1992) Mental Handicap and the Law, Sweet and Maxwell.

Atkins, Norah (1981) 'The Best Possible Start in Life', SWT, 12 (45), 28 July, 14–15.

Audit Commission (1985) Managing Social Services for the Elderly More Effectively, HMSO.

Audit Commission (1986) Making a Reality of Community Care, HMSO.

Bailey, Roy and Lee, Phil (1982) Theory and Practice in Social Work, Blackwell.

Ball, Caroline (1991) Child Care Law, third edition, University of East Anglia, Norwich.

Bamford, Terry (1990) The Future of Social Work, Macmillan.

Banaka, W.H. (1971) Training in Depth Interviewing, Harper and Row.

Barclay Report (1982) Social Workers; their Role and Tasks, Bedford Square Press.

Barnes, Jack and Connelly, Naomi (eds) (1978) Social Care Research, Bedford Square Press.

Barry, Michael (1984) 'Crime Prevention, Community Work and Probation Policy', MA dissertation, University of East Anglia.

Batey, Grace (1979) 'The World of Leslie Wright', CC, 275, 2 August, 24–5.

Bayley, Michael (1973) Mental Handicap and Community Care, Routledge and Kegan Paul.

Bayley, Michael (1978) 'Someone to Fall Back On', CC, 207, 5 April, 42–3.

Bealka, Richard J., psychiatrist, Mental Health Institute, Independence, Iowa, USA; quoted in Compton and Galaway (1975), 203.

Bean, Philip (1980) *Compulsory Admissions to Mental Hospitals*, Wiley.

Bebbington, A. and Charnley, H. (1990) 'Community Care for the Elderly – Rhetoric and Reality', *BJSW*, **20**, 409–432.

Bender, Michael (1983) 'Day Centres – For What and For Whom?', *CC*, **445**, 13 January, 20–21.

Billis, David (1973) 'Entry into Residential Care', *BJSW*, **3** (4), Winter, 447–471.

Bird, Nicholas (1984) *The Private Provision of Residential Care*, Social Work Monographs.

Black, Jim *et al.* (1983) *Social Work in Context*, Tavistock.

Blom-Cooper, Louis (1985) *A Child in Trust*, London Borough of Brent.

Blom-Cooper, Louis (1987) *A Child in Mind*, London Borough of Greenwich.

Boswell, Gwyneth (1985) *Care, Control and Accountability in the Probation Service*, Social Work Monographs.

Boswell, Gwyneth (1989) *Holding the Balance Between Court and Client*, Social Work Monographs.

Bowman, A. (1978) 'Meanwhile Back in Ambridge', *SWT*, **9** (23), 7 February, 8–10.

Brimelow, Mary and Wilson, Judy (1982) 'Ourselves Alone', *SWT*, **13** (21), 2 February, 12–13.

Briscoe, Catherine (1977) 'Community Work and Social Work in the United Kingdom' in Specht and Vickery (1977), 182–94.

British Association of Social Workers (1978) *The Central Child Abuse Register*, BASW Publications.

Brook, Richard (1990) *An Introduction to Disaster Theory for Social Workers*, Social Work Monographs.

Browne, Elizabeth (1978) 'Social Work Activities', In Stevenson and Parsloe (1978), 77–136.

Bulmer, Martin (1987) *The Social Basis of Community Care*, Unwin Hyman.

Burgess, Robin *et al.* (1980) 'Working with Sex Offenders: a Social Skills Training Group', *BJSW*, **10** (2), Summer, 133–42.

Butler, Alan and Pritchard, Colin (1983) *Social Work and Mental Illness*, Macmillan.

Butler, Janet, Bow, Irene and Gibbons, Jane (1978) 'Task-Centred Casework with Marital Problems', *BJSW*, **8** (4), Winter, 393–409.

Butler Report (1975) Committee on Mentally Abnormal Offenders, Cmnd 6244.

Butler-Sloss, E. (1988) *Report of the Enquiry into Child Abuse in Cleveland*, HMSO.

Campbell, T.D. (1978) 'Discretionary "Rights"', in Timms and Watson (1978), 50–77.

Campling, Jo (1980) 'Social Work For the Out Of Work', *SWT* **12** (14), 2 December, 11–12.

Caplan, Gerald (1964) *Principles of Preventive Psychiatry*, Basic Books.

Carter, Jan (1974) *The Maltreated Child*, Priory.

Challis, David and Davies, Bleddyn (1980) 'A New Approach to Community Care for the Elderly', *BJSW*, **10** (1), Spring, 1–18.

Challis, David, Davies, Bleddyn and Holman, Jon (1980) 'Bringing Better Community Care to Fragile Elderly People', *SWT*, **11** (22), 5 February, 14–16.

Chartered Institute of Public Finance and Accountancy (1993) *Personal Social Services Statistics, 1991–92 Actuals*, CIPFA.

Cheetham, Juliet (1980) Personal communication.

Cheetham, Juliet and Learner, Eva (1972) 'Social Workers and Women Requesting a Termination of Pregnancy: Report to the Lane Committee on the Working of the Abortion Act', (Privately circulated report. A summary is contained in the Report of the Committee on the Working of the Abortion Act, Volume II, Statistics. Paras 464–73. HMSO, Cmnd 5579-I, 1974).

Clark, A.T. (1975) 'Volunteers Accredited to the Probation Service: A National Survey', Hertfordshire Probation Service.

Colwell Inquiry: see DHSS (1974).

Compton, B.R. and Galaway, B. (1975) *Social Work Processes*, Dorsey.

Connor, A. and Tibbitt, J. (1988) *Social Workers and Health Care in Hospitals*, HMSO.

Cooper, Michael and Denne, John (1983) 'A Problem of Coordination', *CC*, **456**, 31 March, 16–18.

Cooper, Mike and Stacy, Graham (1981) 'Translating Community Based Care into Action', *CC*, **347**, 12 February, 15–17.

Corby, Brian (1982) 'Theory and Practice in Long-Term Social Work', *BJSW*, **12** (6), December, 619–638.

Corden, John (1980) 'Contracts in Social Work Practice', *BJSW*, **10** (2), Summer, 143–61.

Corney, Roslyn (1981) 'First Time Clients', *CC*, **355**, 9 April, 21–23.

Corob, Alison (1987) *Working With Depressed Women*, Gower.

Cosgrove, Julie (1983) 'Shelter in a Storm', *SWT*, **14** (44), 26 July, 13–15.

Coulshed, Veronica (1988) *An Introduction to Social Work*, Macmillan.

Cree, Gordon, Robertson, Margriet and Short, Maggie (1979) 'Behavioural Casework in Mental Health', *SWT*, **10** (42), 3 July, 22–4.

Crine, Alistair (1982) 'Opus 82', *CC*, **249**, 16 September, 14–17.

Crine, Alistair (1983a) 'Two-Way Squeeze', *CC*, **455**, 24 March, 14–16.

Crine, Alistair (1983b) 'Taking Risks and Making Changes', *CC*, **470**, 21 July, 14–16.

Croft, Suzy and Beresford, Peter (1984) 'Patch and Participation – the Case for Citizen Research', *SWT*, **16** (3), 17 September, 18–24.

Crompton, Margaret (1979) 'Applying to Foster', *CC*, **282**, 20 September, 25.

Crossman, R.H.S. (1976) 'The Role of the Volunteer in the Modern Social Service', in Halsey (1976).

Crowley, Margaret (1982) *Preparation for Foster-Care Practice*, Social Work Monographs.

Curnock, Kathleen and Hardiker, Pauline (1979) *Towards Practice Theory*, Routledge and Kegan Paul.

Davies, Bleddyn and Challis, David (1986) *Matching Resources to Needs in Community Care*, Gower.

Davies, Martin (1969) *Probationers in Their Social Environment*, HMSO.

Davies, Martin (1974) *Social Work in the Environment*, HMSO.

Davies, Martin (1977) *Support Systems in Social Work*, Routledge and Kegan Paul.

Davies, Martin (1984) 'Training – What We Think of it Now', *SWT*, **15** (20), 24 January, 12–17.

Davies, Martin (1989) *The Nature of Probation Practice Today*, Home Office.

Davies, Martin and Wright, Andrew (1989) *The Changing Face of Probation*, Social Work Monographs.

Dawson, Hilton (1983) 'Working with Mr A', *CC*, **451**, 24 February, 17–18.

Department of Health (1988) *Protecting Children*, HMSO.

Department of Health (1989) *Caring for People: Community Care in the Next Decade and Beyond*, HMSO.

Department of Health (1990) *The Care of Children, Principles and Practice*, HMSO.

Department of Health (1991) *Looking after Children: Assessment and Action Record*, HMSO.

DHSS (1971) *Better Services for the Mentally Handicapped*, a White Paper, HMSO.

DHSS (1974) *Report of the Committee of Inquiry into the Care and Supervision Provided in Relation to Maria Colwell*, HMSO.

DHSS (1976) *Guide to Fostering Practice*, a Working Party Report (Chairperson, Janie Thomas), HMSO.

DHSS (1985) *Social Work Decisions in Child Care; Recent Research Findings and their Implications*, HMSO.

DHSS (1987) *The Law on Child Care and Family Services*, a White Paper, HMSO.

Disability Manifesto Group (1989) *An Agenda for the 1990s*, DMG.

Disraeli, Benjamin (1867) Speech in Edinburgh, 29 October.

Doel, M. and Marsh, P. (1992) *Task-Centred Social Work*, Ashgate.

Donnelly, Arnon (1985) *Feminist Social Work with a Women's Group*, Social Work Monographs.

Dorn, Nicholas and South, Nigel (1984) *Drug-Related Social Work in Street Agencies*, Social Work Monographs.

Dyde, Wendy (1987) *Place of Safety Orders*, Social Work Monographs.

Edwards, Carol and Sinclair, Ian (1980) 'Debate: Segregation Versus Integration', *SWT*, **11** (40), 24 June, 19–21.

Fellows, Gill and Marshall, Mary (1979) 'Services for the Homeless Elderly', *SWT*, **10** (35), 8 May, 16–17.

Fisher, M. *et al.* (1984) *Mental Health Social Work Observed*, Allen and Unwin.

Foad, Kathleen (1984) 'Youth Custody Through-Care Practice in Essex', Advanced Certificate dissertation, University of East Anglia.

Folkard, Steven (1974 and 1976) *IMPACT*, Volumes I and II, HMSO.

Ford, Jill and Hollick, Margery (1979) 'The Singer or the Song: An Autobiographical Account of a Suicidal Destructive Person and Her Social Worker', *BJSW*, **9** (4), Winter, 471–88.

Foren, Robert and Bailey, Royston (1968) *Authority in Social Casework*, Pergamon.

Fox, Lorraine M. (1982) 'Two Value Positions in Recent Child Care Law and Practice', *BJSW*, **12** (3), June, 265–290.

Gibbons, Jane (1981) 'Task-Centred Methods of Intervention After Deliberate Self-Poisoning', in Goldberg and Connelly (eds) (1981), 23–44.

Gibbons, Jennifer (1984) 'Live Wires', *SWT*, **15** (24), 20 February, 14–15.

Glassner, Barry and Freedman, Jonathan (1979) *Clinical Sociology*, Longman.

Glendinning, C. (1983) *Unshared Care: Parents and Their Disabled Children*, Routledge.

Goldberg, David and Huxley, Peter (1980) *Mental Illness in the Community*, Tavistock.

Goldberg, E. Matilda *et al.* (1977a) 'Exploring the Task-Centred Casework Method', *SWT*, **9** (2), 6 September, 9–14.

Goldberg, E. Matilda *et al.* (1977b). 'Towards Accountability in Social Work: One Year's Intake to An Area Office', *BJSW*, **7** (3), Autumn, 257–83.

Goldberg, E. Matilda *et al.* (1978) 'Towards Accountability in Social Work: Long Term Social Work in An Area Office', *BJSW*, **8** (3), Autumn, 253–87.

Goldberg, E.M. and Connelly, Naomi (eds) (1981) *Evaluative Research in Social Care*, Heinemann Educational Books.

Goldstein, Joseph, Freud, Anna and Solnit, Albert J. (1973) *Beyond the Best Interests of the Child*, Free Press.

Gosling, Martin (1984) 'Community Programmes in Probation Practice', Advanced Certificate dissertation, University of East Anglia.

The Griffiths Report (1988) *Community Care: Agenda for Action*, HMSO.

Hadley, Roger (1984) 'The Idea of Major Change by Casework Alone Seems Indefensible' *SWT*, **15** (50), 27 August, 16–19.

Hadley, Roger and McGrath, Morag (1983) 'The Normanton Experience', *CC*, **488**, 17 November, 23–4.

Haimes, Erica and Timms, Noel (1984) 'Counselling and the Children Act 1975', *Adoption and Fostering*, **8** (3), 42–46.

Hall, Tony (ed.) (1980) *Access to Birth Records*, Association of British Adoption and Fostering Agencies.

Halsey, A.H. (ed.) (1976) *Traditions of Social Policy*, Blackwell.

Hamilton, Gordon (1940: revised 1951) *Theory and Practice of Social Casework*, Columbia University Press.

Handler, Joel (1973) *The Coercive Social Worker*, Markham.

Hanvey, Christopher (1981) *Social Work with Mentally Handicapped People*, Heinemann Educational Books.

Hare, Edward (1977) Personal communication.

Harman, John (1978) 'A Teamwork Approach at IMPACT', *SWT*, **9** (36), 16 May, 15–17.

Harris, John (1981) 'Christine and Her Shouts', *SWT*, **13** (8), 27 October, 10–11.

Hatch, Stephen (1978) *Voluntary Work: A Report of a Survey*, Volunteers Centre.

Hildebrand, Judith (1977) 'Abortion: with Particular Reference to the Developing Role of Counselling', *BJSW*, **7** (1), Spring, 3–24.

Hoggett, Brenda (1990) *Mental Health Law*, Sweet and Maxwell.

Holbrook, Daphne (1978) 'A Combined Approach to Parental Coping', *BJSW*, **8** (4), Winter, 439–51.

Holdsworth, Lisa (1991) *Empowerment Social Work with Physically Disabled People*, Social Work Monographs.

Home Office (1984) 'Probation Service in England and Wales – Statement of National Purpose and Objectives'.

Home Office (1990) *Crime, Justice and Protecting the Public*, HMSO.

Home Office (1992) *National Standards for the Supervision of Offenders in the Community*, Home Office.

Horsley, Gail (1984) *The Language of Social Enquiry Reports*, Social Work Monographs.

Howe, David, Sawbridge, Phillida and Hinings, Diana (1992) *Half A Million Women*, Penguin.

Hudson, Barbara (1978) 'Behavioural Social Work with Schizophrenic Patients in the Community', *BJSW*, **8** (2), Summer, 159–70.

Hudson, Barbara (1982) *Social Work with Psychiatric Patients*, Macmillan.

Hugman, Bruce (1977) *Act Natural*, Bedford Square Press.

Hunt, Linda (1979) 'Conflict, Pressure and the Psychiatric Emergency', *SWT*, **10** (42), 3 July, 20–1.

Hutchen, Jill (1984) 'Welcome to the World', *CC*, **494**, 12 January, 24–26.

Huxley, Julian (ed.) (1961) *The Humanist Frame*, Allen and Unwin.

Jamieson, John (1978) 'What is an Interview?' *CC*, **199**, 8 February, 18–19.

The Jay Report (1979) *Mental Handicap Nursing and Care*, HMSO.

Jones, Howard (ed.) (1975) *Towards a New Social Work*, Routledge and Kegan Paul.

Jones, Maxwell (1977) *Maturation of the Therapeutic Community*, Human Sciences Press.

Jones, M.A., Neuman, R. and Shyne, A.W. (1976) *A Second Chance for Families*, Child Welfare League of America.

Kahn, A.J. *et al.* (1972) *Child Advocacy*, Columbia University Press.

Keith-Lucas, Alan (1972) *The Giving and Taking of Help*, University of North Carolina Press.

Kent County Council SSD (1993) 'Community Care Plan 1993–96'.

Kerr, Anna *et al.* (1990) *On Behalf of the Child*, Venture Press.

King, J.F.S. (ed.) (1976) *Control Without Custody?*, Institute of Criminology, Cambridge.

Klein, Rudolf (1976) 'The Politics of Public Expenditure: American Theory and British Practice', *British Journal of Political Science*, **6**, 401–32.

Knight, Lindsay (1976) 'Kids they Couldn't Foster', *CC*, **129**, 22 September, 19–21.

Lambeth, London Borough of (1987) *Whose Child?*, The Report of the Panel Appointed to Inquire into the Death of Tyra Henry, Lambeth.

Law Commission (1991) *Mentally Incapacitated Adults and Decision-Making: An Overview*, Law Commission.

Lawson, Colin (1978) *The Probation Officer as Prosecutor*, Institute of Criminology, Cambridge.

Leonard, Peter (1976) 'Marx: the Class Perspective', *CC*, **123**, 11 August, 16–18.

Levy, Leon H. (1976) 'Self-Help Groups: Types and Psychological Processes', *Journal of Applied Behavioural Science*, **12** (3), 311–12.

Lindemann, Erich (1944) 'Symptomatology and Management of Acute Grief', *American Journal of Psychiatry*, **101**, September.

Lishman, Joyce (1978) 'A Clash in Perspective?', *BJSW*, **8** (3), Autumn, 301–11.

Loewenstein, Carol (1974) 'An Intake Team in Action in a Social Services Department', *BJSW*, **4** (2), Summer, 115–41.

MacVeigh, James (1982) *Gaskin*, Jonathan Cape.

Marshall, Mary (1992) *Social Work with Old People*, second edition, Macmillan.

Marshall, Mary and Hargreaves, M. (1979) 'So You Want to Try GP Attachment', *SWT*, **10** (42), 3 July, 25–6.

Mayer, John and Timms, Noel (1970) *The Client Speaks*, Routledge and Kegan Paul.

Millard, D.A. (ed.) (1975 and 1976) 'Shelton 1; and Shelton 2. Papers From a Working Probation Office', Staffordshire Probation and After-Care Service.

Miller, E.J. and Gwynne, G.V. (1972) *A Life Apart*, Tavistock.

Moore, Jean (1992) *The ABC of Child Protection*, Ashgate.

Moroney, Robert M. (1976) *The Family and the State*, Longman.

Morris, Catriona (1984) *The Permanency Principle in Child Care Social Work*, Social Work Monographs.

Morris, Peter (1976) 'House with a View in Havelock Square', *CC*, **121**, 28 July, 14–16.

Nirje, B. (1970) 'The Normalisation Principle', *Journal of Mental Subnormality*, XVI (Pt 2), **31**, December.

Nokes, Peter (1967) *The Professional Task in Welfare Practice*, Routledge and Kegan Paul.

Norman, Alison J. (1980) *Rights and Risk: Civil Liberty in Old Age*, National Corporation for the Care of Old People.

O'Keefe, J. (1988) 'Probation' in *The New Statesman*, 25 November.

Oliver, M. and Hasler, F. (1987) 'Disability and Self-Help', *Disability, Handicap and Society*, **4** (3), 221–239.

Olsen, Rolf (1984) *Social Work and Mental Health*, Tavistock.

Osborn, Julie (1990) *Psychological Effects of Child Sex Abuse on Women*, Social Work Monographs.

Osmond, Robin (1980) Letter to *The Times*, 28 February.

Parker, Paul (1978) 'Reaching Out to a Wider Network', *CC*, **235**, 18 October, 21–2.

Parsloe, Phyllida (1978) 'Some Educational Implications', in Stevenson and Parsloe (1978), 329–59.

Parsloe, Phyllida (1991) 'What is Probation?', *Social Work Education*, **10** (2).

Parton, Nigel (1979) 'The Natural History of Child Abuse', *BJSW*, **9** (4), Winter, 427–51.

Perlman, Helen (1957) *Social Casework: A Problem-Solving Process*, University of Chicago Press.

Perlman, Helen (1970) 'The Problem-Solving Model in Social Casework', in Roberts and Nee (1970), 129–79.

Phillips, Judith (1992a) *Private Residential Care*, Avebury.

Phillips, Judith (1992b) 'The Future of Social Work with Elderly People', *Generations Review* **2** (4), December, 12–14.

Phillips, Judith and McCoy, Peter (1990) 'Public and Private Residential Care for Elderly People' in Juliet Cheetham (ed.) *Research Highlights in Social Work 18*, Jessica Kingsley.

Phillipson, Chris (1988) *Planning for Community Care: Facts and Fallacies in the Griffiths Report*, University of Keele.

Pincus, Allen and Minahan, Anne (1973) *Social Work Practice, Model and Method*, F.E. Peacock.

Plank, M. (1982) *Teams for Mentally Handicapped People*, Campaign for Mentally Handicapped People.

Plant, Raymond (1970) *Social and Moral Theory in Casework*, Routledge and Kegan Paul.

Presland, John and Roberts, Helen (1983) 'Reaching those Who Need Help', *CC*, **487**, 10 November, 19–20.

Prime, Ruth (1977) 'Report on a Method of Workload Management and Weighting', *SWT*, **9** (15), 6 December, 16–18.

Pritchard, Colin (1992) 'Didn't We Do Well?' *SWT*, 23 January, 16–17.

Rapaport, Lydia (1970) 'Crisis Intervention as a Mode of Brief Intervention', in Roberts and Nee (1970), 265–311.

Rashid, Stephen and Ball, Caroline (1991) *Mental Health, Disability, Homelessness, Race Relations*, Social Work Monographs.

Redford, David and Goodenough, Alan (1979) 'Learning Interviewing Skills', *CC*, **279**, 30 August, 27–8.

Rees, Stuart (1974) 'No More than Contact', *BJSW*, **4** (3), Autumn, 255–79.

Rees, Stuart (1978) *Social Work Face to Face*, Edward Arnold.

Rees, Stuart and Wallace, Alison (1982) *Verdicts on Social Work*, Edward Arnold.

Reid, William and Epstein, Laura (1972) *Task Centred Casework*, Columbia University Press.

Reid, William and Epstein, Laura (eds) (1977) *Task Centred Practice*, Columbia University Press.

Reid, William and Hanrahan, Patricia (1982) 'Recent Evaluations of Social Work: Grounds for Optimism', *Social Work (NASW)*, July, 328–40.

Reid, William and Shyne, Anne (1969) *Brief and Extended Casework*, Columbia University Press.

Roberts, R.W. and Nee, R.H. (1970) *Theories of Social Casework*, Chicago University Press.

Rogers, Carl (1967) *The Therapeutic Relationship and its Impact*, University of Wisconsin Press.

Rushton, Andree and Davies, Penny (1984) *Social Work and Health Care*, Heinemann Educational Books.

Russell, Phillippa (1989) 'Handicapped Children' in *Child Care Research, Policy and Practice*, Barbara Kahan (ed.), Hodder and Stoughton.

Sainsbury, Eric (1975) *Social Work with Families*, Routledge and Kegan Paul.

Salmon, Wilma (1977) 'A Service Program in a State Public Welfare Agency', in Reid and Epstein (1977), 113–22.

Scott, Mike (1982) 'Talking to Learn', *SWT*, **13** (37), 8 June, 18–19.

Seebohm Report (1968) *Report of the Committee on Local Authority and Allied Personal Social Services*, HMSO.

Sharron, Howard (1982) 'A Stitch in Time', *SWT*, **13** (18), 12 January, 7–9.

Shaw, Margaret (1974) *Social Work in Prison*, HMSO.

Shaw, Stephen (1983) 'Crime Prevention and the Future of the Probation Service', *Probation Journal*, **30** (4), December, 127–9.

Shearer, Ann (1979) 'The Legacy of Maria Colwell', *SWT*, **10** (19), 9 January, 12–19.

Sheldon, Brian (1977) 'Do You Know Where You're Going?', *CC*, **165**, 8 June, 13–15.

Sheldon, Brian (1981a) 'The Pavlov Inheritance', *SWT*, **13** (9), 3 November, 8–12.

Sheldon, Brian (1981b) 'Crossing the Bridge', *SWT*, **13** (10), 10 November, 10–14.

Sheppard, Michael (1990) *Mental Health – the Role of the Approved Social Worker*, Sheffield University.

Sinclair, Ian *et al.* (1990) *The Kaleidoscope of Care*, HMSO.

Smale, Gerald and Tuson, Graham (1993) *Empowerment, Assessment, Care Management and the Skilled Worker*, HMSO.

Smalley, Ruth (1970) 'The Functional Approach to Casework' in Roberts and Nee (1970), 77–128.

Specht, Harry and Vickery, Anne (eds) (1977) *Integrating Social Work Methods*, Allen and Unwin.

Stein, Mike (1979) 'Children of the State', *SWT*, **10** (28), 13 March, 26–9.

Stevenson, Olive (1974) Editorial, *BJSW*, **4** (1), Spring, 1.

Stevenson, Olive (1976) 'Social Services as Controllers', in King (1976), 1–22.

Stevenson, Olive and Parsloe, Phyllida (1978) *Social Service Teams: The Practitioner's View*, HMSO.

Stone, Karen (1991) *The Integration of Statemented Children in Mainstream Schools*, Social Work Monographs.

Stone, Nigel (1992) 'Pre-Sentence Reports, Culpability and the 1991 Act', *Criminal Law Review*, 558–567.

Thoburn, June (1985) 'What Kind of Permanence?', *Adoption and Fostering*, **9** (4), 29–34.

Thomas, D.N. (1983) *The Making of Community Work*, Allen and Unwin.

Thomlinson, Ray J. (1984) 'Something Works: Evidence from Practice Effectiveness Studies', *Social Work (NASW)*, **29** (1), January/February, 51–6.

Thorpe, David (1982) 'IT in Theory and Practice' in Bailey and Lee (eds), (1982), 78–97.

Tibbitt, John and Connor, Ann (1989) 'Change and Diversity in Hospital Social Work' in Taylor, R. and Ford, J. (eds) *Social Work and Health Care* (1989), Kingsley.

Timms, Judith (1992) *Manual of Practice Guidance for Guardians* ad Litem *and Reporting Officers*, HMSO.

Timms, Noel and Rita (1977) *Perspectives in Social Work*, Routledge and Kegan Paul.

Timms, Noel and Watson, David (eds) (1978) *Philosophy in Social Work*, Routledge and Kegan Paul.

Truax, C.B. and Carkhuff, R. (1967) *Towards Effective Counselling and Psychotherapy*, Aldine.

Truax, C.B. *et al.* (1968) 'Effects of Therapist Persuasive Potency in Individual Psychotherapy', *Journal of Clinical Psychology.*

Vevers, Paul (1981) 'Bringing up Baby', *CC*, **353**, 26 March, 12–13.

Wakefield, C.E. (1976) 'Intake', Supplement to *CC*, **129**, 22 September.

The Warnock Report (1978) *Special Educational Needs*, HMSO.

West, Jenny (1976) 'Community Service Orders' in King (1976), 68–92.

Whitehead, Annette (1993) *Joyriding – Policy, Law and Probation Practice*, Social Work Monographs.

Whittington, Colin (1971) 'Self-Determination Re-Examinied', *BJSW*, **1** (3), Autumn, 293–303.

Wilkin, David (1979) *Caring for the Mentally Handicapped Child*, Croom Helm.

Winter, Karen (1992) *The Day they Took Away our Children: Ritualistic Abuse, Social Work and the Press*, Social Work Monographs.

Wolfensberg, W. (1983) 'Social Role Valorization: a Proposed New Term for the Principle of Normalization', *Mental Retardation*, **21** (6), 234–239.

Wright, Andrew (1984) *The Day Centre in Probation Practice*, Social Work Monographs.

Name index